DIVORCING RESPONSIBLY

This book provides an analysis of the increasing impact on the law in general and divorce law in particular of post-liberalism, which replaces choice with self-discovery. The author shows that post-liberal premises formed the foundation for every aspect of the recent divorce reform proposals. Accordingly, she attributes their failure to the contradictions inherent within post-liberalism. Nevertheless, she concludes that post-liberalism maintains a subtle yet pervasive influence on the law. Specifically, this means that we are held accountable not for what we do but for how we approach our decisions. Accordingly, for the first time ever, it has become possible to divorce responsibly.

D1477818

Divorcing Responsibly

HELEN REECE
Birkbeck College, London

·HART·
PUBLISHING

OXFORD – PORTLAND OREGON
2003

Published in North America (US and Canada) by
Hart Publishing
c/o International Specialized Book Services
5804 NE Hassalo Street
Portland, Oregon
97213-3644
USA

Hart Publishing is a specialist legal publisher based in Oxford, England. To order further copies of this book or to request a list of other publications please write to:

Hart Publishing, Salter's Boatyard, Folly Bridge, Abingdon Rd, Oxford, OX1 4LB
Telephone: +44 (0)1865 245533 Fax: +44 (0) 1865 794882
email: mail@hartpub.co.uk
WEBSITE: http//:www.hartpub.co.uk

British Library Cataloguing in Publication Data
Data Available

ISBN 1–84113–215–2 (hardback)

Typeset by Hope Services (Abingdon) Ltd
Printed and bound in Great Britain by
Biddles Ltd, www.biddles.co.uk

Acknowledgments

I am very grateful to the following people for advice and comments concerning this project, and particularly for having read draft chapters of the manuscript: Jennie Bristow, Professor Richard Collier, Professor Davina Cooper, Alison Diduck, Nissa Finney, Professor Frank Furedi, James Heartfield, Felicity Kaganas, Rachel Napoli, Dr Mike Redmayne, Dr Gordon Reece and Dr Guy Westwell. I am especially grateful to John Gillott, Emily Jackson and Professor Andrew Le Sueur for having read, commented on and criticised several versions of the entire manuscript.

Contents

Introduction

THE LAST 15 years have seen the rise and fall of a post-liberal divorce law. First mooted in the Law Commission Discussion Paper, Facing the Future in 1988,[1] the scheme went through every conceivable legislative stage, accompanied by extensive media discussion, before becoming law in 1996. The main body of the scheme was contained in Part II of the Family Law Act, with the general principles underlying divorce law set down in Part I, legal aid for mediation provided for in Part III and Part V dealing with supplemental matters. (Part IV of the Family Law Act 1996 deals with the separate issue of domestic violence). Parts I, III, IV and V have been implemented. However, after pilot schemes were judged to have failed, the Lord Chancellor announced in early 2001 that implementation of Part II of the Family Law Act would be indefinitely postponed, and that the Government would ask Parliament to repeal it in due course.[2] The Government is currently considering how, if at all, to proceed with divorce reform.[3]

This recent attempt to reform divorce was the first departure from a simple historical trend away from a conservative model towards a liberal model of divorce law. Once marriage had been regulated by Lord Hardwicke's Marriage Act 1753, divorce became a necessity. The most conservative position, adopted up until the Matrimonial Causes Act 1857, was to allow divorce only by way of a Private Act of Parliament. Unsurprisingly, this meant that in this period divorce was exclusively a prerogative of the rich and almost exclusively a male prerogative. Steadily and gradually, the law moved towards greater acceptance of divorce. Gender imbalance in divorce law remained until the Matrimonial Causes Act 1923. However, a far more lasting legacy of the conservative model was (and is) a link between marital fault and

---

[1] Law Commission, *Facing the Future: A Discussion Paper on the Ground for Divorce* (London, HMSO, 1988). See also Booth Committee, *Report of the Matrimonial Causes Procedure Committee* (London, HMSO, 1985) where the principal criticisms of the present law originated.

[2] Lord Chancellor's Department Press Release, 'Divorce Law Reform – Government Proposes to Repeal Part II of the Family Law Act 1996', 16 January 2001. Part II of the Family Law Act 1996 has not been implemented, with the exception of s 22, which provides for funding for marriage support services.

[3] See ch 5, pp 197–99.

entitlement to divorce, which remained practically total, in that divorce was allowed only if fault could be proved, until the Divorce Reform Act 1969.[4] Nor was the connection with fault limited to the divorce itself. Initially, allocation of both responsibility for children and financial resources was heavily dependent on the question of which spouse was in the wrong, in the former case until the Custody of Infants Act 1873 and in the latter case right up until the 1960s.[5]

Prior to the Family Law Act 1996, divorce law was last reformed in the heyday of liberalism; the 1969 Divorce Reform Act was one of a number of 1960s reforms that relaxed moral strictures.[6] In relation to divorce, the form that the relaxation took was to weaken, but not to break, the link between fault and divorce. Most essentially, the ground for divorce was changed to irretrievable breakdown, proved by one of five facts, two of which were based on separation and so did not involve fault.[7] More or less contemporaneous developments rendered fault less important for the division of assets,[8] and by this stage fault was, at least formally, irrelevant to decisions about children.[9] However, the 1969 Divorce Reform Act was just a step towards liberalisation, demonstrated most dramatically by the fact that three out of the five facts available to prove irretrievable breakdown, namely adultery, behaviour and desertion, were still premised on a finding of fault.[10]

Part II of the Family Law Act 1996 contained elements that seemed to take divorce law further in a liberal direction. Crucially, the 1996 Act completely broke the connection between fault and divorce: under the Act, fault would have been irrelevant when deciding whether to grant a divorce. The ground for divorce would have remained the same, namely that the marriage had irretrievably broken down,[11] but instead of being proved by potentially fault-based facts, breakdown would have been proved by a period of reflection and consideration.[12] More controversially, the drive to deregulate divorce in the Family Law Act could be seen as motivated by liberalism. Although more prominent in

[4] See L Stone, *Road to Divorce: England 1530–1987* (Oxford, Oxford University Press, 1990) for a full account.

[5] See *M v M* [1962] 1 WLR 845.

[6] See eg the Abortion Act 1967 and the Sexual Offences Act 1967.

[7] See ss 1(1) and (2)(d) and (e) Matrimonial Causes Act 1973.

[8] See *Wachtel v Wachtel* [1973] Fam 72.

[9] See *S(BD) v S(DJ)* [1977] Fam 109 and *Re K* [1977] Fam 179.

[10] See ss 1(2)(a), (b) and (c) Matrimonial Causes Act 1973.

[11] S 3(1)(a) Family Law Act 1996.

[12] S 5(1)(c) Family Law Act 1996.

the early stages of discussion, such as the Law Commission Discussion Paper and the Law Commission Report, The Ground for Divorce 1990,[13] an element of deregulation was still present in the final Act. The most obvious example of this deregulation was that divorcing couples would have decided themselves, using their own criteria, whether their marriage had broken down;[14] another example was the encouragement to agree rather than litigate arrangements about the finances and the children.[15]

However, there also appeared to be a conservative dimension to the Family Law Act, the most obvious example being that the Act abolished quick divorce. The time taken between petition and decree absolute was under six months for just over one-third of divorces in 2000,[16] the facts of adultery and behaviour theoretically allowing immediate divorce. In contrast, the minimum time between statement of marital breakdown and divorce under the Family Law Act would have been the period of reflection and consideration of nine and a half months.[17] For most divorcing couples, principally those with children, the period would have been automatically extended by six months.[18] Even these time scales had to be read alongside the requirement to wait three months after attending an information meeting before a statement could be made.[19] Less uncontroversially conservative was the emphasis on supporting marriage, visible both in the bald statement in Part I of the Act that 'the institution of marriage is to be supported'[20] and in the (originally fairly muted) encouragement to attempt reconciliation in the scheme.[21]

The conservative and liberal strands of Part II of the Family Law Act are apparent: the principal argument of this book is that there is also a new, post-liberal, strand in the Act.

It is relatively uncontentious that what I will shortly define as post-liberalism has been generally on the ascent. More specifically, it has

[13] Law Commission, *The Ground for Divorce* (London, HMSO, 1990).

[14] See ch 3.

[15] See chs 4 and 5.

[16] See Marriage, divorce and adoption statistics: Review of the Registrar General on marriages, divorces and adoptions in England and Wales, 2000 (London, Office for National Statistics, 2002) 105, Table 4.22.

[17] S 7(3) Family Law Act 1996.

[18] Ss 7(10)–(13) Family Law Act 1996.

[19] S 8(2) Family Law Act 1996.

[20] S 1(a) Family Law Act 1996.

[21] See ch 5 for a full account of the development of an emphasis on marriage-saving.

been argued that liberalism has been losing ground to its critics over the last two decades, in fields as diverse as politics and social policy,[22] political theory[23] and philosophical theory[24] and law.[25] In what follows I take this process as given and treat discussion of its social reasons as beyond the scope of the book. However, the fact that critics of liberalism have come from a range of diverse political perspectives has undoubtedly assisted the demise of liberalism. To name but the few that I will examine in this book, attacks have come from feminism, communitarianism and civic republicanism.[26] The communitarian critique of liberalism in particular has been one of the most notable influences on moral and political debate in the past few decades,[27] so that it can lay claim to being *the* alternative theory. Communitarianism has been seen as 'a ready-made theme' for the Labour Party specifically,[28] as offering something in between the free market and socialism.

[22] A Etzioni, *The New Golden Rule: Community and Morality in a Democratic Society* (New York, Basic Books, 1998) 40; A Crawford, 'The Spirit of Community: Rights, Responsibilities, and the Communitarian Agenda', 23 *Journal of Law and Society* 247 at 249.

[23] A Gutmann, 'Communitarian Critics of Liberalism', 14 *Philosophy and Public Affairs* 308 at 308.

[24] A MacIntyre, *After Virtue: a study in moral theory* (London, Duckworth, 1985).

[25] G Kateb, 'Democratic Individuality and the Meaning of Rights' in N Rosenblum (ed), *Liberalism and the Moral Life* (Cambridge, Massachusetts, Harvard University Press, 1989) 183; E Frazer and N Lacey, *The Politics of Community: A Feminist Critique of the Liberal-Communitarian Debate* (Buffalo, New York, University of Toronto Press, 1994) 103; S Holmes, *The Anatomy of Antiliberalism* (Cambridge, Massachusetts, Harvard University Press, 1993) 2; M Sandel, *Liberalism and the Limits of Justice* (Cambridge, Cambridge University Press, 1998) 186.

[26] See S Benhabib, 'Introduction' in S Benhabib, *Situating the Self: Gender, Community and Postmodernism in Contemporary Ethics* (Cambridge, Polity, 1992); N Rosenblum, 'Introduction' in Rosenblum, above n 25, 4; SM Okin, Justice, *Gender and the Family* (New York, Basic Books, 1989) 43; G Parry, 'Paths to Citizenship' in U Vogel and M Moran (eds), *The Frontiers of Citizenship* (Basingstoke, Macmillan, 1991) 180.

[27] Gutmann, above n 23, 308; Etzioni, above n 22, 40; A Etzioni, 'Introduction' in A Etzioni (ed), *The Essential Communitarian Reader* (Lanham, Rowman & Littlefield, 1998) x; C Cochran, 'The Thin Theory of Community: The Communitarians and their Critics', 37 *Political Studies* 422 at 422.

[28] J Demaine, 'Beyond Communitarianism: Citizenship, Politics and Education' in J Demaine and H Entwistle (eds), *Beyond Communitarianism: Citizenship, Politics and Education* (Basingstoke, Macmillan, 1996) 26. See also E Frazer, *The Problems of Communitarian Politics: Unity and Conflict* (Oxford, Oxford University Press, 1999) 12; Editorial, 'Labour Joins The Right: Divorced From Reality', *The Independent*, 29 May 1996; M Phillips, 'The Race to Wake Sleeping Duty', *The Observer*, 2 April 1995; S Milne, 'Everybody's Talking About', *The Guardian*, 7 October 1994.

However, particularly in its civic republican form, communitarianism has also resonated across the political spectrum.[29] Accordingly, it would be wrong to see a clear progression from conservative to liberal to post-liberal thinking: in fact, it has been argued that it has mainly been right-wing governments that have exploited the rhetoric of community.[30] A more accurate description would be that communitarianism has managed to be all things to all people.[31] Ultimately:

> The way is clear for civic republicans and communitarians to represent themselves as the bearers of vision of a new morality and new society.[32]

Despite the diversity of the political perspectives adopted by critics of liberalism, I believe that it is justifiable to discuss post-liberalism as an entity. Both supporters and detractors of liberalism have suggested that the critics of liberalism share a unity that is deeper than their differences, consisting not of uniformity but in the rejection of the key assumptions of liberalism.[33] Three assumptions in particular stand out. The first is the liberal view of autonomy embodied by the

[29] G Andrews, 'Introduction' in G Andrews (ed), *Citizenship* (London, Lawrence & Wishart, 1990) 12; B Almond, 'The Retreat from Liberty', 8 *Critical Review* 235; 'Just a Social Crowd of Folk', *The Guardian*, 18 February 1995; Phillips, above n 28; Milne, above n 28; J Eekelaar, 'Family Law: The Communitarian Message', 21 *Oxford Journal of Legal Studies* 181 at 181.
[30] Frazer and Lacey, above n 25, 135; Gutmann, above n 23, 309; Frazer, above n 28, 32; Cochran, above n 27, 435; Andrews, above n 29, 12.
[31] See 'Just a Social Crowd of Folk', above n 29; Phillips, above n 28; Milne, above n 28.
[32] N Rosenblum, 'Introduction' in Rosenblum, above n 25, 4.
[33] Holmes, above n 25, 3; S Holmes, 'The Permanent Structure of Antiliberal Thought' in Rosenblum, above n 25, 228; S Gardbaum, 'Why the Liberal State can Promote Moral Ideals After All', 104 *Harvard Law Review* 1350; S Hekman, *Moral Voices, Moral Selves: Carol Gilligan and Feminist Moral Theory* (Cambridge, Polity, 1995) 50; D Cornell, *The Imaginary Domain: Abortion, Pornography and Sexual Harassment* (New York, Routledge, 1995) 38. See also S Benhabib, 'Autonomy, Modernity and Community: Communitarianism and Critical Social Theory in Dialogue' in Benhabib, above n 26; Okin, above n 26, 43; K Martindale and M Saunders, 'Realizing Love and Justice: Lesbian Ethics in the Upper and Lower Case' in C Card (ed), *Adventures in Lesbian Philosophy* (Bloomington, Indiana University Press, 1994) 170; S Benhabib and D Cornell, 'Beyond the Politics of Gender' in S Benhabib and D Cornell (eds), *Feminism as Critique: Essays on the Politics of Gender in Late-Capitalist Societies* (Cambridge, Polity, 1987) 12; P Weiss, 'Feminism and Community' in P Weiss and M Friedman (eds), *Feminism and Community* (Philadelphia, Temple University Press, 1995) 3; P Weiss, 'Feminism and Communitarianism: Comparing Critiques of Liberalism' in P Weiss and M Friedman (eds), *Feminism and Community* (Philadelphia, Temple University Press, 1995); S Sherry, 'Civic Virtue and the Feminine Voice in Constitutional Adjudication', 72 *Virginia Law Review* 543.

centrepiece of liberalism,[34] namely the free and rational individual.[35] The second is the liberal conception of reason, understood as providing universal foundations for truth.[36] The third is the liberal ideal of State neutrality toward different conceptions of the good life.[37]

In this book it is not my purpose to adjudicate between confirmation and rejection of these assumptions; nor do I set out to pass judgment on the debate between liberalism and post-liberalism generally. Given that the conflict between liberals and their critics has been arguably either the explicit or the underlying theme of all recent major debates

[34] Hekman, above n 33, 2.

[35] Holmes, above n 25, 1; G Kateb, *The Inner Ocean: Individualism and Democratic Culture* (Ithaca, New York, Cornell University Press, 1992) 223; S Benhabib and D Cornell, 'Beyond the Politics of Gender' in Benhabib and Cornell, above n 33, 12; J Hewitt, Dilemmas *of the American Self* (Philadelphia, Temple University Press, 1989) 29; T Kitwood, 'Psychotherapy, Postmodernism and Morality', 19 *Journal of Moral Education* 3 at 3; S Williams, 'A Feminist Reassessment of Civil Society', 72 *Indiana Law Journal* 417 at 426; S Gardbaum, 'Law, Politics and the Claims of Community', 90 *Michigan Law Review* 685 at 701; M Griffiths, *Feminisms and the Self: The Web of Identity* (London, New York, Routledge, 1995) 79; Benhabib, above n 26; L McClain, ' "Irresponsible" Reproduction', 47 *Hastings Law Journal* 339 at 426; A Hutchinson and L Green, 'Introduction' in A Hutchinson and L Green (eds), *Law and the Community: The End of Individualism?* (Toronto, Carswell, 1989) 2; J Fudge, 'Community or Class: Political Communitarians and Workers' Democracy' in A Hutchinson and L Green (eds), *Law and the Community: The End of Individualism?* (Toronto, Carswell, 1989) 57–58; Hekman, above n 33, 50; J Weeks, C Donovan and B Heaphy, 'Everyday Experiments: Narratives of Non-Heterosexual Relationships' in E Silva and C Smart (eds), *The New Family?* (London, Sage, 1999) 84; M Friedman, *What are Friends For?: Feminist Perspectives on Personal Relationships and Moral Theory* (Ithaca, New York, Cornell University Press, 1993) 68; P Weiss, 'Feminism and Community' in Weiss and Friedman, above n 33, 3; P Weiss, 'Feminism and Communitarianism: Comparing Critiques of Liberalism', above n 33; Frazer and Lacey, above n 25; G Parry, 'Paths to Citizenship' in Vogel and Moran, above n 26, 180; Gutmann, above n 23, 308; Etzioni, above n 22, 40; Frazer, above n 28, 21; M Minow and ML Shanley, 'Relational Rights and Responsibilities: Revisioning the Family in Liberal Political Theory and Law', 11 *Hypatia* 4 at 13; W Galston, *Liberal Purposes: Goods, Virtues, and Diversity in the Liberal State* (New York, Cambridge University Press, 1991) 74; R Eckstein, 'Towards a Communitarian Theory of Responsibility: Bearing the Burden for the Unintended', 45 *University of Miami Law Review* 843 at 893–94.

[36] Gardbaum, above n 35, 701; S Benhabib, 'Autonomy, Modernity and Community: Communitarianism and Critical Social Theory in Dialogue' in Benhabib, above n 26; A Hutchinson and L Green, 'Introduction' in Hutchinson and Green, above n 35, 2; Okin, above n 26, 43; W Kymlicka, 'Liberalism and Communitarianism', 18 *Canadian Journal of Philosophy* 181 at 186; Frazer and Lacey, above n 25.

[37] Gardbaum, above n 33, 1351; N Rosenblum, 'Introduction' in Rosenblum, above n 25, 4; Okin, above n 26, 43; Friedman, above n 35, 67; Frazer and Lacey, above n 25; Sandel, above n 25, 186; P Weiss, 'Feminism and Communitarianism: Comparing Critiques of Liberalism' in Weiss and Friedman, above n 33, 178.

in legal theory,[38] perhaps also in almost every branch of intellectual life,[39] my doing so could be vainglorious. My aims in this book are rather twofold. First, I aim to show that the rise of post-liberalism in social theory profoundly influenced the development of Part II of the Family Law Bill; accordingly, I set out to explore the elements of post-liberal theory embodied in the Act, alongside the ways in which these elements found expression. Secondly, I aim to suggest that the tensions within post-liberalism formed at least part of the reason that Part II of the Family Law Act was ultimately abandoned; to this end, I examine these tensions and their impact on divorce law. Of course, in claiming that there are tensions within post-liberalism, I recognise that I am, to a limited extent, inevitably passing judgment on its theoretical merits. To summarise, the main contention of this book is that it is impossible to understand fully either the success in passing or the failure in implementing Part II of the Family Law Act without recognising the post-liberal dimension.

To suggest that there was a post-liberal dimension to the Family Law Act is, however, to state my argument in its least provocative form. More ambitiously, I believe that Part II of the Family Law Act is the most perfect example of post-liberal legislation to date. This also helps to explain why Part II of the Family Law Act crumbled when implementation was attempted: the tensions within post-liberal theory mattered more for the Family Law Act than for any other recent reform.

Few would dispute the general proposition, assumed in this book, that changes in law and social policy can be influenced by, but are not slavishly dictated by, changes in social theory. However, the complicating factor in the area of divorce law is that while the relevant social theory has been developed primarily by American academics, as will become apparent the social policy was espoused by such unlikely advocates of post-liberalism as bishops in the House of Lords! Two factors mitigate the improbability of this support for post-liberalism, the first pertaining to awareness of post-liberalism and the second to motivation for supporting post-liberalism. To begin with awareness of post-liberalism, while not all of the theorists to be discussed were familiar to the House of Lords in 1995 and 1996 when they were debating the Family Law Bill, it is indisputable that some were. Clearly, at the time there were (and still are) conduits of post-liberal theory whose life's work was to popularise

---

[38] Gardbaum, above n 35, 1350.
[39] Hekman, above n 33, 2.

the theory to policy-makers. Perhaps the best example is Amitai Etzioni, who, according to the following Guardian article in 1994:

> . . . after three years of touring like an evangelist . . . now influences the power elite. His articles appear in the New York Times, the Wall Street Journal and Time magazine. His book, The Spirit of Community, was recently spotted on Bill Clinton's desk. Housing secretary Henry Cisneros and White House domestic adviser William Galston have come out in favour of the communitarian agenda.[40]

It might be added that William Galston, who co-founded the communitarian movement with Etzioni, was himself a conduit, since he also straddled the line between theorist and policy adviser.[41] Nor was Etzioni's influence exclusive to the United States:

> Amitai Etzioni is no ordinary academic. His ideas are influencing Bill Clinton's domestic policies. European leaders are listening to him. Blair's speeches bear his imprint. Some Labour MPs believe Etzioni represents Labour's new Big Idea.[42]

It has been suggested that Etzioni started to influence thinking among Labour's modernisers around 1990, when his ideas struck a chord with both Tony Blair and Gordon Brown. The following account of the passage of ideas has been given:

> As a self-conscious political movement, communitarianism has its roots in the work of a small group of East Coast American academics—Michael Sandel, Michael Walzer and Alasdair MacIntyre are the essential names for the aficionado—who developed a critique of liberal individualism, its costs and limits. But it was Etzioni, a garrulous Washington sociologist, who popularised the new political philosophy.
>
> In Britain, it was seized on by Geoff Mulgan, trend-spotting director of the think tank Demos, who introduced Etzioni to Tony Blair and Gordon Brown. The pair are now true believers.[43]

Arguably, the popularity of communitarianism in particular was at its peak during the passage of the Family Law Bill through Parliament between 1995 and 1996.

[40] M D'Antonio, 'The Next Big Idea', *The Guardian*, 23 June 1994. See also M Walker, 'Community Spirit', *The Guardian*, 13 March 1995; Phillips, above n 28; Eekelaar, above n 29, 181.

[41] See Walker, above n 40.

[42] M Phillips, 'Father of Tony Blair's Big Idea', *The Observer,* 24 July 1994. See also Phillips, above n 28; Milne, above n 28; J Stacey, 'Families against "The Family": The transatlantic passage of the politics of family values', 89 *Radical Philosophy* 2 at 6.

[43] Milne, above n 28. See also Phillips, above n 42; Eekelaar, above n 29, 181.

Let us turn then to the motivation for supporting post-liberalism, bearing in mind that the Family Law Act was pioneered by the Conservative Party and recognising that much of the description above concerns the influence of post-liberalism on New Labour. The Family Law Act was, however, introduced by the Conservative Party at a stage at which it is universally acknowledged, not least by Conservatives, that the conservative agenda had run out of steam.[44] The Act was introduced into Parliament in 1995, five years after the demise of Thatcherism, and was given Royal Assent in 1996, only a year before the Conservative administration finally collapsed, to be replaced by a Labour Government. The fact that the Family Law Act does not bear the hallmarks of traditional conservatism, let alone Thatcherism, and is actually more akin to New Labour legislation post-1997, can be explained by its date. Introduced in a period in which the Conservative Party was flailing around for new ideas, it is less surprising that post-liberalism held some attraction:

> Similarly desperate for a new vision, they [the Tories] are also sniffing around this territory. Significantly, Etzioni commends not only Gordon Brown but also David Willetts, the MP and Tory thinker, as natural communitarians.[45] . . . Duty, responsibility and community are the fashionable buzz-words on everyone's lips. The Prime Minister claimed them yesterday as the essence of Tory thinking.[46]

Consistent with this interpretation, we will see in Chapter 5 that the post-liberal dimension of the Family Law Act was only reinforced by the 1997 change in administration.

The post-liberal dimension of the Act rests most crucially on the fact that the Act replaces a liberal conception of autonomy with a post-liberal conception of autonomy: Part II of the Family Law Act incorporated a post-liberal approach to autonomy. Accordingly, I begin in chapter one by examining the shift in the meaning of autonomy between liberalism and post-liberalism, alongside the implications of this shift for divorce law. More specifically, I first examine the reasons that post-liberal theory rejects the liberal conception of autonomy and then investigate the difficulties that this rejection poses for post-liberalism. In essence, because post-liberal theory is generally unable to manage without any conception of autonomy for reasons that will be

---

[44] See 'Brutish and Longer', *The Guardian*, 17 February 1999.
[45] Phillips, above n 42.
[46] Phillips, above n 28. See also Milne, above n 28.

discussed, rejecting the liberal model of autonomy creates perhaps the central problem for post-liberal theory, that is, to develop its own conception of autonomy.[47]

In chapter two, the solution to this problem becomes crucial to the argument, because I suggest that Part II of the Family Law Act incorporated a post-liberal conception of autonomy. Essentially, the solution lay in emphasising thought; I therefore examine the various ways in which Part II of the Family Law Act achieved this emphasis. We will discover in this chapter that the theoretical basis for the importance of thought is that self-discovery through reflection, or cognitive autonomy, represents both the predominant and the most coherent post-liberal conception of autonomy. Nevertheless, I consider two difficulties with this approach to autonomy. I conclude chapter two by suggesting that these difficulties can only be resolved if cognitive autonomy abandons its relativism, becoming normative in result as well as method.

In chapter three, I turn to a puzzle thrown up by chapters one and two, namely that while post-liberalism stresses above all else the social nature of the self, the emphasis on self-discovery creates a self who struggles to understand, let alone recognise, social purposes. Specifically, this makes it difficult for post-liberalism to retain the idea of marital obligation, and in chapter three I examine the route it takes to enable it to do so. In essence, the argument is that one's spouse is part of one's self, so that obligations to one's spouse are a species of self-interest and divorce akin to losing an aspect of oneself. The difficulty is that this leads to post-liberal ambivalence towards divorce, an ambivalence which I show was incorporated in Part II of the Family Law Act.

Post-liberal ambivalence towards divorce enables at least a strand of post-liberal thought to adopt a positive attitude to divorce. Chapter four develops this theme, so that by the end of chapter four I suggest that the moral divide is no longer between those who have divorced and those who have stayed married but rather between those who divorce well and those who divorce badly. More strongly put, those who divorce well may leave their marriage with positively enhanced moral standing. I reach this point by examining various themes, principally within civic-republicanism, which together imply the conclusion that post-liberal society must inculcate virtue into adults through education, and crucially that the

---

[47] See Williams, above n 35, 425; McClain, above n 35, 419; Hewitt, above n 35, 150.

virtue is procedural not substantive and the education an end not a means. I argue further in chapter four that these themes were transferred from civic-republicanism into Part II of the Family Law Act.

In this book I am arguing that post-liberalism is on the ascent, and that Part II of the Family Law Act was a post-liberal reform. This raises the question then why Part II has not been implemented, a question that I tackle in chapter five. It is well known that the reform was abandoned because the pilots of the information meetings were viewed as a failure; I argue that they were so viewed because the Government was adopting a post-liberal approach to information provision. Moreover, while the post-liberal dimensions of the Family Law Act explored in the other chapters were present from the inception of the Act, I suggest that the post-liberal approach to information was tacked on later. Accordingly, tensions within post-liberalism, specifically between the more and less coercive varieties, significantly contributed to the collapse of Part II of the Family Law Act.

In the final chapter I return to the starting-point with an examination of post-liberal responsibility, which I argue was the form of responsibility enshrined in Part II of the Family Law Act, and which I suggest develops out of cognitive autonomy. Consistently with the conclusion to chapter four, I suggest that for the first time ever it is possible to divorce responsibly and I examine what this entails. Following the cognitive approach to autonomy explored in chapter two, I argue that responsible divorce is partly based on thought and is wholly a procedural not a substantive achievement. I finish the book with an examination of the implications of post-liberal responsibility, both in relation to divorce law and more generally.

This book in general, and the next two chapters in particular, will be devoted to examining the ways in which Part II of the Family Law Act incorporated the post-liberal approach to autonomy, alongside the implications of the adoption of this approach. However, as a preliminary illustration, let us consider the following commonly observed tension in the Act. The tension is that Part II of the Family Law Act sought to pursue two objectives simultaneously; first, the de-legalisation of divorce, but secondly, behaviour modification, or the use of divorce law and procedure to ensure that divorcing couples were made to hon-

---

[48] J Dewar, 'The Normal Chaos of Family Law' 61 *Modern Law Review* 467 at 476. See also J Dewar, 'Family Law and Its Discontents' 14 *International Journal of Law, Policy and the Family* 59 at 79.

our their responsibilities to each other.[48] In other words, the Family Law Act embodied a belief that the law had a role to play in *pushing* divorcing parties towards settling matters themselves. It has been suggested that this could be viewed either as a form of regulation, in that the legal process was interposing obstacles before it would judge a dispute, or as a retreat from the regulatory role because the law was willing to give priority to the parties' own solutions.[49] In essence:

> ... the 1996 Act seeks both to give the parties greater autonomy while at the same time seeking to influence how they use it.[50]

From a liberal standpoint:

> In seeking to pursue simultaneously the objectives of behaviour modification and of party control or informalisation, the Act creates rich possibilities of potentially unworkable contradictions. This is partly because behaviour modification implies precisely a loss of party control or autonomy.[51]

Looking at the Act through liberal eyes, it is a paradox at best that an emphasis on party control was associated with a more interventionist divorce procedure.[52] However, by the end of this book I will have shown that this coupling makes perfect sense on a post-liberal reading: tempering party control with behaviour modification is almost a definition of the post-liberal approach to autonomy.

---

[49] J Eekelaar, *Regulating Divorce* (Oxford, Clarendon Press, 1991) 154.
[50] Dewar, above n 48, 476.
[51] *Ibid*, 477–78.
[52] *Ibid*, 477–78.

1

The Subject of Divorce

WHY HAS THE LIBERAL VIEW OF AUTONOMY BEEN REJECTED?

... I must emphasize that what the agent is able to say and do intelligibly as an actor is deeply affected by the fact that we are never more (and sometimes less) than the co-authors of our own narratives. Only in fantasy do we live what story we please. ... We enter upon a stage which we did not design and we find ourselves part of an action that was not of our making.[1] ... I can only answer the question 'What am I to do?' if I can answer the prior question 'Of what story or stories do I find myself a part?'[2]

ACCORDING TO LIBERALS, the concept of autonomy is (relatively) straightforward: people can and do make decisions. Indeed, in the liberal account, decision-making is an important aspect of what made people human: within liberalism, what is arguably most essential to the individual's identity is the individual's capacity to choose his or her own roles and identities, and to rethink those choices.[3] The human subject is a sovereign agent of choice, and clearly one such choice can be whether or not to divorce. However, post-liberal theory replaces the atomistic individual of liberal theory with a subject who is embedded in and constituted by context. The context varies with the version of

---

[1] A MacIntyre, *After Virtue: a study in moral theory* (London, Duckworth, 1985) 213.
[2] *Ibid*, 216.
[3] M Sandel, *Liberalism and the Limits of Justice* (Cambridge, Cambridge University Press, 1998); A Oldfield, *Citizenship and Community: Civic Republicanism and the Modern World* (London, Routledge, 1990); S Newman, 'Challenging the Liberal Individualist Tradition in America: "Community" as a Critical Ideal in Recent Political Theory' in A Hutchinson and L Green (eds), *Law and the Community: The End of Individualism?* (Toronto, Carswell, 1989); MC Regan, *Family Law and the Pursuit of Intimacy* (New York, New York University Press, 1993); C Berry, *The Idea of a Democratic Community* (Hemel Hempstead, Harvester Wheatsheaf, 1989); J Hewitt, *Dilemmas of the American Self* (Philadelphia, Temple University Press, 1989) especially 27; M Sandel, *Democracy's Discontent: America in Search of a Public Philosophy* (Cambridge, Massachusetts, Belknap Press, 1996) 12; D Phillips, *Looking Backward: A Critical Appraisal of Communitarian Thought* (Princeton, New Jersey, Princeton University Press, 1993) 182.

post-liberal theory, but is always an aspect of social relations.[4] The basis for the post-liberal challenge to autonomy is therefore that post-liberal theory rests on social constructionist foundations.[5] In particular, an emphasis on gender as social construction characterises most current feminist scholarship.[6] Within post-liberalism, the subject can no longer straightforwardly make a decision whether or not to divorce, because this decision depends in one way or another on the context in which he or she finds himself or herself.

Social construction must be distinguished from recognition of the social nature of man, which is 'too trite to count as an insight'.[7] Failure to do so 'foists upon liberals an implausible conception of autonomy.'[8] Liberal theory does not need to, and could not, maintain that the content of people's beliefs and attitudes are unaffected by social relations, which would be 'manifestly false, ignoring the most mundane facts of socialisation.'[9] When critics of liberalism attack a 'hopelessly naïve'[10] version of liberalism, liberals are justified in being dismissive.[11] However, it has been suggested that an unfortunate corollary of the naïve interpretation of liberalism is that liberals mistakenly suppose

---

[4] S Hekman, *Moral Voices, Moral Selves: Carol Gilligan and Feminist Moral Theory* (Cambridge, Polity, 1995) 2; P Weiss, 'Feminism and Community' in P Weiss and M Friedman (eds), *Feminism and Community* (Philadelphia, Temple University Press, 1995) 3; P Weiss, 'Feminism and Communitarianism: Comparing Critiques of Liberalism' in P Weiss and M Friedman (eds), *Feminism and Community* (Philadelphia, Temple University Press, 1995); E Frazer and N Lacey, *The Politics of Community: A Feminist Critique of the Liberal-Communitarian Debate* (Buffalo, New York, University of Toronto Press, 1994); A Gutmann, 'Communitarian Critics of Liberalism', 14 *Philosophy and Public Affairs* 308 at 308; A Etzioni, *The New Golden Rule: Community and Morality in a Democratic Society* (New York, Basic Books, 1998) 21.

[5] S Williams, 'A Feminist Reassessment of Civil Society', 72 *Indiana Law Journal* 417 at 427; E Frazer, *The Problems of Communitarian Politics: Unity and Conflict* (Oxford, Oxford University Press, 1999) 111.

[6] SM Okin, *Justice, Gender and the Family* (New York, Basic Books, 1989) 6.

[7] S Holmes, 'The Permanent Structure of Antiliberal Thought' in N Rosenblum (ed), *Liberalism and the Moral Life* (Cambridge, Mass, Harvard University Press, 1989) 231. See also S Holmes, 'The Ku Klux Klan are a Close-knit Bunch Too', *The Guardian*, 18 February 1995; S Holmes, 'The Community Trap', *The New Republic*, 28 November 1988, 26.

[8] S Caney, 'Liberalism and Communitarianism: A Misconceived Debate', 40 *Political Studies* 273 at 277.

[9] P Neal and D Paris, 'Liberalism and the Communitarian Critique: A Guide for the Perplexed', 23 *Canadian Journal of Political Science* 419 at 425. See also N Rosenblum, *Another Liberalism: Romanticism and the Reconstruction of Liberal Thought* (Cambridge, Massachusetts, Harvard University Press, 1987) 161; S Gardbaum, 'Liberalism, Autonomy and Moral Conflict', 48 *Stanford Law Review* 385 at 394.

[10] Neal and Paris, above n 9, 425.

[11] *Ibid*, 426.

that there is nothing more to the post-liberal critique than this mis-guided sociological objection. In fact, what post-liberals are attacking is the liberal idea that there must always remain a deep core of selfhood that defines the essential identity of the self, and that this deep core can never be reached by particular social relations, which are only ever contingent features.[12] Post-liberal theory holds the opposite to be the case, disputing the liberal disjuncture between the self and its ends. Examining the reasons that post-liberal theory fuses the self with its ends thereby disputing the liberal conception of selfhood forms a use-ful entry-point into an investigation of the reasons that post-liberalism rejects the liberal view of autonomy.

The Self Constituted By Its Ends

The argument that the self cannot be distinguished from its ends is most commonly associated with Michael Sandel. Sandel argues that the liberal emphasis on freedom of choice requires the liberal view of self-hood, in particular the priority of the self over ends because:

> The priority of the self over its ends means that I am not merely the passive receptacle of the accumulated aims, attributes, and purposes thrown up by experience, not simply a product of the vagaries of circumstances, but always, irreducibly, an active, willing agent, distinguishable from my sur-roundings and capacity of choice. To identify any set of characteristics as my aims, ambitions, desires, and so on, is always to imply some subject 'me' standing behind them, and the shape of this 'me' must be given prior to any of the ends or attributes I bear.[13]

However, Sandel believes that unless the subject's ends are part of its self, the self is empty. This point can be illustrated with respect to mar-riage and divorce. Construing the subject's relationship with his or her spouse as separate from the self may miss the role that it plays for those for whom the marital relationship is essential to their well-being and an irreducible part of their identity. These people are 'encumbered selves', claimed by duties they cannot choose to renounce.[14] More generally, Sandel argues that within the liberal conception of selfhood, the self becomes so distanced and dissociated from its ends that it becomes

---

[12] *Ibid*, 426.
[13] Sandel, *Liberalism*, above n 3, 19.
[14] *Ibid*, xii–xiii.

increasingly unclear in what sense the ends belong to the self.[15] Being free to question all the given limits of one's situation is self-defeating because if the chooser is sufficiently distanced from his or her choices to do so then he or she is lifeless and impoverished: there is simply nothing left of the subject:

> To imagine a person incapable of constitutive attachments . . . is not to conceive an ideally free and rational agent, but to imagine a person wholly without character, without moral depth.[16]

The roots of this argument lie in Charles Taylor's work. Taylor argues that we cannot answer the question, 'who am I?' without establishing which of our characteristics are of central importance to us, because these characteristics will be part of our identity. These properties so centrally touch that which we are that it is difficult, if not impossible, for us to repudiate them, because we would be repudiating our selves.[17] If our relationship with our spouse is essential to our identity then far from being a rational decision, either marrying or divorcing may represent self-denial, or even self-destruction.

Questioning the Internal/External Split

We can continue with Charles Taylor as an exemplar of perhaps the most common reason that post-liberals reject the liberal view of autonomy, namely a questioning of the internal/external split. Taylor argues that one of the most powerful motives behind the modern

---

[15] See also Hekman, above n 4, 50; W Kymlicka, 'Liberalism and Communitarianism', 18 *Canadian Journal of Philosophy* 181 at 186; W Galston, *Liberal Purposes: Goods, Virtues, and Diversity in the Liberal State* (New York, Cambridge University Press, 1991) 74.

[16] Sandel, *Liberalism*, above n 3, 179. See also M Sandel, 'Morality and the Liberal Ideal', *New Republic*, 7 May 1984, 15 at 17; S Benhabib, 'The Generalized and the Concrete Other: The Kohlberg-Gilligan Controversy and Moral Theory' in EF Kittay and D T Meyers (eds), *Women and Moral Theory* (Totowa, New Jersey, Rowman & Littlefield, 1987) 166; D Cornell, 'Institutionalization of Meaning, Recollective Imagination and The Potential for Transformative Legal Interpretation', 136 *University of Pennsylvania Law Review* 1135; R Beiner, *What's the Matter with Liberalism?* (Berkeley, California, University of California Press, 1992) especially 16; S Benhabib, 'Autonomy, Modernity and Community: Communitarianism and Critical Social Theory in Dialogue' in S Benhabib, *Situating the Self: Gender, Community and Postmodernism in Contemporary Ethics* (Cambridge, Polity, 1992); B Jordan, M Redley, S James, *Putting the Family First: Identities, Decisions, Citizenship* (London, UCL Press, 1994) 4.

[17] C Taylor, 'What is Human Agency?' in T Mischel (ed), *The Self: Psychological and Philosophical Issues* (Oxford, Blackwell, 1977) 124–25.

defence of freedom is the post-Romantic idea that each person's form of self-realisation is original. In other words, to be a person, the individual's life-plan, choices and sense of self must be attributable to the individual as their point of origin.[18] But if freedom includes something like the freedom of self-realisation then this form of freedom can plainly fail for inner reasons as well as external obstacles. Someone will not be free on a self-realisation view if he or she is totally unrealised. He or she will not be free if he or she is wholly unaware of his or her potential, or paralysed by the fear of breaking some social norm that he or she has internalised but which does not authentically reflect him or her:

> . . . where this happens, where, for example, we are quite self-deceived, or utterly fail to discriminate properly the ends we seek, or have lost self-control, we can quite easily be doing what we want in the sense of what we can identify as our wants, without being free; indeed, we can be further entrenching our unfreedom.[19]

Once we have adopted a self-realisation view, then being able to do what we want can no longer be accepted as a sufficient condition of being free, because you are 'not free if you are motivated through fear, inauthentically internalized standards, or false consciousness to thwart your self-realization.'[20] On this conception of freedom, we are only free if what we want is authentic. Some desires are experienced as fetters, as even not our own, because they incorporate an erroneous idea of what matters to us:

> A man who is driven by spite to jeopardise his most important relationships, in spite of himself, as it were, or who is prevented by unreasoning fear from taking up the career he truly wants, is not really made more free if one lifts the external obstacles to his venting his spite or acting on his fear. Or at best he is liberated into a very impoverished freedom.[21]

On this view inauthentic desires must dent our autonomy, because we could not otherwise explain such common human responses to decision-making as inner turmoil, emptiness or regret. So autonomy

---

[18] C Taylor, 'The Concept of a Person' in C Taylor, *Human Agency and Language: Philosophical Papers 1* (Cambridge, Cambridge University Press, 1985) 97.

[19] C Taylor, 'What's Wrong with Negative Liberty?' in C Taylor, *Philosophy and the Human Sciences: Philosophical Papers 2* (Cambridge, Cambridge University Press, 1985) 215.

[20] *Ibid*, 215–16.

[21] *Ibid*, 227.

must be more complex than the maximisation of desire satisfaction. People feel that they have acted unautonomously, not only when they have failed to achieve their aims but also, and more profoundly, when they feel that their lives are out of kilter with their selves. This indicates that the threat to autonomy is not merely external.[22] Nevertheless, the traditional notion of autonomy focuses on a distinction between action originating within the person and action in response to external forces. This notion breaks down if action from within is in some meaningful sense not the person's own.[23]

This point has been made even more forcefully. It has been argued that both communitarianism and liberalism seek to free us from constraints on our wills, but while liberalism sees the threat as coming from external forces, communitarianism sees the *principal* obstacles as emanating from inside ourselves.[24] For the post-liberal, it is no longer sufficient to establish whether the subject *wants* to divorce: instead, we need to discover whether divorce would help him or her to realise himself or herself, or whether remaining married would more authentically reflect him or her.

The Self Constituted By Oppression

Feminist critics of liberalism tend to regard these internal obstacles as even less benign than do communitarians: it would not be an exaggeration to say that many feminists see them as alien forces entering the self through the pathway of socialisation.[25] This is because feminists have long argued that male superiority is founded on differences between men and women that are caused at least partly by the different social experiences that they have.[26] Consequently, most feminists feel that they need to claim that at least some of women's desires are not truly autonomous, because they are the fruits of this social conditioning.[27] It

[22] DT Meyers, *Self, Society, and Personal Choice* (New York, Oxford, Columbia University Press, 1989).
[23] Williams, above n 5.
[24] B Frohnen, *The New Communitarians and the Crisis of Modern Liberalism* (Lawrence, University Press of Kansas, 1996) 161.
[25] See M Griffiths, *Feminisms and the Self: The Web of Identity* (London, New York, Routledge, 1995) 79.
[26] See P Weiss, 'Feminism and Communitarianism: Comparing Critiques of Liberalism' in Weiss and Friedman, above n 4, 165.
[27] Williams, above n 5. See also Berry, above n 3, 28–29.

would be hard to find a feminist theorist, even a liberal feminist, who did not minimally accept that the *exercise* of women's autonomy was impaired or impeded by their social position. But while a liberal feminist will see a female subject formed prior to experiencing oppression, a social constructionist feminist will accord at least a part played by oppression in shaping the female subject. One example is the belief that sustained exposure to dominant images shapes women's vision of themselves, by limiting their sense of their options through making some choices seem more plausible than others.[28]

Structuralist feminism allots the greatest formative role to oppression.[29] Most commonly associated with MacKinnon's work, structuralist feminism emphasises the pervasiveness of sexually associated domination in shaping both society's image of women and women's images of themselves:[30]

> Feminism . . . has grasped the completeness of the incursion into who one really becomes through growing up female in a male-dominated society. This effect can be understood as a distortion of the self . . . understanding women's conditions leads to the conclusion that women are damaged.[31]

It has been suggested that patriarchal oppression causes women to experience incoherence in reason and desire, rather than a unified active core self, because women internalise and value what they also reject, an example being the contradictory feelings that many women have toward romantic fiction.[32] The problem of developing a feminist perspective is exacerbated by the fact that theory and language are necessary to do so, both of which may be inherently masculine.[33]

Lesbian feminist theorists have provided similar accounts that differ mainly in identifying the predominant structure as heterosexualism not patriarchy. They argue that within the structure of heterosexualism, men dominate and deskill women in ways that vary from outright attack to paternalistic care, while women devalue female bonding and

---

[28] K Abrams, 'Title VII and the Complex Female Subject', 92 *Michigan Law Review* 2479 at 2530.

[29] See V Schultz, 'Room to Maneuver (f)or a Room of One's Own? Practice Theory and Feminist Practice', 14 *Law and Social Inquiry* 123 at 129.

[30] Abrams, above n 28; L McClain, ' "Irresponsible" Reproduction', 47 *Hastings Law Journal* 339 at 425.

[31] C MacKinnon, *Toward a Feminist Theory of the State* (Cambridge, Massachusetts, Harvard University Press, 1989) 103.

[32] Griffiths, above n 25, 77–78.

[33] *Ibid.*

value an ethos of dependence. Unsurprisingly, this structure undermines female agency and moral ability:

> . . . heterosexualism . . . is a particular economic, political, and emotional
> relationship between men and women: men must dominate and women
> must subordinate themselves to men . . .[34]

According to this standpoint, the function of traditional ethics is social
control, and the value at its heart that of dominance and subordination. Here too, oppression constructs rather than merely impedes
actions:

> Oppression functions, not just by those in power limiting our options . . .
> domination is totally successful when someone . . . internalizes those oppres-
> sive values, comes to believe those values are good and right – or even that
> they are fact (reality).[35]

This discussion raises the question of whether impaired autonomy is
seen as a generalised consequence of socialisation, or as a specific result
of occupying an inferior position within the social hierarchy. Many
feminist critiques focus exclusive attention on the impact on women or
other oppressed groups. For example, MacKinnon tells us that if the
damage done to women is accepted then 'women are in fact not full
people in the sense men are allowed to become.'[36] Other critiques
identify the problem as being that rationality and autonomy have been
defined in an exclusively masculine form, so that feminine counterparts
such as caring have been left out.[37] In these accounts, men's agency is
left intact and the liberal ideal of autonomy retained, but women are
denied this freedom.[38] Recent feminist theory tends more, though,
towards questioning the meaningfulness of the liberal model of autonomy for men as well as women.[39] It has been suggested that this is simply a matter of degree: women's autonomy is more limited and
precarious than men's as a result of their differential socialisation, but
men's autonomy is also problematic.[40] For people from powerful

---

[34] SL Hoagland, 'Why *Lesbian* Ethics?' in C Card (ed), *Adventures in Lesbian Philosophy* (Bloomington, Indiana University Press, 1994) 201.

[35] *Ibid*, 210. See also B Houston, 'In Praise of Blame' in Card, above n 34, 145.

[36] MacKinnon, above n 31, 103.

[37] Hekman, above n 4, 50; P Weiss, 'Feminism and Communitarianism: Comparing Critiques of Liberalism' in Weiss and Friedman, above n 4, 165; M Minow and ML Shanley, 'Relational Rights and Responsibilities: Revisioning the Family in Liberal Political Theory and Law', 11 *Hypatia* 4 at 13–14.

[38] Williams, above n 5.

[39] *Ibid*.

[40] Meyers, above n 22.

groups as well as marginalised groups, social imagery establishes their position in the hierarchy and shapes their opinions.[41]

If women's desires are the products of oppression then respecting a woman's decision to marry or divorce without further investigation becomes positively dangerous. Although historically, feminism has focused more on the pitfalls of marriage than divorce for women, we will see in chapter three that the fact that this view of the self makes the decision to divorce as questionable as the decision to marry has not escaped feminists' attention, particularly recently.

The Self Constituted By Community

In contrast to the last view, I turn now to a much more positive view of social influences on the self, in which autonomy is not only unattainable but also undesirable. This attack on liberal autonomy holds that liberalism relies on 'a notion of abstract and atomistic individualism deeply at odds with the constitutive role of communities in a person's identity.'[42] Here, the separate and independent individual envisaged by the liberal conception of autonomy is impossible if the most fundamental structures of identity are formed in relation to other people.[43] Instead, the creation of identity is viewed as collective, in that the individual can only exist through the various communities of which he or she is a member, and is continually constructed by those communities.[44] More strongly put, individuation does not proceed association, rather it is the kinds of associations that we have that define the kinds of individuals that we become.[45]

This reason to reject liberal autonomy is prominent within both communitarianism and feminism. In relation to communitarianism specifically, the idea that we cannot conceive of personhood without reference to the person's role as a citizen and participant in communal

---

[41] Abrams, above n 28, 2530.

[42] D Greschner, 'Feminist Concerns with the New Communitarians: We Don't Need Another Hero' in Hutchinson and Green, above n 3, 120. See also Hekman, above n 4, 50; A Etzioni, 'The Good Society', 7 *Journal of Political Philosophy* 88 at 94; P Weiss, 'Feminism and Community' in Weiss and Friedman, above n 4, 3; Neal and Paris, above n 9, 419.

[43] Williams, above n 5.

[44] Griffiths, above n 25, 92.

[45] S Benhabib, 'Autonomy, Modernity and Community: Communitarianism and Critical Social Theory in Dialogue' in Benhabib, above n 16, 71.

life can be regarded as one of the central communitarian claims about autonomy.[46] The conflict between communitarianism and liberalism arises because liberalism and communitarianism have different conceptions of shared relations: while liberalism envisages contingently shared relations, communitarianism endorses essentially shared relations. The former is a relationship between separate selves that may profoundly affect the content of the selves' beliefs but does not penetrate their identity. In contrast, the latter is constitutive of the selves' identities, so that it is meaningful to speak of two or more selves' becoming one, or even of one self's splitting.[47] This means much more than simply that humans will of course encounter each other; it means that there are no human beings in the absence of relations with others and the content of autonomy makes sense only in this context.[48] People acquire their identity through their relations with others in their communities, so that we discover who we are by examining our attachments to our communities.[49]

This criticism of liberal autonomy is perhaps most famously associated with Alasdair MacIntyre, who argues that because we are what we inherit, we find ourselves bearers of a tradition. The story of our life is always embedded in the story of the communities from which we derive our identity:

> I am someone's son or daughter, someone else's cousin or uncle; I am a citizen of this or that city, a member of this or that guild or profession; I belong to this clan, that tribe, this nation. Hence what is good for me has to be the good for one who inhabits these roles. As such, I inherit from the past of my family, my city, my tribe, my nation, a variety of debts, inheritances,

---

[46] S Gardbaum, 'Law, Politics and the Claims of Community', 90 *Michigan Law Review* 685 at 691. See also B Barber, *Strong Democracy: Participatory Politics for a New Age* (Berkeley, University of California Press, 1984); W Kymlicka, *Contemporary Political Philosophy: An Introduction* (Oxford, Oxford University Press, 1990) 199; Kymlicka, above n 15, 186; G Parry, 'Paths to Citizenship' in U Vogel and M Moran (eds), *The Frontiers of Citizenship* (Basingstoke, Macmillan, 1991); W Kymlicka, *Liberalism, Community, and Culture* (Oxford, New York, Clarendon Press, 1991) 1.

[47] Neal and Paris, above n 9. See also J Fudge, 'Community or Class: Political Communitarians and Workers' Democracy' in Hutchinson and Green, above n 3, 58; Berry, above n 3, 116.

[48] J Nedelsky, 'Reconceiving Autonomy: Sources, Thoughts and Possibilities' in Hutchinson and Green, above n 3.

[49] Sandel, *Liberalism*, above n 3, 63; D Greschner, 'Feminist Concerns with the New Communitarians: We Don't Need Another Hero' in Hutchinson and Green, above n 3, 134.

rightful expectations and obligations. These constitute the given of my life, my moral starting point. This is in part what gives my life its own moral particularity.[50]

These determinate characteristics are essential not accidental features of the person's identity, so that to lack a particular place in the pre-ordained social matrix is to lack a concrete sense of who you are.[51] It has been suggested that MacIntyre's account is a particularly strong version of the claim that the self is socially constituted, to the extent that there is no space left for the individual, because there is no content to the self outside of the roles assigned by custom and tradition.[52] A different interpretation is that while MacIntyre's subjects have a largely ascribed status, room is left for the individual because the roles that society provides for individuals are open to a range of definitions.[53]

Of course, MacIntyre's reliance on pre-modern communities has attracted voluminous criticism from feminists, since his society of tradition and static identities fosters élitism and covers up relations of domination, meaning that women in particular are provided with only one possible role, namely one in which reproduction and nurturing are central.[54] Some feminists have accordingly suggested that MacIntyre's communitarianism represents little improvement on liberalism.[55] Others have argued for broader identity-creating groups, so that an emphasis on family, neighbourhood and nation has been supplemented, and sometimes replaced, by one on sex, race or sexuality.[56] This leads to a related feminist argument that while the separate self may reflect the reality of men's lives, oppressed groups bound together through sub-cultures are more likely to experience their selves as inter-subjective.[57]

To turn to feminism in particular now, it has been argued that the rise of social constructionism has both been accelerated by and has

---

[50] MacIntyre, above n 1, 220.

[51] S Newman, 'Challenging the Liberal Individualist Tradition in America: 'Community' as a Critical Ideal in Recent Political Theory' in Hutchinson and Green, above n 3, 258.

[52] *Ibid*, 258.

[53] Hekman, above n 4, 54–56.

[54] *Ibid*, 60; Okin, above n 6; S M Okin, 'Humanist-Liberalism' in Rosenblum, above n 7, 48; Gutmann, above n 4, 309.

[55] Hekman, above n 4, 60.

[56] Weiss, 'Feminism and Communitarianism: Comparing Critiques of Liberalism' in Weiss and Friedman, above n 4, 165. See further ch 3.

[57] *Ibid*, 165.

accelerated the emphasis on the inter-subjective nature of women's sense of self.[58] Within feminism, it is perhaps Carol Gilligan who has articulated the most famous version of relational subject, which has been regarded as removing the very possibility of a self-legislating agent.[59] Some feminists have seen the relational subject as reflecting women's experiences of connection through motherhood.[60] On this view, women's lives are profoundly relational, because women physically transcend the individuation of the biological self through sharing a physical identity with their foetus and an emotional bond with their child.[61] A different version agrees that women are particularly enmeshed in relations that blur the boundaries between self and other, but attributes this to women's identities more generally as sisters, wives and friends, rather than simply as mothers.[62] Similarly to the view discussed above that the self is constituted by oppression, feminists differ on whether this concept of selfhood is exclusively concerned with women or whether there is no such thing as a separate self for anyone.[63]

If the subject is constituted by community then it becomes even more meaningless for him or her to claim that he or she has made the decision to divorce. The person's identity is constructed from relationships with others, and for the spouse, perhaps the most important identity-forming relationship is with his or her marital partner. Deciding to divorce therefore involves disentangling the halves of the self. This Herculean task can be viewed as either assisted or complicated by other identity-forming relationships with children, family and friends. The implications for divorce of the view that the self is formed in relation to others will be explored in detail in chapter three.

---

[58] Hekman, above n 4, 2–3; S Sherry, 'Civic Virtue and the Feminine Voice in Constitutional Adjudication', 72 *Virginia Law Review* 543 at 582.

[59] Carol Gilligan, *In a Different Voice: Psychological Theory and Women's Development* (Cambridge, Massachusetts, Harvard University Press, 1982). See also Hekman, above n 4, 2–3; Sherry, above n 58, 582.

[60] McClain, above n 30, 420.

[61] R West, 'The Difference in Women's Hedonic Lives: A Phenomenological Critique of Feminist Legal Theory' in MA Fineman and NS Thomadsen (eds), *At the Boundaries of Law: Feminism and Legal Theory* (New York, London, Routledge, 1991) 130.

[62] C Keller, *From a Broken Web: Separation, Sexism and the Self* (Boston, Beacon Press, 1986) 1–2.

[63] *Ibid*, 1–2.

Instrumental Communitarianism

There is an inconsistency that arises from the argument in the previous section. It is that even if we accept that the self is encumbered, it is illegitimate to move from the encumbered self to the self with the particular encumbrance of community values;[64] this move has been described as 'one of the central fallacies of communitarianism.'[65] Rather, it is more consistent to believe that if we are constituted by our communities then our characteristics will depend upon the nature of our community, and:

> [o]ne obvious implication of this principle would seem to be that liberal societies 'produce' liberal individuals, with liberal outlooks and values . . .[66]

On this view, individual identity depends significantly upon the values embedded in society, autonomy is a central value in our society, therefore '[i]n liberal societies, individuals choose their ends, but they canot be said to choose to choose them.'[67] To put it simply, we are programmed by liberal society to be (or believe that we are) autonomous.[68]

Post-liberal theorists respond to this inconsistency in three different ways. One way is to claim, as Sandel does, that the picture of the freely choosing individual is simply false: social relations are constitutive.[69] However, a second response is provided by *instrumental communitarians* who agree, and lament, that we are autonomous.[70] Indeed, it has been suggested that they despise autonomy precisely because its ascendance was a crucial historical factor in the decline of community life as

---

[64] Gardbaum, above n 46, 702; Rosenblum, 'Pluralism and Self-Defense' in Rosenblum, above n 7, 218; Kymlicka, above n 15, 188.

[65] Kymlicka, above n 15, 188.

[66] Gardbaum, above n 46, 703.

[67] *Ibid*, 703.

[68] S Holmes, 'The Permanent Structure of Antiliberal Thought' in Rosenblum, above n 7, 234. Conversely, Gardbaum makes the point that *choosing* to follow tradition or social norms does not violate the principles of liberalism: above n 9, 394.

[69] Sandel, *Liberalism*, above n 3. See also P Weiss, 'Feminism and Communitarianism: Comparing Critiques of Liberalism' in Weiss and Friedman, above n 4, 172.

[70] For discussion of instrumental communitarianism, see Gardbaum, above n 46, 703; Hekman, above n 4, 50; N Rosenblum, 'Pluralism and Self-Defense' in Rosenblum, above n 7, 219; Frazer and Lacey, above n 4, 108; L Hirshman, 'The Virtue of Liberality in American Communal Life' 88 *Michigan Law Review* 983 at 989; P Weiss, 'Feminism and Communitarianism: Comparing Critiques of Liberalism' in Weiss and Friedman, above n 4, 169; Berry, above n 3, 94; M D'Antonio, 'The Next Big Idea', *The Guardian*, 23 June 1994; Phillips, above n 3, 4.

the central identity-forming social practice.[71] On this view, liberal theory has an unfortunate but real impact on liberal society, so that the liberal concept of the subject reinforces the loneliness and alienation that characterises liberal society,[72] rewarding selfishness and fostering egoism.[73] Autonomy becomes descriptively correct but normatively regrettable.[74] The third response combines the previous two. A person's self-understanding affects his or her behaviour, so the belief that we are atomistic individuals will not make us into atomistic individuals but will make us behave as if we were. Liberal theory is thus simultaneously true and false. It both distorts our behaviour and denies us access to our true communal selves.[75]

This third response is perhaps the most common communitarian approach. Indeed, it has been suggested that a dominant theme of communitarian writings is the insensitivity of liberalism to the virtues and importance of our membership in a community and a culture.[76] It has also been argued that it is in part this aspect of communitarianism that has led to its resurgence in political theory, connecting as it does with contemporary fears about the disintegration and alienation of the modern world.[77] On this view, liberalism is identified with philistine impersonality by communitarians concerned with the frustration of romantic sentiment.[78] In practice, the influential communitarians, Amitai Etzioni and Robert Bellah, have adopted this approach.[79] Etzioni argues that communitarianism can serve as a corrective in societies in which individualism has gained too much ground since the 1960s.[80] Bellah argues that liberal ideology has propagated the myth

[71] Gardbaum, above n 46, 703.

[72] For discussion, see Hekman, above n 4, 50; N Rosenblum, 'Pluralism and Self-Defense' in Rosenblum, above n 7, 219; Hirshman, above n 70, 989.

[73] For discussion, see P Weiss, 'Feminism and Communitarianism: Comparing Critiques of Liberalism' in Weiss and Friedman, above n 4, 169; Berry, above n 3, 94; D'Antonio, above n 70.

[74] See Phillips, above n 3, 4; P Weiss, 'Feminism and Communitarianism: Comparing Critiques of Liberalism' in Weiss and Friedman, above n 4, 165.

[75] For discussion, see S Holmes, 'The Permanent Structure of Antiliberal Thought' in Rosenblum, above n 7, 234–35.

[76] Kymlicka, *Liberalism*, above n 46, 1. For criticism, see S Holmes, 'The Permanent Structure of Antiliberal Thought' in Rosenblum, above n 7; Holmes, The Community Trap, above n 7, 26.

[77] Frazer and Lacey, above n 4, 130. See also A Crawford, 'The Spirit of Community: Rights, Responsibilities, and the Communitarian Agenda', 23 *Journal of Law and Society* 247 at 249.

[78] Rosenblum, above n 9, 163.

[79] Etzioni, above n 4; R Bellah *et al*, *The Good Society* (New York, Knopf, 1991).

[80] Etzioni, above n 4, 40. See also D'Antonio, above n 70.

that individuals can be autonomous from social institutions, forgetting that autonomy depends for its existence on a social network to which individuals correspondingly have a moral duty to subordinate their autonomy. In elevating autonomy over other virtues such as responsibility and care that can only be exercised through social networks, autonomy becomes not meaningless but hollow, because the virtue in autonomy can only be realised alongside these more social virtues. Autonomy therefore makes sense but exacts a high moral and political price.[81] This point has been made more strongly:

> . . . without the 'thick' attachments provided by the kind of ethos that builds meaningful character, free choice between abstractly posited alternatives hardly seems worth the bother.[82]

We can see how common this response is by recognising that the implications that the response holds for divorce represent the prevalent communitarian attitude to divorce law. On this view, it is undeniable that people can and do (believe they can) choose to divorce, and make this choice in their hundreds of thousands, but whether or not they realise it at the time, they will suffer for it.

A final and opposite argument is that the main flaw in liberal autonomy is not theoretical but practical,[83] so that the liberal theoretical response has little bearing on the practical and political implications of the communitarian critique.[84] One version of this argument is that the individual in liberal society has little autonomy because control has been handed over to large-scale bureaucracies.[85] Another is that liberal autonomy is an élitist notion which may be possible for 'a few rare artists or intellectuals',[86] but is certainly not realistic for the populace who are 'simply socialized to given roles':[87]

---

[81] Bellah, above n 79, 12 and 50.

[82] R Beiner, 'What's the Matter with Liberalism?' in Hutchinson and Green, above n 3, 55.

[83] U Beck and E Beck-Gernsheim, *The Normal Chaos of Love* (Cambridge, Polity Press, 1995) 41.

[84] D Greschner, 'Feminist Concerns with the New Communitarians: We Don't Need Another Hero' in Hutchinson and Green, above n 3, 140.

[85] See Neal and Paris, above n 9, 436.

[86] Ronald Beiner, *What's the Matter with Liberalism?* (Berkeley, University of California Press, 1992) 43.

[87] *Ibid*, 43.

My suspicion is that the actual substance of autonomy and diversity in liberal society is in inverse ratio to the vigor and enthusiasm with which liberals celebrate it.[88]

While less prevalent, this approach is also apparent in attitudes to divorce, particularly in the argument that the children of divorcees are 'programmed' to enter marriages which will fail.

THE POST-LIBERAL PROBLEM OF AUTONOMY

I have reviewed the principal reasons that post-liberalism rejects the liberal view of autonomy and briefly highlighted the implications each one holds for interpreting the spouse's decision to divorce. Post-liberal theory is thus faced with two options, either to develop a different conception of autonomy or to abandon the whole concept. We can appreciate that resolving this dilemma is particularly critical when we realise that there is a strand of post-liberal theory that holds that choice has become *both* more problematic *and* more obligatory. The individual is confronted with an increasingly complex diversity of choices, almost unaided.[89] We will see throughout this book that post-liberalism generally chooses the former option, and we will discover the consequences that this holds for divorce law. But in this section, I examine why post-liberalism rarely chooses the latter route.

To begin with feminism, it has been argued that structuralist feminism does dispense entirely with the ideal of autonomy.[90] Even here however, a strategic element has been postulated, namely that it is in

---

[88]   Beiner, above n 86, 43.

[89]   A Giddens, *Modernity and Self-Identity: Self and Society in the Late Modern Age* (Cambridge, Polity Press, 1991) 80; A Giddens, 'Living in a Post-Traditional Society' in U Beck, A Giddens and S Lash, *Reflexive Modernization: Politics, Tradition and Aesthetics in the Modern Social Order* (Cambridge, Polity Press, 1994) 77; Beck and Beck-Gernsheim, above n 83; J Rodger, *Family Life and Social Control: A Sociological Perspective* (Basingstoke, Macmillan, 1996) 85; J Nolan, *The Therapeutic State: Justifying Government at Century's End* (New York, New York University Press, 1998) 4.

[90]   S Benhabib, 'Autonomy, Modernity and Community: Communitarianism and Critical Social Theory in Dialogue' in Benhabib, above n 16, 196; McClain, above n 30, 425 and 427; D Cornell, *The Imaginary Domain: Abortion, Pornography and Sexual Harassment* (New York, Routledge, 1995) 144. For examples, see C Card, 'The Feistiness of Feminism' in C Card (ed), *Feminist Ethics* (Lawrence, Kansas, University Press of Kansas, 1991) 25; J Singer, 'The Privatization of Family Law', 71 *Wisconsin Law Review* 1443 at 1538.

order to confront the hegemony of the liberal version that structuralist feminism emphasises the systematic character of constraint, re-interpreting even those choices subjectively experienced as free as really the product of oppression.[91] Undoubtedly, most feminists feel that they cannot afford to give up autonomy completely. If feminism loses the potential for individuals to move beyond their social conditioning, feminism renders itself impossible in a sexist society, in two senses. First, feminism would be an epistemological impossibility because people shaped by traditional society could never come to hold feminist beliefs.[92] Secondly, feminism would be a political impossibility because there would be no notion of resistance or social change.[93] This makes a nonsense out of feminism, because feminists' central concern is arguably to free women from the definition of themselves given by men and male-dominated society so that they may shape their own lives and identities.[94] Moreover, on a personal level, it has been argued that the view of women as hapless victims of social conditioning reduces women's complex identities to one aspect of their experience and excludes women who see themselves as social actors.[95] There are also positive reasons to re-interpret autonomy. For example, it has been argued that giving strength back to the concept of autonomy on one level threatens feminism, since it makes it possible to recognise consent in relations of domination, but on another level it is liberating because it allows women's creativity and joy to be celebrated.[96]

> The problem, of course, is how to combine the claim of the constitutiveness of social relations with the value of self-determination.[97]

According to Nedelsky, because liberalism has been the source of our language of freedom and self-determination, the values of freedom and self-determination are embedded in a theory that denies the centrality

[91] Abrams, above n 28.

[92] Williams, above n 5; Schultz, above n 29, 129.

[93] Williams, above n 5; Schultz, above n 29, 129; Christopher Berry, above n 3, 28–30.

[94] Williams, above n 5; J Nedelsky, 'Reconceiving Autonomy: Sources, Thoughts and Possibilities' in Hutchinson and Green, above n 3, 221; S Benhabib and D Cornell, 'Beyond the Politics of Gender' in S Benhabib and D Cornell (eds), *Feminism as Critique: Essays on the Politics of Gender in Late-Capitalist Societies* (Cambridge, Polity, 1987) 12; Phillips, above n 3, 181.

[95] Williams, above n 5; M Minow, 'Surviving Victim Talk', 40 *UCLA Law Review* 1411 at 1432.

[96] A Harris, 'Race and Essentialism in Feminist Legal Theory', 42 *Stanford Law Review* 581 at 614.

[97] J Nedelsky, 'Reconceiving Autonomy: Sources, Thoughts and Possibilities' in Hutchinson and Green, above n 3, 221.

of relationships in constituting the self.[98] But the values themselves cannot be lost.[99] Feminists have argued that autonomy remains a valuable liberal accomplishment of the Enlightenment, explaining the revolutionary potential of liberalism.[100] A central dilemma in feminist work is therefore to articulate a non-liberal conception of agency and responsibility.[101] Feminists believe that they need their own language of freedom in order to express feminist concern with self-direction.[102] Feminism:

> . . . must develop a model of personhood that includes some capacity to redefine ourselves and make self-conscious change in the oppressive conditions that have shaped us.[103] . . . Feminism requires a new conception of autonomy. . . . The basic value of autonomy is, however, central to feminism. Feminist theory must retain the value, while rejecting its liberal incarnation.[104]

To turn to communitarianism, it has been suggested that ultimately there is no communitarian or feminist prepared to abandon autonomy because we all share a deep attachment to freedom, and freedom is only meaningful if coupled with the capacity for self-determination.[105] However, some feminists see the need for transformative potential as more important within feminism than communitarianism: communitarians 'may become either complacent or resigned, but feminists cannot afford to adopt either of these positions.'[106] It is true that communitarian theorists come closest to abandoning autonomy altogether.[107] Occasionally this occurs explicitly; for example, Ronald

---

[98] J Nedelsky, 'Reconceiving Autonomy: Sources, Thoughts and Possibilities' in Hutchinson and Green, above n 3, 221.

[99] *Ibid*; D Greschner, 'Feminist Concerns with the New Communitarians: We Don't Need Another Hero' in Hutchinson and Green, above n 3, 140; McClain, above n 30, 432.

[100] D Greschner, 'Feminist Concerns with the New Communitarians: We Don't Need Another Hero' in Hutchinson and Green, above n 3, 140.

[101] McClain, above n 30, 432; Giddens, above n 89, 216.

[102] J Nedelsky, 'Reconceiving Autonomy: Sources, Thoughts and Possibilities' in Hutchinson and Green, above n 3.

[103] Williams, above n 5, 429.

[104] J Nedelsky, 'Reconceiving Autonomy: Sources, Thoughts and Possibilities' in Hutchinson and Green, above n 3, 221.

[105] *Ibid*, 221; Berry, above n 3, 94.

[106] Williams, above n 5, 428. See also Griffiths, above n 25, 79; Frazer and Lacey, above n 4, 141; S Benhabib and D Cornell, 'Beyond the Politics of Gender' in Benhabib and Cornell, above n 94, 13; P Weiss, 'Feminism and Communitarianism: Comparing Critiques of Liberalism' in Weiss and Friedman, above n 4; M Friedman, *What are Friends For?: Feminist Perspectives on Personal Relationships and Moral Theory* (Ithaca, New York, Cornell University Press, 1993) 63.

[107] See Cornell, above n 16, 1139.

Beiner tells us that 'liberals are wrong because we are not essentially choosers, autonomous agents, or framers of our own individual destiny.'[108] Sometimes the complete absence of autonomy is implicit, in that the theory does not allow for dissent; for example, feminists accuse MacIntyre in particular of preserving the unity of the subject by evoking a pre-modern world of homogeneity and coherence and suppressing all diversity.[109]

Nevertheless, other communitarian theorists, such as Sandel, evince concern about abandoning autonomy.[110] When Sandel replaces the unencumbered self, whose personhood is antecedent to particular ties or attachments, with a self who is constituted by its choices he worries that this self could become a 'radically situated subject'. Because such a subject would be fully constituted by his or her attributes, the distance between subject and situation would completely collapse. Sandel sees a need to recover and preserve a space between the self and its ends, because without this space, *any* change in the person's situation, however slight, would change the person. Taken literally, given that the situation changes all the time, this would mean that identity would blur indistinguishably into situation:

> Crowded by the claims and pressures of various possible purposes and ends, all impinging indiscriminately on my identity, I am unable to sort them out, unable to mark out the limits or the boundaries of my self, incapable of saying where my identity ends and the world of attributes, aims, and desires begins. I am disempowered in the sense of lacking any clear grip on who, in particular, I am. Too much is essential to my identity. Where the ends are given prior to the self they constitute, the bounds of the subject are open, its identity infinitely accommodating and ultimately fluid. Unable to distinguish what is mine from what is me, I am in constant danger of drowning in a sea of human circumstance.[111]

So the simple response to rejecting the liberal view of autonomy, namely to abandon autonomy altogether, is discarded in favour of the attempt to develop a post-liberal conception of autonomy: the decision to divorce must mean *something*. But the question is whether there can be a social constructionist conception of autonomy:

[108] R Beiner, 'What's the Matter with Liberalism?' in Hutchinson and Green, above n 3, 51.

[109] See Frazer and Lacey, above n 4, 155.

[110] Sandel, *Liberalism*, above n 3. See also A Buchanan, 'Assessing the Communitarian Critique of Liberalism', 99 *Ethics* 852 at 871.

[111] Sandel, *Liberalism*, above n 3, 57–58. See also Regan, above n 3; R Unger, *Knowledge and Politics* (New York, Free Press, 1975) 204; Berry, above n 3, 102.

To acknowledge the profound impact of socialization continuing from infancy into adulthood is to raise the question of whether people have any traits, beliefs, or capabilities that can be called their own and, therefore, whether the direction of their lives is not merely an outcropping of acculturation.[112] . . . if people are products of their environments, it seems fatuous to maintain that the agency of individuals has any special importance, for personal choice dissolves into social influence.[113] . . . This move toward a socially constructed conception of the self undermines the internal / external distinction on which the traditional notion of autonomy rests. If sources of action that appear to be (and are experienced as) internal were in fact externally generated, it is difficult to see why we should regard them as privileged or especially valuable or a form of freedom at all. . . . In other words, in a world characterized by social construction, autonomy – understood in this way – becomes both incoherent and irrelevant.[114]

A COERCIVE SOLUTION

There is a way to develop a post-liberal conception of autonomy, and that is to retain social constructionism but to abandon relativism.[115] For most feminist and communitarian theorists, social constructionism entails some version of relativism, meaning that at least explicitly there is no true autonomy, except possibly from within the self.[116] In contrast, on the view to be explored now, our decisions are socially constructed and therefore not genuine, but there is a truly autonomous decision that we could make, which plainly cannot come from within. The advantage of this solution is that it is coherent, but the drawback is that its consequences are straightforwardly coercive, and this brings post-liberalism back too close for comfort to conservatism for most communitarians and feminists. But it is perhaps because communitarianism has a slightly freer hand, given feminism's concern with women's liberation, that this solution, while clearly present within strands of feminism, is most commonly espoused within the civic republican strand of communitarianism.[117]

[112] Meyers, above n 22, 25.

[113] *Ibid*, 26.

[114] Williams, above n 5, 427. See also Frazer and Lacey, above n 4; Phillips, above n 3, 181; Rosenblum, above n 9, 163.

[115] See S Gey, 'The Unfortunate Revival of Civic Republicanism', 141 *University of Pennsylvania Law Review* 801.

[116] See further ch 2.

[117] See C R Sunstein, *Free Markets and Social Justice* (New York, Oxford, Oxford University Press, 1997); C R Sunstein, 'Preferences and Politics', 20 *Philosophy and*

Civic republicans share the belief that our decisions are socially constructed. 'Choices are a function of context,'[118] the context being social norms, our particular social role and the social and expressive meaning of acts. People's conception of the right actions to take, and even of their own self-interest, is a function of their particular social position. When social norms do not appear to be present, this is only because they are so deeply internalised as to seem natural. Therefore it is hard to know what people want, because their judgements are entangled with norms, meanings and roles that are not chosen but (within limits) imposed.[119] To make these ideas concrete:

> People are socially constituted and continually penetrated by culture, by social and moral influences, and by one another. Businesses advertise products in ways that motivational research has shown will appeal to their customers' infantile and impulsive urges. The youth culture promotes risky, irrational behavior. Social bonds tug at people unconsciously. In short, the choices made by individuals are not free from cultural and social factors.[120]

In order to understand people's behaviour better, we have to look behind choices to preferences, which are internal mental states. But social construction cannot be escaped in this way. Preferences are extraordinarily complex, because they are determined by:

> . . . an unruly amalgam of things – aspirations, tastes, physical states, responses to existing roles and norms, values, judgments, emotions, drives, beliefs, whims.[121]

The interaction of these forces produces particular outcomes depending on the context. Preferences are neither fixed nor stable.[122] Therefore preferences as well as choices are constructed by social situations[123] and may be products of:

Public Affairs 3; CR Sunstein, 'Legal Interference with Private Preferences', 53 *University of Chicago Law Review* 1129; M Galston, 'Taking Aristotle Seriously: Republican-Oriented Legal Theory and the Moral Foundation of Deliberative Democracy', 82 *California Law Review* 331.

[118] Sunstein, *Free Markets*, above n 117, 6.
[119] *Ibid.*
[120] Etzioni, above n 4, 21.
[121] Sunstein, *Free Markets*, above n 117, 38.
[122] *Ibid.*
[123] Sunstein, 'Preferences', above n 117, 5.

... such things as biology, inaccurate appraisals of available possibilities, or a socialization process that assumes the legitimacy of the existing, and often questionable, status quo.[124]

It is not possible to rescue autonomy from social norms by imagining what people would do in a state of nature because any state of nature would include its own prevailing norms.[125]

Crucially, certain norms are objectively autonomy-diminishing. In some cases this will be because they compromise autonomy itself, for example, norms discouraging people from educating themselves or exposing themselves to diverse conceptions of the good, often by stigmatising education or diversity. These norms prevent people from:

... giving critical scrutiny to their own conceptions, in such a way as to make it impossible for them to be, in any sense, masters of the narratives of their own lives.[126]

Therefore autonomy is more fundamental in preference formation than in preference satisfaction.[127] The view that freedom involves an opportunity to choose among options is supplemented by the view that people should not be constrained in the free development of their preferences and beliefs.[128]

However, in other cases autonomy diminishing norms are substantive not procedural. The clearest example is when preferences are produced by past acts of consumption, in other words addiction, but the point is much broader. For example, both myopic behaviour, where minor short-term benefits of an activity eclipse major long-term costs,[129] and weakness of will diminish autonomy:[130]

Unjust institutions can breed preferences that produce individual and collective harm. Severe deprivation – including poverty – can be an obstacle to the development of good preferences, choices and beliefs. For example, a society in which people 'prefer' to become drug addicts, or violent criminals has a serious problem. Such preferences are likely to be an artifact of existing social norms, and those norms may disserve human freedom or well-being.[131]

[124] Galston, above n 117, 348.
[125] Sunstein, *Free Markets*, above n 117.
[126] *Ibid*, 59.
[127] Sunstein, 'Preferences', above n 117, 12.
[128] *Ibid*, 13.
[129] On this point see also R Goodin, 'Permissible Paternalism: In Defence of the Nanny State' in A Etzioni (ed), *The Essential Communitarian Reader* (Lanham, Rowman & Littlefield, 1998) 117.
[130] Sunstein, 'Preferences', above n 117, 26.
[131] Sunstein, *Free Markets*, above n 117, 5.

Civic republicans believe that where these norms are in operation the choices and preferences resting on them will not necessarily be connected with human well-being, 'even if there is neither force nor fraud, and whether or not there is "harm to others".'[132] The resulting choices and preferences are not genuinely autonomous. In essence:

> The only way toward an account of individual rationality, or rational self-interest, that is separate from social norms is through an inquiry that is frankly normative and defended as such. Such an account must include an understanding of what people's ends *should* be.[133]

On this view, there are truly autonomous choices and decisions;[134] there is a difference between actual interests and interests as subjectively perceived,[135] because the latter may be the product of some kind of cognitive distortion.[136] Taylor recognises that his argument that there can be internal as well as external obstacles to freedom lends itself to autonomy stemming from outside the person. The subject cannot be the final arbiter on the question whether he or she is free, because he or she may be profoundly mistaken about his or her purposes.[137] But he leaves it to others to draw out the most sinister implications of his argument:

> We are purposive in that we have goals whose attainment seems desirable and attainable – in some measure, anyway – through our striving. And freedom is valuable because it permits us to pursue our good.
>
> But, *ex hypothesi*, the real good and the apparent good are not identical. Negative freedom allows us to pursue the apparent good even at the cost of losing the real good. But the real good is what we really want. It is the goal we would pursue if we had full intellectual clarity and emotional receptivity.[138]

Miriam Galston reaches a similar result by returning to the Aristotelian routes of civic republicanism.[139] Beginning with the apparent tension between the civic republican views that man is virtuous by nature and that virtue demands sacrifice, she argues that the tension can be resolved by examining what Aristotle meant by man's nature. While in popular usage, 'nature' or 'natural' refers to something spontaneous

---

[132] *Ibid*, 36.
[133] *Ibid*, 54.
[134] *Ibid*.
[135] Galston, above n 117.
[136] Sunstein, *Free Markets*, above n 117.
[137] Taylor, above n 19, 216.
[138] Galston, above n 15, 86.
[139] Galston, above n 117.

that does not have to be worked at, Aristotle uses 'nature' as a term of art. To Aristotle, a thing's nature is the thing when its being has completely unfolded – its end, in the sense of best state. So a person is fulfilling his or her nature when his or her existence is perfected. The dichotomy between the popular usage of nature and nature as a term of art parallels the distinction between what a person pursues spontaneously and the ideal state that a person must first correctly identify and then actively nurture. In simpler terms, the distinction is between nature as a descriptive and normative concept. Our natures (in the Aristotelian sense) are not natural (in the popular sense) in two distinct respects: first, we must positively work towards our best state; secondly, we must fight against countervailing impulses and appetites.[140] The distinction between the interpretations of nature accords with the distinction between preferences and interests, which is a predominant theme in civic republicanism. Preferences describe people's spontaneous desires while interests refer to desires that have been subjected to a critical process. Accordingly, civic republican theorists should favour interests over preferences as a normative measure for evaluating individual choices. The conclusion is that an individual has an interest in, among other things, the non-satisfaction of preferences that are antithetical to his or her interests. The original tension is resolved, because virtue only requires sacrifice of our well-being while we misconceive what our well-being requires. There are two consecutive purposes to the sacrifice of restraining spontaneous desires: first, in order to discover one's nature and secondly, to implement the discovery. But the reward is assured: sacrifice may be necessary for the initial attainment of civic virtue, but not for its ultimate exercise.[141]

There is a strong teleological strand to MacIntyre's theorising as well. Within his theory, it is fixed social identity that supplies a sense of purpose. To know oneself as a member of the community is to accept life as a journey with set goals, moving toward a given end. In contrast, the modern liberal self has lost its traditional boundaries and therefore its sense of direction, having no alternative standard to guide the self's development.[142]

---

[140] For discussion of this point, see P Weiss, 'Feminism and Communitarianism: Comparing Critiques of Liberalism' in Weiss and Friedman, above n 4, 168.

[141] Galston, above n 117.

[142] MacIntyre, above n 1. See S Newman, 'Challenging the Liberal Individualist Tradition in America: "Community" as a Critical Ideal in Recent Political Theory' in Hutchinson and Green, above n 3, 258–59.

Although less prominent, it would be wrong not to recognise that this more authoritarian strain exists within feminism as well. It is perhaps most prominent in structuralist feminism, because:

> MacKinnon depicts women's purportedly unencumbered choices as ideologically infused acts which contribute to their own subordination, and suggests that women's perceptions of their experiences are less reliable than her own.[143]

Therefore the only hope for the exercise of agency is that 'by radical enlightenment they are somehow empowered to act for themselves.'[144] This more coercive tone is present in other strands of feminism apart from structuralist feminism. For example, Jana Singer in her examination of family-related choices argues that there is no necessary link between expanding choice and enhancing autonomy, because people may consent to family arrangements that neither foster autonomy nor improve well-being out of deference to authority or a sense of social obligation. Furthermore, she casts doubt on whether preferences and choices can be said to exist independently of either the legal system or prevailing gender structures.[145]

The problem here for feminism is of course that this leads feminism back to the objectivity that it has rejected. When a feminist scholar argues that her explanations of a woman's choices should be categorically preferred to the woman's own, the argument appeals to the idea of unsituated knowledge that feminism has decried.[146] Other feminists have accordingly set their faces against this more authoritarian strand of feminism, arguing for the freedom for women to claim themselves as the self-authenticating source of what the good life is for them:[147]

> No one woman should be allowed to say that her symbolic translation is the only authentic one. We want contest and struggle, as well as joy and celebration, as we engage with one another to find our own language.[148]

So to return to civic republicanism as the principal residence of this solution, if there is true autonomy to which some norms pose an obstacle, the question becomes how to achieve true autonomy.[149] The ideal

---

[143] K Abrams, 'Ideology and Women's Choices', 24 *Georgia Law Review* 761 at 765.
[144] Harris, above n 96, 613.
[145] Singer, above n 90, 1539.
[146] Abrams, above n 143, 770. See also Gey, above n 115, 810.
[147] D Cornell, *At the Heart of Freedom: Feminism, Sex and Equality* (Princeton, New Jersey, Princeton University Press, 1998) 37.
[148] Cornell, above n 90, 145.
[149] Sunstein, *Free Markets*, above n 117.

solution is to change the norms.[150] This can sometimes be achieved because socially constructed choices are seen as fragile and therefore malleable, since they depend on social norms to which people do not have deep allegiance and which they may actually deplore. The next question is who can change the norms. There are three possibilities, of which the first is the individual. However, despite the strong antipathy that individuals may hold towards the norms, civic republicanism, here resembling structuralist feminism, tends to regard the norms which shape people's choices as 'set by forces that are emphatically human but that are largely outside of the control of the individual agent'.[151] This is partly because people cannot help indulging in myopic behaviour. The second possibility is dissident groups. When norms are socially contested, this can lead to the formation of diverse norm communities, such as religious organisations or feminist groups, so that people who are dissatisfied with the prevailing norms can enter a different and more congenial norm community. But this is not a complete solution because the social construction of choices runs too deep: the dissident community may seem unthinkable or may be too costly for someone raised in the dominant community; it may also be merely reactive to or even defined by the dominant norm community. Sometimes, the dominant norms are too damaging to human wellbeing to leave their overthrow to dissident communities. The third and most satisfactory solution therefore lies in a collective response stemming from government to change the norms.

'Under this view, private preferences are, by virtue of their status as such, entitled at most to presumptive respect.'[152] If changing the norms proves too cumbersome then there is an easier solution. The constructed nature of our preferences casts doubt on the notion that government ought generally to respect private desires and beliefs:[153]

> To invade negative freedom in the name of the real good is to promote the individual's benefit over his or her harm, rationality over irrationality, truth over error.[154]

---

[150] On this point, see also Etzioni, above n 42, 93–94.
[151] Sunstein, *Free Markets*, above n 117, 50.
[152] Sunstein, 'Legal Interference', above n 117, 1133.
[153] For discussion, see Gey, above n 115, 823; K Abrams, 'Kitsch and Community', 84 *Michigan Law Review* 941 at 953; Frohnen, above n 24, 11; Unger, above n 111, 278.
[154] Galston, above n 15, 86.

The case for paternalism is that public officials might better respect a person's preferences than the person would have done through his or her own actions. The blow is softened slightly by the suggestion that when paternalistic action is justified as being in the person's interest, we should look for a warrant within the person's own value system. Even so, paternalistic action is justified whenever the state is not convinced that a person is acting on preferences that are relevant, settled, preferred, and his or her own:[155]

> Individual choice is important both as a manifestation of individuality and as a sign of the species nature, a nature never fully represented by any set of shared values. But one may be mistaken about mankind or about oneself, choose wrongly, and thus become less rather than more free: value, though revealed by choice, always transcends it.[156]

The implications of civic republicanism for divorce law are straightforward. Rather than the communitarian or feminist approach of attempting to ensure that the decision to divorce is authentic, civic republicanism feels comfortable with substituting what it views as the right decision. In later chapters, particularly chapter five, I will argue that while initially Part II of the Family Law Act incorporated a gentle communitarian or feminist approach, a more coercive civic republican approach was added later, and that the tension between these approaches contributed significantly to the collapse of the scheme.

THE POST-LIBERAL PULL

Before I turn to an examination of post-liberal attempts to develop a conception of autonomy, I should examine one complicating factor in exposing the post-liberal dimension of the Family Law Act, which also demonstrates the extent to which the liberal critique has fallen from favour. This is that it is rare to find a liberal theorist who has not given some ground to post-liberalism. Often, the ground-giving takes the form of denying any discrepancy:

> It is odd that the argument often involves claims, particularly by liberals, that there is no real dispute at all; liberalism, it is argued, is perfectly consistent

---

[155] R Goodin, 'Permissible Paternalism: In Defence of the Nanny State' in Etzioni, above n 129, 116–17.

[156] Unger, above n 111, 278.

with the communitarian critique and can readily accept it. This kind of accommodation is an odd response to criticisms which are offered as crucial and even paradigmatic.[157]

For example, from the liberal perspective comes the argument that where critics of liberalism go wrong is not in their concerns, but in failing to appreciate that their concerns can be addressed within the terms of the liberal tradition. On this view, liberalism can be a theory of citizenship as well as individualism and a theory about the interdependence of people as well as their separateness. These amendments are 'an initial step toward a liberalism more complete, sufficient, and coherent than what has been previously available.'[158]

A common area for concessions is in respect of relationships. For example, communitarianism is viewed not as a fundamental challenge to liberalism but rather as a corrective that can remind us of the importance of relationship, association and community in preserving the communal ties that make liberal society possible. On this view, there is much that liberals can gain from the communitarian critique: while liberalism should reject coercive imposition of communitarian norms, it should not remain neutral as to their social value but should adopt a 'soft communitarian perspective'.[159]

The theorist who has been most successful in bridging the gap between liberalism and communitarianism is probably Will Kymlicka,[160] whose liberalism has been described as 'quasi-communitarian liberal pluralism'[161] and has prompted the concession that it would satisfy all the radical aspirations of communitarians and feminists.[162] Kymlicka admits that liberal social science has often been sociologically naïve compared with, for example, feminist gender-analysis.[163] In relation to four principal communitarian claims, he argues that we can distinguish a stronger and a weaker version. The

---

[157] Neal and Paris, above n 9, 421.

[158] A Damico, 'Introduction' in A Damico (ed), *Liberals on Liberalism* (Totowa, New Jersey, Rowman & Littlefield, 1986) 2. See also J Reiman, 'Liberalism and its Critics' in C F Delaney (ed), *The Liberalism-Communitarianism Debate: Liberty and Community Values* (Lanham, Rowman & Littlefield, 1994).

[159] B Woodhouse, '"It All Depends on What You Mean By Home": Toward a Communitarian Theory of the "Nontraditional" Family', 1996 *Utah Law Review* 569 at 586. See also Caney, above n 8, 277.

[160] See Kymlicka, *Liberalism*, above n 46; Kymlicka, above n 15.

[161] R Beiner, 'Revising the Self', 8 *Critical Review* 247 at 255.

[162] *Ibid*, 252. See also C Taylor, 'Can Liberalism be Communitarian?', 8 *Critical Review* 257 at 259.

[163] Kymlicka, *Liberalism*, above n 46, 74.

weaker versions advance true and important claims, but ones that are already recognised by liberal theories and are not in conflict with liberal premises, while the stronger versions, which are inconsistent with liberalism, are mistaken and potentially repressive.

The first communitarian claim is that liberals have misconstrued the relationship between the self and social roles and relationships. Kymlicka responds:

> . . . the liberal view is sensitive to the way our individual lives and our moral deliberations are related to, and situated in, a shared social context. The individualism that underlies liberalism isn't valued at the expense of our social nature or our shared community. It is an individualism that accords with, rather than opposes, the undeniable importance to us of our social world.[164]

Secondly, Kymlicka closes the gap between liberal and communitarian views of the relationship between the self and its ends. He suggests that Sandel essentially makes two arguments for holding that the self is not prior to its ends.[165] The first is that the liberal view does not correspond with our deepest self-perception and the second is that the self is constituted by community values. Kymlicka agrees with Sandel on both of these arguments but maintains that they do not matter. In relation to the first, Kymlicka responds that it is not necessary for liberalism to maintain that we can *perceive* a self prior to its ends but only that there is one, because what is important to liberalism is that none of our ends is exempt from possible re-examination.[166] In relation to the second, Kymlicka argues that even if we accept that the self is constituted, this is not fatal to liberalism so long as the self can reconstitute itself, which Sandel and even MacIntyre occasionally acknowledge.[167] Kymlicka concludes that Sandel agrees with liberals that the *person* is prior to his or her ends and simply disagrees over where precisely, within the person, to draw the boundaries of the self:

> . . . this question, if it is indeed a meaningful question, is one for the philosophy of mind, with no definite relevance to political philosophy[168] . . . at

---

[164] Kymlicka, *Liberalism*, above n 46, 2–3. See also C Taylor, 'Cross-Purposes: The Liberal-Communitarian Debate' in Rosenblum, above n 7.

[165] Sandel, *Liberalism*, above n 3.

[166] Kymlicka, above n 15, 190. For discussion, see Beiner, above n 161; S M Okin, 'Humanist-Liberalism' in Rosenblum, above n 7.

[167] See MacIntyre, above n 1.

[168] Kymlicka, above n 15, 192.

this point it's not clear whether the whole distinction between the two views doesn't collapse entirely.[169]

Kymlicka suggests that we clearly can reject our commitments, since people do abandon even their dearest attachments, and he adds that it is not clear which, if any, communitarians really believe that we cannot re-examine our ends. But without this belief:

> ... the advertised contrast with the liberal view is a deception, for the sense in which communitarians view us as 'embedded' in communal roles incorporates the sense in which liberals view us as independent of them[170] ... The differences would be merely semantic.[171]

The third communitarian claim that Kymlicka examines is that liberals erroneously believe that individuals escape society in order to escape social influence when they revise their beliefs. Here Kymlicka agrees with communitarianism:

> We all question, at various points in our lives, the projects we have adopted, but we don't go outside society to do this, nor do we suppose we transcend any social conditioning in so doing. Nor do we need to exist outside of, or prior to, society for it to be morally important that we have the ability to question our chosen ends.[172]

Finally, he turns to what he believes critics of liberalism, from socialists and conservatives to communitarians and feminists, have argued is the foundational flaw of liberalism, namely that liberal theory prioritises the right over the good. He suggests that there is no real issue here either, because the difference is not over the relative priority of the right and the good but over competing accounts of what the good is and how best to promote it.[173] When communitarians accuse liberals of prioritising the right over the good, other liberals have argued that liberals make three distinct replies. While one reply is to proclaim the virtue of neutrality, the other two more common replies open up new ground. The first is to argue that liberalism contains moral resources that have been overlooked and the second pays attention to evidence of moral life in everyday practices. Accordingly, communitarian attacks have not demoralised liberals but instead have inspired them to rethink whether

---

[169] Kymlicka, above n 15, 191.
[170] *Ibid*, 194.
[171] *Ibid*, 195.
[172] Kymlicka, *Liberalism*, above n 46, 15.
[173] *Ibid*, 35. For a similar view, see Gutmann, above n 4, 317.

and how liberalism supports a defensible view of moral life, giving them an opportunity to affirm a connection between liberalism and moral life. Rather than defend neutrality, liberals reply with moral arguments on behalf of distinctly liberal virtues.[174] On this interpretation, there is a middle path between liberal neutrality and antiliberalism, namely a non-neutral, substantive liberalism committed to its own conception of the good.[175]

With such tentative defences of liberalism abounding, it becomes even less surprising that the Family Law Act at the very least contained a post-liberal dimension. The ground has been laid to begin to examine this dimension more closely. In the next chapter I will examine the post-liberal approach to autonomy and the consequences of adopting this approach for divorce law.

---

[174] N Rosenblum, 'Introduction' in Rosenblum, above n 7. See also C Taylor, 'Cross-Purposes: The Liberal-Communitarian Debate' in Rosenblum, above n 7.

[175] Galston, above n 15, 44. See also Minow and Shanley, above n 37.

2

Reflecting on Divorce

IN CHAPTER ONE, I examined the reasons that post-liberalism rejects the liberal view of autonomy, and I suggested that Part II of the Family Law Act reflected this rejection of liberal autonomy. I then claimed that because post-liberalism is unable to manage without the concept of autonomy, for reasons that were discussed, rejection of the liberal view of autonomy creates perhaps the central problem for post-liberal theory, namely to develop a post-liberal conception of autonomy. In this chapter the solution to this problem becomes crucial because I argue that Part II of the Family Law Act incorporated a post-liberal conception of autonomy.

Rejection of the liberal approach to autonomy meant that under the structure of the Act, a spouse's decision to divorce could not just be taken at face value: the fact that a spouse *wanted* a divorce could not in itself be taken as sufficient reason to allow divorce. Equally however, for reasons that will be fully explored in chapter three, any substantive basis for divorce would not have made sense under the post-liberal approach to autonomy, and accordingly the Family Law Act removed any such ground. Paradoxically, *only* the spouse's internal state *could* provide a basis for divorce.

The solution lay in emphasising thought. In October 1995 Lord Mackay described his mission to Marriage Care as follows:

> I want them [divorcing couples] to be able to think through the consequences of divorce before it happens, not after. I want them to think about what their marriage has to offer both them and their children before they decide whether or not to throw it away[1]

This mission was to be achieved most fundamentally by requiring couples to undertake a period of reflection and consideration prior to

---

[1] Lord Mackay, quoted in P Toynbee, 'Lord Mackay's Well-Intentioned Fiasco', *The Independent*, 25 October 1995.

divorce.[2] Moreover, the period of reflection itself could not begin until the spouse initiating divorce had spent three months thinking about the information received at the compulsory information meeting.[3] By way of these and other mechanisms which will be explored later in this chapter,[4] reflection was right at the heart of Part II of the Family Law Act. The theoretical basis for this emphasis is that self-discovery through reflection represents both the predominant and the most coherent post-liberal conception of autonomy. To understand why this is the case, we need to pick up the theoretical story where we left it at the end of chapter one, namely how post-liberalism develops a conception of autonomy distinct from the liberal approach.

So in this chapter, I turn to three attempts to develop a post-liberal conception of autonomy, the first two of which are drawn exclusively from feminism. The first is the search for middle ground and the second is the concept of socially constructed autonomy. After considering these two methods, I suggest that their internal inconsistency rendered them unsuitable for implementation in Part II of the Family Law Act. I then turn to the third method, the cognitive approach to autonomy, and I argue that this is the approach that we can see adopted in the Family Law Act. I next suggest that not only is the post-liberal subject unable to make decisions except through reflection, but that making decisions through reflection is also what he or she *should* do: this is the subject's life goal, both generally and in divorce law. Despite the fact that cognitive autonomy is the most coherent post-liberal conception of autonomy, I consider two difficulties with the approach, which I conclude this chapter by suggesting can only be resolved if cognitive autonomy abandons its relativism, becoming normative in result as well as method.

POST-LIBERAL CONCEPTIONS OF AUTONOMY

The Search for the Middle Ground

Just as liberals have conceded ground to communitarianism, the simplest solution for post-liberals is to add a small dose of liberal autonomy to their theory, so that although we are socially constituted, we are still to some limited extent able to make decisions.[5] It has been argued that many post-liberal theorists do not take their conception of autonomy much further than this.[6] However, more sophisticated versions of the search for the middle ground bifurcate into partial agency and limited agency.

Partial Agency

For feminists, middle ground clearly means moving away from structuralist feminism, because structuralist feminism views women as totally constituted by a singular gender structure, leaving no room for manoeuvre.[7] It has been argued that structuralist feminism contains the seeds of its own demise.[8] When different structuralist accounts are juxtaposed, even though they all concentrate on the constructive force of gender, the juxtaposition reveals that identity as a woman could be shaped by multiple images. This can be illustrated in relation to two structuralist accounts, dominance feminism and difference feminism. Because difference feminism sees women as constituted primarily by their domestic commitments and the social expectations that

---

[5] For examples, see M Sandel, *Liberalism and the Limits of Justice* (Cambridge, Cambridge University Press, 1998) 21; R Fallon, 'Two Senses of Autonomy', 46 *Stanford Law Review* 875 at 887–88; SL Hoagland, *Lesbian Ethics: Toward New Value* (Palo Alto, California, Institute of Lesbian Studies, 1988) 12; L McClain, ' "Irresponsible" Reproduction', 47 *Hastings Law Journal* 339 at 419 and 422; M Griffiths, *Feminisms and the Self: The Web of Identity* (London, New York, Routledge, 1995) 1; D Greschner, 'Feminist Concerns with the New Communitarians: We Don't Need Another Hero' in A Hutchinson and L Green (eds), *Law and the Community: The End of Individualism?* (Toronto, Carswell, 1989) 141; M Friedman, *What are Friends For?: Feminist Perspectives on Personal Relationships and Moral Theory* (Ithaca, New York, Cornell University Press, 1993) 63; A Gutmann, 'Communitarian Critics of Liberalism', 14 *Philosophy and Public Affairs* 308; M C Regan, *Alone Together: Law and the Meanings of Marriage* (New York, Oxford University Press, 1998) 12 and 15. For discussion, see C Berry, *The Idea of a Democratic Community* (Hemel Hempstead, Harvester Wheatsheaf, 1989) 102–4; E Frazer and N Lacey, *The Politics of Community: A Feminist Critique of the Liberal-Communitarian Debate* (Buffalo, New York, University of Toronto Press, 1994) 152.

[6] N Rosenblum, *Another Liberalism: Romanticism and the Reconstruction of Liberal Thought* (Cambridge, Massachusetts, Harvard University Press, 1987) 163; C Cochran, 'The Thin Theory of Community: The Communitarians and their Critics', 37 *Political Studies* 422 at 432; S Hekman, *Moral Voices, Moral Selves: Carol Gilligan and Feminist Moral Theory* (Cambridge, Polity, 1995) 50–56.

[7] See V Schultz, 'Room to Maneuver (f)or a Room of One's Own? Practice Theory and Feminist Practice', 14 *Law and Social Inquiry* 123 at 129.

[8] K Abrams, 'Title VII and the Complex Female Subject', 92 *Michigan Law Review* 2479.

accompany them while dominance feminism describes women created by their subjection to sexualisation, their juxtaposition implicitly raises the question whether women could not be shaped by both domestic commitments and sexualisation. It is inevitable that the further question emerges of why women are not subject to other constructive influences as well as gender.[9] The upshot is post-structuralist feminism, which distinguishes itself from structuralist feminism by moving from a description of a singular structure to one of multiple structures, and from liberalism by regarding people not as under-determined but as over-determined by multiple and overlapping structures.[10] Kathryn Abrams puts post-structuralist feminism into a more concrete context, juxtaposing constraint and agency in different ways to develop three different forms of what she describes as partial agency.[11]

The first type is transcendent agency, in which agency is achieved simply by unambiguous self-assertion. Women easily achieve such agency, either by just being exposed to a contrary view or by simply recognising the social construction of women's vulnerability. So a close friend's decision to divorce, or reading a book in which the heroine divorces, could allow a woman to make the autonomous decision to divorce. Abrams suggests that the ease with which transcendent agency is achieved fits unhappily with the original power accorded to dominance feminism. She concludes that this theory is therefore more consistent with the liberal subject formed prior to social influences than with the socially constructed subject who has internalised dominant forces. Accordingly, transcendent agency theory is arguably an example of liberal feminism rather than partial agency theory.

The second type is psychological or internal agency. We can begin here by posing the tension between accepting that a woman can resist constituents of her very self and the reality that we know that there are social critics and deviants. The tension is resolved by seeing the potential for deviation in the complexity of selves and the diversity of ways in which we are constituted, so that we can depart from any one social influence because of the combined effects of the various constituents.[12]

---

[9] Abrams, above n 8, 2482–83.
[10] Schultz, above n 7, 132; S Benhabib, 'Autonomy, Modernity and Community: Communitarianism and Critical Social Theory in Dialogue' in S Benhabib, *Situating the Self: Gender, Community and Postmodernism in Contemporary Ethics* (Cambridge, Polity, 1992) 196.
[11] Abrams, above n 8.
[12] On this point, see also Friedman, above n 5, 76; McClain, above n 5.

Abrams suggests that this potential is most crucial to black feminists, who have argued that since black women have been faced with relentlessly negative images from mainstream society, they have had to construct positive self-images from other sources, for example from art, literature and their own communities.[13] The potential is amplified because social norms are themselves irregular, contradictory and chaotic in two senses. First, because norms are general they do not dictate the specific way that they are to be realised in a particular case. Secondly, social norms are ambiguous and send mixed messages, as witnessed for example in the concurrent condemnation of and condonation of sexualising children.[14]

On this view, women are not born with a *self* but are composed of a collection of *selves*, which are partial and sometimes contradictory or even antithetical.[15] Therefore identity is not an essence but a construction from fragments of experience, under the guidance but not the control of the self and only partly understood by the self, so that the self may be surprised as different selves take precedence. Fragmentation is an ordinary condition of human selves, but a coalition of the fragments may be possible.[16] Women forge unity among these multiple voices by an act of will: although women cannot escape the voices that they hear, some of which will inevitably be the voices of oppression, they can decide how to shuffle them. Ultimately:

> . . . authenticity is more likely to be reached by an acceptance of the fragmentary nature of the self, than by clinging hopelessly to a dream of unity.[17]
> . . . The acceptance of fragmentation is the relinquishing of an inappropriate dream of purity, as well as a relinquishing of the wish for the unity of the subject.[18] . . . It is essential to acknowledge that there exists no unity of the self, no unchanging core of being. Such a belief is a fancy and will mislead the self into seeking to establish it. Being true to oneself does not mean seeking after such a core. It means undertaking the difficult business of assessment and transformation within a changing context of self. Authenticity requires re-assessing the changing self, not preserving a sameness.[19]

---

[13] Abrams, above n 8. See eg A Harris, 'Race and Essentialism in Feminist Legal Theory', 42 *Stanford Law Review* 581.

[14] Friedman, above n 5, 77.

[15] Griffiths, above n 5.

[16] On this point, see also C Smart and B Neale, *Family Fragments?* (Cambridge, Polity Press, 1999) 139.

[17] Griffiths, above n 5, 181.

[18] *Ibid*, 182.

[19] *Ibid*, 185.

Consciousness is never fixed or permanently attained but always a process. Not only is the self fragmented, but it is also relational, a function of surroundings. Therefore the self is always an invention.[20] So a woman can make the decision to divorce by drawing on various contrasting and counteracting influences, whether taken from literature or friendships. However, in contrast to the decision that she could make if she could achieve transcendent agency, a decision to divorce based on internal agency is hard-won and inevitably incomplete. To make a decision based on internal agency, a woman will constantly struggle to define herself in untainted terms.[21]

The final type of partial agency is political agency.[22] This occurs when women attempt individual resistance or collective change by applying their powers of interpretation not just to their self-images but also to their social circumstances. Political agency is promoted by, among others, feminists who agree with the fundamental insight of dominance feminism but worry about its political consequences. Therefore rather than downplaying, they highlight the examples that they find of women's self-determination and resistance. A common illustration is the re-interpretation of the responses of battered women as forms of resistance. The theoretical quarrel here with dominance feminism is with the idea that there is only one interpretation of mainstream practices, a common example being feminist re-interpretations of pornography. An example of political agency with respect to divorce could involve reclaiming what is commonly regarded as the plight of the abandoned wife as really her liberation. Abrams agrees that it is preferable for women to explore rather than ignore oppressive practices, with a view to placing their own distinctive mark on them. But she suggests that, given that this strategy places the woman's action in opposition to the accumulated force of entrenched norms, it is more significant where the norms are so entrenched as to make their opposition unintelligible rather than merely implausible. Clearly, the increasing number of divorces, the availability of divorce and the existence of different narratives about divorce ensure that divorce is universally intelligible as an option. In general, Abrams believes that re-interpretation is more likely to foster internal agency than produce political agency.[23]

---

[20] Griffiths, above n 5, 185; Harris, above n 13; Hekman, above n 6, 82.
[21] Abrams, above n 8.
[22] *Ibid.*
[23] *Ibid.*

Other feminists have been less positive about the impact of post-structuralism on agency.[24] The argument is that since post-structuralist accounts still view the human subject as in some sense produced by a multiplicity of structures, the human actor is still nothing more than the site at which these discourses come together. On this view, post-structuralism 'seems to involve an ironic sort of "neo-determinism" '.[25] But paradoxically, the relation between these discourses and the human subject is also no more than random, so that it cannot even explain how an individual's consciousness is configured. Ironically, the randomness of post-structuralism swallows up women's particularity just as much as the pre-social subject of liberalism. Taken to its logical conclusion, the chaos of post-structuralism would wipe out feminism just as surely as the rigidity of structuralism. Structuralism and post-structuralism are seen as sharing an inability to account for either social change or differences in women's consciousness. In simple terms, neither theory can account for feminism or feminists according to this argument:

> If the arrival of any particular permutation of discourses at any given human 'site' is 'random', does one 'become' either a feminist or not through a process no more 'determinate' than a coin flip? Without some plausible account of how consciousness may be transformed, post structuralist feminism, too may be politically paralyzing. At least ideally, our theories should provide some way of talking about how and why people – women and men – are moved, politicized, transformed.[26]

If post-structuralism cannot account for feminists any more than can structuralism, the question remains of how women can be enabled to become feminists. An alternative approach is that the best hope lies in providing powerful stories.[27] The conclusion that follows from this is striking: it is that the dilemma highlighted above between structuralist feminism and post-structuralist feminism is less real than is often thought because both approaches may be used to convince people that what is doesn't have to be. Different audiences may be moved by different accounts. So some audiences will not experience structuralist feminist accounts as paralysing but rather as so systematic as to demand resistance, and as they resist, their sense of their own ability to

[24] Schultz, above n 7.
[25] *Ibid*, 133.
[26] *Ibid*, 134.
[27] *Ibid*.

change things grows. Similarly other women will not find post-structuralist accounts unsettling but liberating, in that they are suddenly free to select from the overlapping structures to create something new.[28]

Ultimately, all of these approaches end up blurring the distinction between the accuracy and political viability of different social constructionist accounts. What is important for these theorists is the effect that a description has rather than whether it is an accurate reflection of the situation. So for example, Abrams sees the main problem with dominance feminism as being that it is unwise rather than inaccurate.[29] In conclusion, it could be argued that these are all theories of double social construction: women are constructed first, by oppressive circumstances and secondly, by feminist interpretations of those oppressive circumstances.

Limited Agency

Our main theorist here is Sarah Hoagland, who has developed 'moral agency under oppression' as the appropriate ethical theory for lesbians.[30] She argues that oppressed people need a moral theory that will enable them to avoid de-moralisation. When someone has been de-moralised, although she is still a moral agent, her ability to make choices and even to perceive herself as able to make choices is undermined. Hoagland suggests that the way that traditional ethics poses the problem of agency as a conflict between free will and determinism is unhelpful, particularly to people living under oppression:

> For my purposes, considerations about 'freedom' as it relates to 'moral agency' involve considerations about our day-to-day moral choices from where we stand – as finite beings . . . who live within boundaries of a finite world as well as under significant restrictions, including oppression: That is, my interest concerns what we as lesbians face, as we make choices given the parameters of this life. And it is from such a day-to-day, mundane perspective, rather than from a grandiose theory of free will, that I wish to proceed.[31]

[28] Schultz, above n 7.
[29] Abrams, above n 8. For other examples, see Harris, above n 13, 613; M Minow, 'Surviving Victim Talk', 40 *UCLA Law Review* 1411 at 1429.
[30] Hoagland, above n 5; S L Hoagland, 'Why *Lesbian* Ethics?' in C Card (ed), *Adventures in Lesbian Philosophy* (Bloomington, Indiana University Press, 1994). See also K Martindale and M Saunders, 'Realizing Love and Justice: Lesbian Ethics in the Upper and Lower Case' in C Card (ed), *Adventures in Lesbian Philosophy* (Bloomington, Indiana University Press, 1994) 171.
[31] Hoagland, above n 5, 203–4.

She sees moral agency as limited in present circumstances, currently occupying a moral space in between responsibility and powerlessness. She argues that the traditional approach, which regards the only proper moral decision as one in which the person is in control and could have done otherwise, and in which there are no constraints, boundaries, or limits, obscures the important distinction between control and choice. While lesbians do not control situations, they do affect, engage and act in them. Moral agency accordingly involves acting *within* the existing oppressive structure:

> Oppression is . . . a dimension within which we make our choices, a dimension which involves constructed ignorance, coercion, exploitation, and at times, enslavement. My concern is with our going on and making choices within this dimension.[32]

She suggests that moral agency involves enacting choice in limited circumstances, and working within boundaries rather than trying to rise above them. This is inevitable because:

> . . . to state the obvious, it is not likely that in our lifetime we will understand what it is like to act without the constraints of oppression.[33]

However, even outside the context of oppression, decisions are still made in specific situations that create specific boundaries or limits:

> Perhaps my central point about 'moral agency' is this: choice is at the very core of the concept of 'moral agency'. *It is not because* we are free and moral agents that we are able to make moral choices. Rather, it is because we make choices, choose from among alternatives, act in the face of limits, that we declare ourselves to be *moral beings*. That is what it *means* to be a moral being. Just as choice is a matter of creation, not sacrifice, so making choices within limited situations is a matter of affirming moral agency, not undermining it.[34]

One step towards developing moral agency is therefore to embrace the idea of working within limits and acknowledging boundaries. Rather than boundaries or limits being a drawback or something to be overcome, boundaries and limits are the context which help to give meaning to our choices.

---

[32] *Ibid*, 212.
[33] *Ibid*, 230.
[34] *Ibid*, 231.

To use Abrams' terminology,[35] there is a transcendental aspect to Hoagland's thesis, since she suggests that it is only through understanding boundaries and limits that we can ever hope to change them, and there is also an element of political agency:

> Moral agency . . . becomes a question of, not how we are going to stop all the injustice, but rather what our part is and what we are going to do next. In this way, acknowledging our boundaries does not detract from our interactions but rather locates us in a context wherein we act.[36]

Clearly, this adds little to the liberal account of autonomy, certainly in the context of the decision to divorce. A woman can make the decision to divorce, but she is inevitably making it within the confines of her circumstances and experiences.

Socially Constructed Autonomy

Here I turn to Diana Meyers' argument.[37] Meyers begins by defining autonomy as living in harmony with one's authentic self.[38] The problem is therefore posed as locating and understanding the authentic self, or knowing what one really wants, and the chief task of a theory of autonomy as being to forge a distinction between real and apparent desires. Meyers argues that people often experience desires as alien to their identity, and that when this happens suspicion falls on socialisation. On this hypothesis, the authentic self would be the self stripped of the socialisation process that instilled these false desires, and the problem one of how to rescue the authentic self from the effects of socialisation. Meyers examines attempts to do this, but, like Hoagland, she concludes that it is wrong to regard the problem of personal autonomy as an aspect of the problem of free will. Although socialisation is responsible for rendering the concept of the authentic self suspect, removing all taint of socialisation is probably impossible, and in any case is neither necessary nor sufficient for personal autonomy because:

---

[35] Abrams, above n 8.

[36] Hoagland, above n 5, 241. See also B Houston, 'In Praise of Blame' in Card, above n 30, 145; S L Hoagland, 'Why *Lesbian* Ethics?' in Card, above n 30.

[37] D T Meyers, *Self, Society, and Personal Choice* (New York, Columbia University Press, 1989).

[38] See also S Williams, 'A Feminist Reassessment of Civil Society', 72 *Indiana Law Journal* 417; Hekman, above n 6, 75.

Though it is reasonable to suppose that socialization poses a threat to autonomy and therefore that people cannot be autonomous unless they exert some sort of control over their socialization, the stronger claim that people are autonomous once they have rid themselves of social influences is not reasonable. Not only is it doubtful that people can accomplish this goal, but also privileging a self purged of social influence places the individual at the mercy of that self, regardless of what it turns out to be like.[39]

Even if we could strip away the effects of socialisation to reveal a free agent then we would be left with either a set of attributes or a pure will. If we uncovered a set of attributes, then the person would be stuck with those attributes, whether they were positive or negative, and all our experience tells us that innate attributes are even less conducive to free agency than is socialisation.[40] If we were left with a pure will then we would have returned full circle to the liberal subject and particularly to Sandel's criticisms of it, principally that decision-making is an exercise in arbitrariness.[41] Meyers concludes that autonomy must be a dynamic process, but removing all taint of socialisation from the subject would leave us with an inescapably static conception of the self.

So what is her solution? She argues that a primarily ontological view of the authentic self must give way to a primarily procedural view, in which the main task of a theory of autonomy is to explain the procedure by which people make decisions. Her conception of autonomy is essentially skills-based:

> Autonomous people must be disposed to consult their selves, and they must be equipped to be able to do so. More specifically, they must be able to pose and answer the question 'What do I really want, need, care about, value, etcetera?'; they must be able to act on the answer; and they must be able to correct themselves when they get the answer wrong. The skills that enable people to make this inquiry and to carry out their decisions constitute what I shall call *autonomy competency*.[42]

An authentic self is therefore a self that has autonomy competency, alongside the collection of attributes that emerges through the successful exercise of this competency. This competency is learnt through social experience. So not only is it unnecessary to remove socialisation from an account of agency but it is in fact essential to retain socialisation, not least to create social criticism: capacities for doubting,

[39] Meyers, above n 37, 44.
[40] On this point, see also Griffiths, above n 5, 76.
[41] See ch 1, pp 15–16.
[42] Meyers, above n 37, 52–53.

criticising or resisting are socially learnt to varying degrees. These tech-
niques can be generalised and deployed against the conventional as
well as the unconventional:[43]

> When someone finds out that she can 'just say no' to drug dealers, she is also
> learning how to say no to other demands.[44]

These demands could of course be those of her husband's and the solution could be to divorce him.

What is intriguing about all the accounts of autonomy examined so
far is that while they begin by posing the conundrum of how autonomy
can be retained within social constructionism, they conclude that not
only our characters but even our autonomy is socially constructed. In
all these accounts, we end up being doubly socially constructed: the
control that we exercise over both our decisions and our capacity to
make decisions is procedural not substantive.[45] In essence, the accounts
either find autonomy through their retention of elements of liberal
theory or they lapse into double social construction, and sometimes do
both. It is hard to see how these approaches could have been incorporated into a legislative framework: ultimately they fall back on liberalism for their accounts of autonomy. In any case, these post-liberal
approaches to autonomy were not implemented in Part II of the Family
Law Act, so I turn now to the approach that was adopted there.

THE COGNITIVE APPROACH TO AUTONOMY

The cognitive approach to autonomy, which essentially replaces the
liberal emphasis on choice with an emphasis on self-discovery, represents the most coherent post-liberal conception of autonomy. Within
communitarianism, Michael Sandel provides the clearest account of
this approach, which he develops out of his rejection of the liberal conception of autonomy.[46]

To turn to his argument for rejecting liberal autonomy, the liberal
subject cannot ultimately choose the wants on which his or her choices
rest, because in order to avoid recursion the wants must at some point
be the product of circumstances. Therefore, once the liberal subject has

---

[43] Meyers, above n 37, 52–53.
[44] Friedman, above n 5, 77.
[45] See S Macedo, *Liberal Virtues: Citizenship, Virtue, and Community in Liberal
Constitutionalism* (Oxford, Clarendon Press, 1990) 216–23.
[46] Sandel, above n 5.

ascertained what his or her wants actually are, there is nothing left for him or her to choose: all he or she needs to do is to match his or her wants to the best means of achieving them. Sandel describes this as factual accounting, not an exercise of will. The decision the agent makes:

> . . . amounts to nothing more than an estimate or psychic inventory of the wants and preferences he already has, not a choice of the values he would profess or the aims he would pursue.[47]

This decides nothing except how accurately the agent has perceived and heeded his or her pre-existing desires: choice is illusory.

Rather than choosing, what the liberal subject is doing is praying in aid a superficial form of introspection, which is just inward enough to survey his or her motives and desires uncritically. This introspection is restricted to the relative intensities of his or her wants and desires and how likely his or her plans are to achieve them. The subject's immediate wants and desires are transparent to him or her, so nothing recognisably deliberative occurs since he or she knows everything that he or she needs to know straightaway. The connection between fulfilment of the desire and the agent's identity cannot be a subject for introspection since, as we have seen, no desires are essential to identity, because identity is fixed in advance.[48] Sandel concludes that for the liberal subject, 'deliberation about ends can only be an exercise in arbitrariness'.[49]

If agency is to be anything more than an exercise in prudential accounting then the subject needs to be capable of a deeper, superior form of introspection.[50] However, this deeper type of reflection is possible if and only if the self is constituted by its desires, so that the subject can change his or her self.[51] Only a thickly constituted self, shaped in its very being by traditions, attachments and more or less irrevocable moral commitments, can distinguish among options in a way that counts.[52] Conversely and crucially, if the self is constituted by

---

[47] *Ibid*, 162.

[48] *Ibid*, 159. See also R Beiner, 'What's the Matter with Liberalism?' in Hutchinson and Green, above n 5, 38.

[49] Sandel, above n 5, 179. For a similar view, see C Taylor, 'The Concept of a Person' in C Taylor, *Human Agency and Language: Philosophical Papers 1* (Cambridge, Cambridge University Press, 1985) 113. For discussion, see Meyers, above n 37, 94. For a contrary view, see S Gardbaum, 'Liberalism, Autonomy and Moral Conflict', 48 *Stanford Law Review* 385 at 395.

[50] Sandel, above n 5, 172.

[51] For discussion of this point, see Meyers, above n 37, 94; Berry, above n 5, 101.

[52] For a similar view, see R Beiner, 'What's the Matter with Liberalism?' in Hutchinson and Green, above n 5, 38.

its ends, then it is impossible for it to choose: instead, the self must distinguish among options through a process of self-discovery.[53] In essence, the subject does not choose his or her ends; he or she finds them out:

> Where the ends of the self are given in advance, the relevant agency is not voluntarist but cognitive, since the subject achieves self-command not by choosing that which is already given (this would be unintelligible), but by reflecting on itself and inquiring into its constituent nature, discerning its laws and imperatives, and acknowledging its purposes as its own.[54]

The aim of cognitive agency is to achieve a distance between the self and its ends, that is, to disentangle the person from his or her desires.[55] This is essential to ensure continuity of identity, because otherwise, as we have seen, the self would be transformed when faced with any contingency. Establishing this distance requires self-knowledge: in order to distinguish between self and ends the subject needs to find out who he or she is.[56]

> In reflexivity, the self turns its lights inward upon itself, making the self its own object of inquiry and reflection.[57]

When the post-liberal subject reflects, he or she examines different possible modes of being. This takes him or her into the heart of his or her existence. In considering his or her preferences, in addition to weighing their intensities, this subject has to assess their suitability to the person he or she is. This enables the subject to discriminate among his or her immediate wants and desires, because some now seem essential to his or her identity while others seem merely incidental:[58]

> I ask, as I deliberate, not only what I really want but who I really am, and this last question takes me beyond an attention to my desires alone to reflect on my identity itself.[59]

---

[53] For a similar view, see C Taylor, *The Ethics of Authenticity* (Cambridge, Massachusetts, Harvard University Press, 1991) 29. For discussion, see Berry, above n 5, 101.

[54] Sandel, above n 5, 162.

[55] For a similar view, see R Unger, *Knowledge and Politics* (New York, Free Press, 1975) 200.

[56] Sandel, above n 5, 56.

[57] *Ibid*, 58.

[58] *Ibid*, 179.

[59] *Ibid*, 172. For similar views, see Fallon, above n 5, 887; Unger, above n 55, 204.

In developing the cognitive approach to agency, Sandel draws heavily on Charles Taylor's distinction between the simple weigher and the strong evaluator.[60] The simple weigher, who corresponds with Sandel's liberal subject, weighs up the desirability of different options, defined with reference to his or her existing desires. The strong evaluator, who becomes the socially embedded subject in Sandel's work, also examines different possible modes of being, distinguishing options against the backdrop of those characteristics that are part of his or her identity.[61] He or she does not make choices but attempts to formulate what is initially inchoate. Therefore, options not only count in relation to desires but also in virtue of 'the quality of life, the kind of beings we are or want to be.'[62] Strong evaluation is deeper than simple weighing because it takes us to the centre of our existence.

The snag for Taylor is that these formulations do not leave their object unchanged. In other words, formulating or re-formulating how we feel usually changes how we feel. For example, if we perceive that we have been deluding ourselves when we feel love for someone else then we will experience that emotion differently, perhaps as infatuation. Even if the emotion otherwise stays the same, as a minimum we will in future experience it as irrational, which will in itself change our experience of the feeling:[63]

> We can say therefore that our self-interpretations are partly constitutive of our experience. For an altered description of our motivation can be inseparable from a change in this motivation.[64]

If description completely captured emotion then the causal influence would operate only in this direction, so that 'thinking simply made it so'.[65] Taylor thinks that there are some domains of feeling where that may be the case, for example tastes in food. But with more complicated emotions, our descriptions can be incomplete, representing a deluded or imperfect understanding of our feelings.[66]

---

[60] C Taylor, 'What is Human Agency?' in T Mischel (ed), *The Self: Psychological and Philosophical Issues* (Oxford, Blackwell, 1977).

[61] For a similar view, see V Davion, 'Integrity and Radical Change' in C Card (ed), *Feminist Ethics* (Lawrence, Kansas, University Press of Kansas, 1991) 185.

[62] Taylor, above n 60, 115.

[63] Taylor, above n 49, 100–1.

[64] Taylor, above n 60, 127.

[65] Taylor, above n 49, 101.

[66] *Ibid*, 101.

Description and experience are therefore bound together in a constitutive relationship, allowing for causal influences in both directions. We alter our experiences by interpreting them differently. More fundamentally however, insight is limited by the socially embedded nature of our experience, that is, our insight takes place within social constraints, with the self using the culturally available building blocks to create itself.[67] Therefore, our descriptions are neither simple, in that the objects they describe are not independent of the description, nor arbitrary, in that the description can be more or less adequate. It follows that 'an articulation can be *wrong*, and yet it shapes what it is wrong about'.[68] Accordingly, the pattern that strong evaluation takes is a search for the true form of our emotions,[69] and because our insights are distorted by our experiences, there is always room for re-evaluation.[70]

However, the fact that our experiences distort our insights means that we can be wrong even about our most fundamental characteristics, which form the backdrop against which we evaluate. In fact, Taylor argues that we are most likely to be wrong about these characteristics because they are the least articulated. Therefore we ought to re-evaluate even our most basic characteristics. This radical re-evaluation is peculiar because it is not carried out within the terms of a more fundamental undisputed evaluation: no meta-language is available. Therefore, all that we can do is to look at our commitments in a stance of openness and all that we have to take the place of a yardstick is our deepest unstructured sense of what is important:

> ... this stance of openness is very difficult. It may take discipline and time. It is difficult because this form of evaluation is deep in a sense, and total in a sense, that other less than radical ones are not.[71] ... The obstacles in the way of going deeper are legion. There is not only the difficulty of such concentration, and the pain of uncertainty, but also all the distortions and repressions which make us want to turn away from this examination: and which make us resist change even when we do re-examine ourselves.[72]

---

[67] For a similar view, see M Dan-Cohen, 'Responsibility and the Boundaries of the Self', 105 *Harvard Law Review* 959 at 968.

[68] Taylor, above n 60, 127.

[69] Taylor, above n 49, 114.

[70] Taylor, above n 60.

[71] *Ibid*, 132. For a similar view, see Griffiths, above n 5.

[72] Taylor, above n 60, 133.

This deep reflection is truly a reflection about the self, engaging the whole self.[73]

Taylor claims that the capacity for strong evaluation is both essential to our conception of the human subject[74] and indispensable for freedom. This is because once we have recognised that freedom can be compromised because of internal as well as external obstacles,[75] freedom involves being able to recognise our more important purposes and overcome or at least neutralise our motivational fetters. But these conditions:

> . . . require me to have become something, to have achieved a certain condition of self-clairvoyance and self-understanding. I must be actually exercising self-understanding in order to be truly or fully free.[76]

There are strong connections between Sandel's theory of cognitive agency and Giddens' view of the self as a reflexive project.[77] Giddens explains that although we need to understand ourselves, self-understanding is subordinated to the more fundamental aim of creating a coherent and satisfying sense of self. This sense of self presumes a narrative, the moral thread of which is authenticity, which is based on being true to oneself. The material form that the narrative takes is the adoption of a lifestyle, that is, a more or less integrated set of practices. To be true to oneself involves finding oneself through an active process of self-construction,[78] a project carried out amid a profusion of resources to aid reflection, such as 'therapy and self-help manuals of all

---

[73] *Ibid.*

[74] For discussion of this point, see also B Frohnen, *The New Communitarians and the Crisis of Modern Liberalism* (Lawrence, University Press of Kansas, 1996) 42.

[75] See ch 1, pp 16–18.

[76] C Taylor, 'What's Wrong with Negative Liberty?' in C Taylor, *Philosophy and the Human Sciences: Philosophical Papers 2* (Cambridge, Cambridge University Press, 1985) 229. For other accounts of deep reflection, see V Davion, 'Integrity and Radical Change' in Card, above n 61, 185; Dan-Cohen, above n 67, 965–68; W Kymlicka, *Liberalism, Community, and Culture* (Oxford, New York, Clarendon Press, 1991) 12–13; W Kymlicka, 'Liberalism and Communitarianism', 18 *Canadian Journal of Philosophy* 181 at 190.

[77] Sandel, above n 5; A Giddens, *Modernity and Self-Identity: Self and Society in the Late Modern Age* (Cambridge, Polity Press, 1991); A Giddens, *The Transformation of Intimacy: Sexuality, Love and Eroticism in Modern Societies* (Cambridge, Polity, 1992). See also J Rodger, *Family Life and Social Control: A Sociological Perspective* (Basingstoke, Macmillan, 1996) 85.

[78] Giddens, *Modernity*, above n 77; C Smart, 'Wishful Thinking and Harmful Tinkering? Sociological Reflections on Family Policy', 26 *Journal of Social Policy* 301; J Hewitt, *Dilemmas of the American Self* (Philadelphia, Temple University Press, 1989) 6.

kinds, television programmes and magazine articles'.[79] Personal growth therefore depends on disentangling the true from the false self, partly by conquering emotional barriers that inhibit us from understanding ourselves. If we fail to conquer these barriers then we will be imprisoned by traits that are inauthentic, because they stem from feelings and situations that have been imposed on us. Our life-plan involves rethinking and reconstructing the past,[80] alongside a more or less continuous interrogation of past, present and future.[81] Life transitions are integrated within and overcome by means of the narrative of self-development.[82]

The implications of Giddens' approach have been considered in relation to divorce specifically.[83] The upshot of his approach is that divorce law needs to give importance to the emotional significance of revisiting and reinterpreting the past, as a route to reconstructing the self and imagining a future after divorce, because this is crucially important for biographical repair and integrating experience. Making sense of the past is a prerequisite for letting go and moving on:

> Divorcing people do not only have to construct for themselves a new vision of the future, but also a new vision of the past, as the whole meaning of the past alters in the light of the marriage breakdown. Without a past, it is hard to maintain a sense of self.[84]

We have already seen that the post-liberal subject can only make decisions by finding out who he or she is. We now see the corollary, namely that the choices that the subject does make, even the small everyday ones such as what to wear or what to eat, are not only about how to act but who to be.[85] The more post-traditional the settings in

---

[79] Giddens, *Intimacy*, above n 77, 30. See also Giddens, *Intimacy*, above n 77, 64; Rodger, above n 77, 85.

[80] Giddens, *Modernity*, above n 77.

[81] Giddens, *Intimacy*, above n 77, 30.

[82] Giddens, *Modernity*, above n 77.

[83] SD Sclater, *Divorce: A Psychosocial Study* (Aldershot, Ashgate, 1999).

[84] *Ibid*, 161.

[85] Giddens, *Modernity*, above n 77; U Beck, 'The Reinvention of Politics' in U Beck, A Giddens and S Lash, *Reflexive Modernization: Politics, Tradition and Aesthetics in the Modern Social Order* (Cambridge, Polity Press, 1994); A MacIntyre, *After Virtue: a study in moral theory* (London, Duckworth, 1985); D Morgan, 'Risk and Family Practices: Accounting for Change and Fluidity in Family Life' in E Silva and C Smart (eds), *The New Family?* (London, Sage, 1999) 23; J Weeks *et al*, 'Everyday Experiments: Narratives of Non-Heterosexual Relationships' in E Silva and C Smart (eds.), *The New Family?* (London, Sage, 1999) 84; Unger, above n 55, 204.

which a person moves, the more his or her lifestyle is concerned with the very core of self-identity, its making and remaking.[86] In a post-liberal era, the question 'Who shall I be?' is inextricably bound up with 'How shall I live?'.[87]

The cognitive approach to agency is, as already stated, also the predominant feminist response to the problem of autonomy.[88] A clear example is the narrative model of agency.[89] In this model, the hallmark of autonomous action is that the agent experiences the action as consistent with, or even demanded by, her identity and life story; this is evident in the commonsense notion that autonomy involves integrity, or being true to oneself. Autonomy takes place through narrative construction, which involves shifting from the general, that is, values and narratives available in the particular culture, to the particular, namely the person's own life experiences. Self-conscious reflection is key to narrative construction: while the model does not privilege rationality over emotional responses, it does privilege self-conscious reflection over instinctive integrity. Spontaneous decisions are inevitable, and can be justified through being retrospectively subjected to critical reflection. But engaging in self-conscious reflection is essential to being autonomous, or even to choosing, because 'to choose is to assess one's options for action in terms of one's identity, as understood through critical reflection'.[90]

This reference to spontaneity highlights a clear tension within post-liberal theory in relation to this model of agency, because paying heed to instinct and feeling is emphasised by feminism in particular[91] but

[86] Giddens, *Modernity*, above n 77, 81; John Rodger, above n 77, 85.

[87] Giddens, *Intimacy*, above n 77, 198.

[88] See eg D Cornell, *The Imaginary Domain: Abortion, Pornography and Sexual Harassment* (New York, Routledge, 1995); D Cornell, *At the Heart of Freedom: Feminism, Sex and Equality* (Princeton, New Jersey, Princeton University Press, 1998) 38; D Cornell, 'Institutionalization of Meaning, Recollective Imagination and The Potential for Transformative Legal Interpretation', 136 *University of Pennsylvania Law Review* 1135; M Minow and ML Shanley, 'Relational Rights and Responsibilities: Revisioning the Family in Liberal Political Theory and Law', 11 *Hypatia* 4 at 13; Friedman, above n 5, 63; J Nedelsky, 'Reconceiving Autonomy: Sources, Thoughts and Possibilities' in Hutchinson and Green, above n 5, 223; Frazer and Lacey, above n 5, 198–99; I M Young, 'The Ideal of Community and the Politics of Difference' in L Nicholson (ed), *Feminism/Postmodernism* (London, Routledge, 1989) 301; Griffiths, above n 5, 76.

[89] Williams, above n 38.

[90] *Ibid*, 436. For discussion, see K Abrams, 'Redefining Women's Agency: A Response to Professor Williams', 72 *Indiana Law Journal* 459 at 461.

[91] Griffiths, above n 5, 95; R Colker, 'Feminism, Sexuality and Authenticity' in MA Fineman and NS Thomadsen (eds), *At the Boundaries of Law: Feminism and Legal Theory* (New York, London, Routledge, 1991) 136.

also by the more romantic strains of communitarianism.[92] One attempt to resolve this tension is to argue that while authentic feelings and emotions can come unbidden and unforced, this cannot possibly be the whole story because it would give insufficient weight to the social construction of the self. Being authentic requires acting at one's own behest both on the level of feelings and at an intellectual, reflective level. Feelings are the spontaneous enactment of agency but intellectual reflection is the wider context, which may well change what future feelings arise spontaneously.[93]

According to the narrative model,[94] autonomy is neither a given for everyone nor an end-state to be achieved, but rather a continuing process, only possible if the person has developed three capacities. The first is self-knowledge: the person has to know herself so that she can identify the life story that will guide her actions. The second is self-esteem, which allows the person to do the necessary exploration and tell her story.[95] Finally, we need the ability to understand and appreciate others' evaluative standards.

The argument is that the narrative model of autonomy avoids the difficulty that the post-liberal view of the connection between self and others posed for the liberal model of autonomy because in the narrative model, autonomy is dependent on the self's relations to others in three ways. First, the necessary capacities can only be produced and maintained in a particular social context. More profoundly, the capacities cannot even be conceived or described in isolation from social relations; for example, the concept of social esteem has no meaning for the hermit. Finally, the content of identity is generated from social categories, for example the identity of being a good mother.

More fundamentally, and just like the cognitive approach to autonomy, the narrative model is designed to solve the internal/external problem specifically and the problem of social construction generally. Under the narrative model the fact that decisions are shaped by social forces does not make them any less our own because:

[92] M C Regan, *Family Law and the Pursuit of Intimacy* (New York, New York University Press, 1993) 45; Rosenblum, above n 6; J Nolan, *The Therapeutic State: Justifying Government at Century's End* (New York, New York University Press, 1998) 5–7.
[93] Griffiths, above n 5, 174–79.
[94] Williams, above n 38.
[95] On this point, see also Frohnen, above n 74, 166.

The central issue for the narrative model is not where the motives for action come from in some causal sense, but whether the actor has gone through the narrative process of examination and retelling necessary to make them her own before she acts on them.[96]

Because feminism is more wary of the socially determined subject and consequently more concerned about freeing women from the effects of social conditioning than is communitarianism,[97] feminism has paid far more attention than communitarianism to the practical question of how reflective agency could actually work.[98] The feminist practice of consciousness raising is the most concrete illustration of the cognitive approach to agency:[99]

As marxist method is dialectical materialism, feminist method is consciousness raising: the collective critical reconstitution of the meaning of women's social experience, as women live through it.[100] . . . The key to feminist theory consists in its *way* of knowing. Consciousness raising is that way.[101]

The method is that as multiple experiences are exchanged, new interpretations emerge and find strength and validity from the collective practice.[102] To elaborate:

First, a woman discovers the 'falsity' of her felt pleasures and desires in consciousness-raising *when she discovers that they are not her own* – when she discovers quite literally, that she has been seeking the pleasure of others, not herself. Second, she discovers the 'falsity' of her desires when she discovers, again quite literally, that she has been lying, either to herself or others. The desire (or the pleasure) is discovered to be 'false' when she discovers that what she has been calling 'desirable' is *not* in fact – *to her* – desirable. And third, and perhaps most centrally, she discovers the 'falsity' of her desires when *she herself* – not outside observers – feels their falsity.[103] . . . Consciousness-raising, more than any other feminist methodology, has given women a means by which to break the chain of deception in which we

[96] Williams, above n 38, 436.
[97] See ch 1, pp 18–21.
[98] P Weiss, 'Feminism and Communitarianism: Comparing Critiques of Liberalism' in P Weiss and M Friedman (eds), *Feminism and Community* (Philadelphia, Temple University Press, 1995) 168; Griffiths, above n 5, 94.
[99] Frazer and Lacey, above n 5.
[100] C MacKinnon, *Toward a Feminist Theory of the State* (Cambridge, Massachusetts, Harvard University Press, 1989) 83.
[101] *Ibid*, 84. For a contrary view, see R Colker, 'Feminism, Sexuality and Authenticity', 143, in Fineman and Thomadsen, above n 91.
[102] Frazer and Lacey, above n 5.
[103] R West, 'The Difference in Women's Hedonic Lives: A Phenomenological Critique of Feminist Legal Theory' in Fineman and Thomadsen, above n 91, 128.

live. By learning to identify the falsehoods we utter, we have learned to create a self who can assert a truth.[104]

Many feminists make the point that consciousness-raising is a *method*, rather than a *situation*, very few women actually being actively engaged in formal consciousness-raising groups but many more engaging in intimate conversations with study groups or small groups of friends:[105]

> . . . we should be clear that the self-conscious consciousness-raising group of the women's movement is an illustration of this process and not the only or even a privileged medium in which it takes place . . . consciousness-raising is not confined to a self-conscious institutional practice relating to a very specific historical moment. It takes place also in casual discussion, and even without the meeting of two persons, via the internal dialogue that we as critically reflective subjects are not only capable of but engage in when we try to make sense of our lives or formulate our views . . . A chance scene in a film or passage in a novel; reflection on a dream; recollection of one's past feelings and behaviour in certain situations; an argument at work; all these are capable of generating reinterpretations and reconceptualisations of the world.[106] . . . Consciousness raising is the process through which the contemporary radical feminist analysis of the situation of women has been shaped and shared. As feminist method and practice, consciousness raising is not confined to groups explicitly organized or named for that purpose. In fact, consciousness raising as discussed here was often not practiced in consciousness-raising groups. Such groups were, however, one medium and forum central to its development as a method of analysis, mode of organizing, form of practice, and technique of political intervention.[107]

Consciousness-raising is not the only practical example of reflective agency however. Critical autobiography, that is, autobiography that makes use of individual experience, theory, and a process of reflection and re-thinking, has also been suggested as providing a basis for approaching autonomy,[108] as have leaps of imagination, as expressed in Utopian dreams.[109]

[104] *Ibid*, 129. For discussion, see also Berry, above n 5.
[105] R Colker, 'Feminism, Sexuality and Authenticity' in Fineman and Thomadsen, above n 91, 143.
[106] Frazer and Lacey, above n 5, 208–9. For a similar view, see M Friedman, 'Feminism and Modern Friendship: Dislocating the Community', 99 *Ethics* 275. For discussion, see Berry above n 5, 25–30. For a contrary view, see R Colker, 'Feminism, Sexuality and Authenticity' in Fineman and Thomadsen, above n 91, 143.
[107] MacKinnon, above n 100, 84.
[108] Griffiths, above n 5, 72.
[109] *Ibid*, 191.

In conclusion, rather than summoning his or her will, the post-liberal subject must seek to understand himself or herself, because he or she is the concatenation of his or her desires:

> The relevant question is not what ends to choose, for my problem is precisely that the answer to this question is already given, but rather who I am.[110]

The self comes by its ends not by choice but by reflection.[111] Choice, the imperative for the liberal individual, has been reconstructed as a project of personal growth,[112] which becomes the imperative for the post-liberal self.[113] The life-goal of the post-liberal subject is to find himself or herself.[114]

Cognitive Autonomy in the Family Law Act

According to the cognitive approach to autonomy, the only way that we could find out whether our decision to divorce is authentic is through deep reflection. As Baroness Scotland assured the House of Lords in the debates on the Act, there is little doubt that 'the Act tries to put the emphasis back on . . . thought'.[115] There were three main mechanisms used to encourage thought. First, there were formal settings, akin to consciousness-raising sessions within feminism. These

---

[110] Sandel, above n 5, 59.

[111] *Ibid*, 152; Fallon, above n 5, 887.

[112] Giddens, *Modernity*, above n 77; U Beck and E Beck-Gernsheim, *The Normal Chaos of Love* (Cambridge, Polity Press, 1995); Sandel, above n 5; Hewitt, above n 78, 217; F Michelman, 'Law's Republic', 99 *Yale Law Journal* 1493 at 1528; Cornell, 'Institutionalization of Meaning', above n 88, 1228; C Schneider, 'Moral Discourse and the Transformation of American Family Law', 83 *Michigan Law Review* 1803; Rodger, above n 77, 85; M Galston, 'Taking Aristotle Seriously: Republican-Oriented Legal Theory and the Moral Foundation of Deliberative Democracy', 82 *California Law Review* 331 at 363; Griffiths, above n 5; MacIntyre, above n 85; Regan, above n 5, 11; J Nedelsky, 'Law, Boundaries, and the Bounded Self', 30 *Representations* 162 at 168; Smart and Neale, above n 16, 139.

[113] W Kymlicka, *Contemporary Political Philosophy: An Introduction* (Oxford, Oxford University Press, 1990) 213; Kymlicka, 'Liberalism and Communitarianism', above n 76, 190; P Weiss, 'Feminism and Communitarianism: Comparing Critiques of Liberalism' in Weiss and Friedman, above n 98, 176; Rosenblum, above n 6, 51; Hewitt, above n 78, 27.

[114] Regan, above n 92.

[115] Baroness Scotland, Hansard, House of Lords, 6 July 1999, Col 788. See also Lord Chancellor's Department, *Looking to the Future: Mediation and the Ground for Divorce* (London, HMSO, 1995) 8.

began with the information meeting, compulsory for anybody wishing to make a statement of marital breakdown.[116] This gave the opportunity and encouragement to have a meeting with a marriage counsellor. It also provided information on marriage counselling, other marriage support services and mediation, the importance of child welfare and how the divorcee could learn how to help any children cope with the divorce, and protection, support and assistance available with respect to violence.[117]

The Labour Government's 1998 Consultation Document on the family, Supporting Families, suggested that there should be two meetings.[118] The first meeting, which would have replaced the information meeting, would have concentrated on information to help the couple decide whether their marriage was over. The second meeting would have been a group presentation at which the couple would have been given detailed information about issues concerning their children, finances, property and mediation at a time when the Government believed that the couple would have been ready for this information. This would have been at the very least after they had already embarked on the divorce.[119]

At any time after the divorcee had made a statement of marital breakdown, the court could order him or her to attend another meeting to have mediation explained and to provide an opportunity for him or her to agree to take advantage of those facilities. The mediator had to report back to the court as to whether the divorcee had attended the meeting and whether he or she had agreed to take part.[120]

The second mechanism was the use of time to encourage thought. The heart of the scheme was the period of reflection and consideration, but even before this period could be entered, the prospective divorcee was obliged to take at least three months to think over the information that he or she had been given in the information meeting.[121] Only after thinking for three months was the spouse allowed to make a statement that his or her marriage had broken down, which signalled the begin-

[116] S 8(2) Family Law Act 1996.
[117] S 8(9) Family Law Act 1996.
[118] Home Office, *Supporting Families: A Consultation Document* (London, HMSO, 1998), 35–36.
[119] *Ibid*, 35.
[120] S 13 Family Law Act 1996. See ch 4, pp 150–52 for discussion of the significance of this meeting.
[121] S 8(2) Family Law Act 1996.

ning of the period of reflection itself.[122] The post-liberal conception of decision-making as a process was also reflected in the discussion that preceded the Family Law Act. The Law Commission Report, *The Ground for Divorce*, suggested that the proposed reform reflected 'the recognition that divorce is not a single event but a social, psychological and only incidentally a legal process.'[123]

Finally, the divorcee was instructed in the Family Law Act debates on how to think. He or she was told to 'think hard;[124] think more thoroughly;[125] think very seriously;[126] think it through;[127] stop and think;[128] stop and think clearly;[129] consider properly,[130] consider carefully,[131] stop and think very very carefully;[132] think once, think twice,[133] think many times;[134] have second thoughts,[135] draw back and think again,[136] think again right up to the moment when the divorce is granted.'[137]

THE OBLIGATION TO REFLECT

In this chapter we have seen that if the subject is socially constituted then he or she has no alternative but to make decisions through a process of self-discovery. Conversely, we have seen that if the subject is to be able to make decisions through a process of self-discovery then he or she must be socially constituted. Crucially, however, this is not just

---

[122] S 7(3) Family Law Act 1996.

[123] Law Commission, *The Ground for Divorce* (London, HMSO, 1990) 16.

[124] Lord Mackay, 'Champions of Marriage Should Back Me', *The Independent*, 26 April 1996; Viscount Cranbourne, Hansard, House of Lords, 5 July 1996, Col 1774.

[125] J Corston, Hansard, House of Commons, 17 June 1996, Col 447.

[126] Lord Mackay quoted in A Thomson, 'Mackay Fails to Pacify Peers on Divorce Reforms', *The Times*, 23 February 1996.

[127] Lord Mackay addressing Marriage Care, quoted in Toynbee, above n 1; Lord Mackay quoted in C Brown, 'Mackay Seeks to Calm Unease on Divorce Bill', *The Independent*, 25 October 1995.

[128] Lord Bishop of Oxford, Hansard, House of Lords, 29 February 1996, Col 1653.

[129] Baroness Park, Hansard, House of Lords, 11 January 1996, Col 344.

[130] Lord Chancellor's Department, above n 115, 9.

[131] Lord Mackay, Hansard, House of Lords, 22 January 1996, Col 875; Lord Mackay, Hansard, House of Lords, 23 January 1996, Col 955.

[132] Lord Bishop of Oxford, Hansard, House of Lords, 29 February 1996, Col 1653.

[133] Lord Jakobovits, Hansard, House of Lords, 29 February 1996, Col 1658.

[134] Lord Stoddart, Hansard, House of Lords, 22 January 1996, Col 817.

[135] Lord Stoddart, Hansard, House of Lords, 29 February 1996, Col 1705.

[136] Lord Chancellor's Department, above n 115, 31.

[137] Baroness Young, Hansard, House of Lords, 29 January 1996, Col 1704.

a matter of description: discovering himself or herself is what the post-liberal subject *should* do:

> According to communitarians we seek, and should seek, to fulfil ourselves. Developing our own life plans and putting them into action, we exercise our faculties and our faculty for moral choice in particular. Acting on our spontaneous feelings and desires we create a unique life for ourselves. We follow the voice that is inside us, and the better we do this, the more fulfilled and more fully human we become.[138]

Charles Taylor is very concerned to stress the normative dimension.[139] He argues that being in touch with our inner selves has taken on an independent and crucial moral significance. In the heyday of liberalism, the inner voice was important only because it helped us do the right thing: it was a means to the end of acting in the right way. With the demise of liberalism, there has been a 'displacement of the moral accent': rather than using our inner voice to connect with an external source, the source we have to connect with is now deep inside us.[140] As a result of the shift in the centre of gravity of moral demands, authenticity becomes the end in itself:[141]

> . . . self-truth and self-wholeness are seen more and more not as means to be moral, as independently defined, but as something valuable for their own sake.[142]

But the inner voice has a far greater moral significance than so far accorded. One idea that communitarianism has retained from liberalism is the idea that each of us has an original way of being human. There is a certain way of living that is my way, and I am called upon to live my life in this way, not in imitation of anyone else's way; each of our voices has something of its own to say.[143] Within communitarianism, it is this principle of originality that gives crucial moral significance to being true to oneself: 'If I am not, I miss the point of my life, I

[138] Frohnen, above n 74, 42.
[139] Taylor, above n 53.
[140] On this point, see also Beck and Beck-Gernsheim, above n 112, 5; Hewitt, above n 78, 6; Nolan, above n 92, 2–3.
[141] On this point, see also C Taylor, *Sources of the Self: The Making of the Modern Identity* (Cambridge, Cambridge University Press, 1989) 507; Giddens, *Intimacy*, above n 77, 198; Frohnen, above n 74; D Morgan, 'Risk and Family Practices: Accounting for Change and Fluidity in Family Life' in Silva and Smart, above n 85, 23; Rosenblum, above n 6, 45; Beck and Beck-Gernsheim, above n 112, 40; Hewitt, above n 78, 6.
[142] Taylor, above n 53, 64–5.
[143] On this point, see Rosenblum, above n 6, 45.

miss what being human is for *me*.'[144] The notion that each one of us has an original way of being human demands that each of us has to discover what it is to be ourselves, and we can only do this by articulating afresh. This principle of originality gives moral force to what Taylor calls the culture of authenticity.

Although less prevalent, the obligation to reflect is present in feminism as well in that unreflective opinions cannot be accorded much respect because they simply exhibit and confirm conventional practices.[145] Moreover, while the strand of feminism known as standpoint feminism suggests that the standpoint of women provides the most accurate account of the workings of patriarchal society:

> . . . standpoint feminism does not celebrate the vision of all women, only those who have collectivized and reinterpreted their experiences through processes of consciousness-raising or similar political activity.[146]

The Obligation to Reflect in the Family Law Act

We have already seen a strong obligation to reflect in Part II of the Family Law Act: anyone initiating divorce was obliged to attend at least one meeting and some divorcees were obliged to attend several additional meetings. However, in the early stages of the discussion that preceded the Family Law Act, it is arguable that only an opportunity to reflect was envisaged. For example, the Law Commission recommended a 'reasonably long period of delay, where each party has every opportunity to reflect upon the position and explore the alternatives'.[147] As late as 1993 the Government Green Paper suggested mildly that the proposals might give couples 'the space and peace to reflect on what has gone wrong in their marriage.'[148]

Even the 1995 White Paper, Looking to the Future, could be viewed as endorsing only an opportunity to reflect.[149] Looking to the Future

---

[144] Taylor, above n 53, 29.

[145] Friedman, above n 5, 50.

[146] C Smart, 'Unquestionably a moral issue: Rhetorical devices and regulatory imperatives' in L Segal and M McIntosh (eds), *Sex Exposed: Sexuality and the Pornography Debate* (London, Virago Press Ltd, 1992) 197.

[147] Law Commission, above n 123, 19. See also Law Commission, above n 123, 16.

[148] Lord Chancellor's Department, *Looking to the Future: Mediation and the Ground for Divorce* (London, HMSO, 1993) 17. See also Lord Chancellor's Department, *Looking to the Future: Mediation and the Ground for Divorce* (London, HMSO, 1993) 16 and 40.

[149] Lord Chancellor's Department, above n 115.

suggested that the current system provided little incentive to reflect as to whether the marriage had broken down and perhaps even actively discouraged such consideration. Correspondingly, the White Paper regarded it as important that the new process allow the parties to consider this question properly, by providing mechanisms to create an opportunity for reflection and consideration as well as time to consider marriage guidance. The Government promised: 'There will be every opportunity to draw back and think again.'[150] A similarly gentle tone was present in Lord Mackay's suggestion during the Parliamentary debates on the Family Law Act that the reform gave 'a chance for people to think very seriously'.[151]

However, a harsher tone was present as well in the White Paper, an example being its proclamation that the key aspect of the proposals was that 'the system should require divorcing couples to consider carefully the consequences and implications of divorce before dissolution.'[152] Indeed, the Paper went so far as to regard the proposed reform as the implementation of a 'divorce process based on a requirement to reflect'.[153]

Obligation was also emphasised by several of the legislators during the debate. Jean Corston claimed: 'The Bill is going to make divorce harder, and make people think about it more thoroughly'.[154] Viscount Cranbourne hoped that:

> . . . the Family Law Bill will strengthen the institution of marriage. By making people think hard about the consequences of divorce . . . I believe that it will do so.[155]

The obligation to reflect was similarly welcomed by the media. An Independent leader argued:

> The most significant failing in the current legislation is that there is no requirement for divorcing parents to give thought to the consequences of their actions on their children.[156]

---

[150]   Lord Chancellor's Department, above n 115, 31.
[151]   Thomson, above n 126. For a similar tone, see Baroness Young, Hansard, House of Lords, 29 January 1996, Col 1704.
[152]   Lord Chancellor's Department, above n 115, 17.
[153]   *Ibid*, 31.
[154]   J Corston, Hansard, House of Commons, 17 June 1996, Col 447.
[155]   Viscount Cranbourne, Hansard, House of Lords, 5 July 1996, Col 1774. See also Toynbee, above n 1.
[156]   'Labour Joins the Right: Divorced from Reality,' *The Independent*, 29 May 1996.

The leader took the view that the Act would remedy this, to 'achieve one of the central goals of any reform: to make divorcing parents think'.[157]

TWO PROBLEMS WITH COGNITIVE AUTONOMY

The cognitive approach to agency is the most coherent post-liberal conception of autonomy, as a result of which it is the approach that we have found incorporated in Part II of the Family Law Act. Nevertheless, it is hard to see how this approach avoids the following two problems: first, the infinite regress and secondly, the impossibility of self-improvement.

Infinite Regress

We have seen that despite feminist ambivalence towards the socially constituted subject, post-liberals generally believe that removing all taint of the socialisation process is neither possible nor desirable.[158] Yet if we are thoroughly socially conditioned so that there is no core below, it is difficult to escape the conclusion that all that we are doing when we reflect is peeling off never-ending layers of social conditioning:[159]

> Introspection may find a thoroughly conditioned self. Likewise, a decision to change may reflect socially instilled values and preferences, and a meta-decision confirming that decision may again reflect socially instilled values and preferences. In sum, self-administered checks on the autonomy of the individual may themselves be products of socialization, and any review of these reviews may be socially tainted, as well.
>
> The search for the authentic self thus appears to set in motion an infinite regress.[160]

Prior socialisation may determine the outcome of self-examination, and this socialisation may operate unconsciously. Once we concede that unconscious forces are at work then it follows that no-one can ever

---

[157] *Ibid.*
[158] See pp 54–56.
[159] Frazer and Lacey, above n 5, 157; S Gey, 'The Unfortunate Revival of Civic Republicanism', 141 *University of Pennsylvania Law Review* 801 at 831.
[160] Meyers, above n 37, 20.

be satisfied that he or she has brought all of these forces to the surface. A plausible conclusion is that we cannot rely on the concept of a mastered social background to provide a tenable account of autonomy.[161]

This infinite regress may be more worrying to feminists than communitarians because, as we saw in chapter one, feminists recognise a broader range of social forces with a deeper and more destructive impact on identity than do communitarians.[162] Feminists have argued that traditions such as sexism and racism may be particularly 'pervasive, constant, intimate, and unconscious.'[163] Accordingly, they have recognised the need for a measuring rod to gauge the extent to which social forces have been avoided, but have had little to say about how to develop one.[164] The troubling nature of the infinite regress, coupled with the absence of a solution, perhaps explains why it has even been argued that blind faith that we are moving towards an authentic self must be a fundamental tenet of feminist struggle.[165]

More cynically:

> . . . we are skeptical of the idea that people have anything like a 'core self,' a bedrock of character and belief where, if we can just reach it, we can stand with confidence. Instead, we more and more suppose that we are quantum selves – just spin, all the way down. . . . The ironic stance invites us to be self-absorbed, but in selves that we cannot believe to be especially interesting or significant.[166]

In relation to marriage or divorce, reflection may only lead us to endorse a decision based on various aspects of our socialisation, so that even a decision based on deep thought is suspect. Moreover, the infinite regress means that reflection is endless: we can never achieve self-knowledge, so we can never proclaim that we have reflected sufficiently; instead, reflection is a life-long process, never completely achieved.[167]

---

[161] Meyers, above n 37, 28–29.

[162] See pp 18–21.

[163] P Weiss, 'Feminism and Communitarianism: Comparing Critiques of Liberalism' in Weiss and Friedman, above n 98, 165. See also SM Okin, *Justice, Gender and the Family* (New York, Basic Books, 1989) 42–43.

[164] R Colker, 'Feminism, Sexuality and Authenticity' in Fineman and Thomadsen, above n 91, 136.

[165] *Ibid.*

[166] J Purdy, 'Age of Irony', 39 *The American Prospect* 84 at 86.

[167] C Schneider, 'Marriage, Morals and the Law', 1994 *Utah Law Review* 503; Regan, above n 92, 44. See ch 6 for further discussion.

The Impossibility of Self-Improvement

Despite the difficulty and pain associated with deep reflection, it is arguable that even the most radical re-evaluation of one's most fundamental characteristics involves merely finding oneself rather than actually changing oneself. A possible post-liberal response to this simple but profound argument is to accept its validity, but to contend that the self-knowledge obtained through reflection is still liberating because knowledge of the sources of characteristics is in itself sufficient to loosen their hold over the person. Consciousness of the socialisation process thus enables us to accept or reject our characteristics.[168] However, the rejoinder to this is that people often know why they have certain traits yet remain unable to alter them, so that self-knowledge is necessary but not sufficient for autonomy,[169] self-definition being essential as well.[170] To be autonomous, we need the capacity to conceive and institute changes in our true selves; otherwise, people afflicted with unfortunate characteristics are doomed. For at least some people, self-definition is crucial. On any other view:

> . . . the true self is like a sunken treasure – a pre-existing, hidden entity. Though there are diving procedures, fortune-hunters can follow to locate it and float it, there is no guarantee that any given expedition will succeed in retrieving the treasure. The true self may elude a well-equipped seeker of autonomy, yet it remains intact awaiting the day when its secrets will be brought to light.[171]

If cognitive agency does not allow us to change ourselves then it does not solve the problem of autonomy because:

> If people were so completely determined by their social context that their 'retelling' of their stories consisted of nothing more than a parroting back of the cultural elements they were given, it would be difficult to see why this version of 'autonomy' would be worth protecting at all.[172]

Post-liberal theorists, particularly feminists for the reasons already discussed, have recognised that unless reflective autonomy gives us the capacity to change ourselves, the approach simply moves the problem

---

[168] Meyers, above n 37, 27–28.
[169] *Ibid*, 33.
[170] *Ibid*.
[171] *Ibid*, 45.
[172] Williams, above n 38, 436.

to a new location. Instead of worrying about how a socially determined subject can be free, we now worry about how to explain creativity in the process of re-telling a social script. Post-liberals have accepted that if autonomy is to mean anything, it is essential to find some scope for individual creativity.[173]

Feminists have accused the leading communitarian theorists of indeed leaving little scope for change.[174] MacIntyre is a common culprit here.[175] Feminists argue that MacIntyre's conception of the subject presupposes a community of fixed roles, where status is allotted rather than achieved. The society that he describes is a hierarchical society in which everyone knows his or her place, and in which women's and other disadvantaged groups' place is particularly lowly. The conclusion is that the 'narrative selfhood that MacIntyre lauds can be achieved only at a high price: the ascription of traditional roles.'[176]

At first glance, Sandel leaves more scope for change, describing the bounds of the self as possibilities rather than fixtures, with contours that are at least partly unformed.[177] He argues that through reflection, this flexible perimeter enables the self to participate in constituting its own identity,[178] so that the subject's identity is the product rather than the premise of his or her agency.[179] However, a closer analysis shows that this is essentially a process of excluding or including pre-existing desires and ends:

> Unlike the capacity for choice, which enables the self to reach beyond itself, the capacity for reflection enables the self to turn its lights inward upon itself, to inquire into its constituent nature, to survey its various attachments and acknowledge their respective claims . . .[180]

While Sandel's subject is self-interpreting, and so through reflecting on his or her history is able to distance himself or herself from it, Sandel

---

[173] Williams, above n 38, 436; S Benhabib, 'Autonomy, Modernity and Community: Communitarianism and Critical Social Theory in Dialogue' in Benhabib, above n 10, 73.

[174] Hekman, above n 6, 55; Meyers, above n 37, 93.

[175] MacIntyre, above n 85.

[176] Hekman, above n 6, 55. For a different view, see A Ferrara, 'universalisms: procedural, contextualist and prudential' in D Rasmussen (ed), *Universalism vs. Communitarianism: Contemporary Debates in Ethics* (Cambridge, Massachusetts, MIT Press, 1990) 26; Kymlicka, 'Liberalism and Communitarianism', above n 76, 193–94; Berry, above n 5, 109.

[177] Sandel, above n 5, 59.

[178] *Ibid*, 144.

[179] *Ibid*, 152.

[180] *Ibid*, 153.

himself acknowledges that the distance between the self and its history is always precarious, with the point of reflection never secured outside the history itself.[181] It would not be too harsh to conclude in relation to Sandel's conception of the self that:

> Since social experience implants ends in the self, the self is maximally open to the vicissitudes of circumstances and, conversely, minimally under the control of the individual. While its powers of critical reflection endow this self with a rational basis for change, change is limited to orchestrating pre-existing elements.[182]

Another approach is to accept that since our identities are largely constituted by learnt or inherited patterns of behaviour, 'the consciousness that struggles against these patterns is nevertheless implicated in them,'[183] but to suggest that there is still a way that we can change. This is not for the self to struggle against its character but rather for the self to mobilise certain character traits against others. So ambition can be made to counteract sloth, and courage can overcome shame.[184] Clearly, this approach merely involves re-organising characteristics that are already present in the self.

Even Kymlicka believes that communitarians cannot resolve the problem of self-improvement and that only liberalism really allows for revision of the self:[185]

> For liberals, the question about the good life requires us to make a judgment about what sort of a person we wish to be or become. For communitarians, however, the question requires us to discover who we already are.[186]

According to Kymlicka, communitarianism allows us to interpret the *meaning* of our constitutive attachments but not to reject them. He argues that this approach is implausible, since we can and do reject even our most basic commitments. His characteristic conclusion is that either communitarianism is implausible or it is no different from liberalism.[187]

---

[181] *Ibid*, 179.
[182] Meyers, above n 37, 93. See also Kymlicka, above n 113, 213.
[183] W Galston, *Liberal Purposes: Goods, Virtues, and Diversity in the Liberal State* (New York, Cambridge University Press, 1991) 58.
[184] *Ibid*, 58.
[185] Kymlicka, above n 113, 213; Kymlicka, 'Liberalism and Communitarianism', above n 76, 194. See R Beiner, 'Revising the Self', 8 *Critical Review* 247 at 248.
[186] Kymlicka, above n 113, 213.
[187] Kymlicka, 'Liberalism and Communitarianism', above n 76, 194.

Feminists have acknowledged that they are also unable to provide a complete solution to the problem of self-improvement.[188] When they try, they often fall back on the unsatisfactory solution of partial agency. The argument is that since the self is fragmented, finding oneself is interpreted as finding a self, or selves, which is, or are, acceptable to the self, rather than finding a coherent, transparent, unity to the self.[189] Moreover, fragmentation assists the search for the true self because awareness of our incoherence is the catalyst for re-assessment; each fragment can reflect on the other fragments, or a person can even 'try on' one fragment at a time, discovering herself in different ways. On this view, acknowledgement of our complexity is a pre-condition of self-transformation, because creativity is produced by the complex nature of causal factors. This renders change not just possible but inevitable: each repetition of the social script is a reinterpretation not a replication.[190] Critical reflection does not necessarily aim at any more than a baseline of coherence, because we are able to hold multiple and even conflicting views and interpretations, so that most people's experience of themselves is not of stable coherence but rather of intrapersonal dialogue.[191] It has even been argued that any stability that the post-liberal self achieves is defined by and founded on an acceptance of constant inconsistency and change.[192] The resulting suggestion is that attention should turn to an explanation of the conditions that encourage this beneficial complexity.[193] Clearly, this takes us no further than the point that we reached at the end of our discussion of partial agency.[194]

So even after careful reflection, on this approach when we decide whether or not to divorce, we will only be making a decision based on our combination of pre-existing characteristics, whether those are flirtatiousness or cowardice, adventurousness or loyalty.

RESULT-ORIENTED REFLECTION

There are two problems with the cognitive approach to autonomy. First, the hunt for the true self collapses into an infinite regress.

---

[188] Williams, above n 38.
[189] Griffiths, above n 5, 77.
[190] Williams, above n 38, 438.
[191] Frazer and Lacey, above n 5, 198–99; Griffiths, above n 5, 183–85.
[192] Regan, above n 92, 50.
[193] Griffiths, above n 5, 185.
[194] See pp 47–52.

Secondly, even if the cognitive approach allowed us to *find* our true self, it would not allow us to *change* ourselves. Because of these problems and although cognitive autonomy starts from relativist premises, the only way that it can achieve internal consistency is to abandon its relativism and follow the more coercive track laid in chapter one, mainly by civic republicans.[195] On this account, there is still a firm obligation to reflect, but there is an additional duty to reach the right result from the reflection.

There is no contradiction between reflection and coercion within civic republicanism; rather, reflection is necessary but not sufficient. Even the strongest advocates of an overtly coercive approach retain the emphasis on reflection. A person is not free if he or she merely attempts to satisfy whatever ends he or she already has: reflection is a necessary condition of freedom, which should be understood to refer to a deliberative process in which a person chooses his or her own ends.[196] A citizen's degree of autonomy can even be measured by the extent to which he or she is reflective and deliberative about his or her choices.[197]

However, '[u]nder this view, private preferences are, by virtue of their status as such, entitled at most to presumptive respect.'[198] The need for reflection goes hand in hand with the need for coercion. Government should not pay too much respect to people's simple choices because these choices depend on norms that people may not endorse on reflection.[199] But even after people have reflected, as we have just seen, people have a difficult struggle to disentangle the social forces to find out what their characters are. Therefore, coercion can be justified on the basis that it implements the decisions that people would make if their ends and desires were apparent to them. Moreover, as we have also just seen, because people's characters are socially determined, changing these characters is completely beyond them. If the social forces are undesirable then they will mould people's characters in an unfortunate manner, preventing people from making the truly authentic choices and living the truly autonomous lives that they otherwise could.[200] Therefore, if people with unfortunate characters caused

---

[195] See pp 32–39.
[196] CR Sunstein, 'Legal Interference with Private Preferences', 53 *University of Chicago Law Review* 1129 at 1132.
[197] CR Sunstein, *Free Markets and Social Justice* (New York, Oxford, Oxford University Press, 1997) 62.
[198] Sunstein, above n 196, 1132.
[199] Sunstein, above n 197, 51.
[200] Frohnen, above n 74, 161.

by these undesirable social forces are not to be left without hope of change, then social forces need to be changed on their behalf, in order to give them more satisfactory characters.[201] Governmental action is the only solution, because often most people, or even everyone, would like to see a change in a particular norm but cannot bring about the change individually.[202]

> . . . communitarians are convinced that they would free us by enrolling us into these various totally managed organizations. These organizations would 'free our minds.' They would dissolve our improper prejudices and replace them with liberating prejudices . . .[203] Their goal is to unchain our wills and desires from unexamined beliefs they deem harmful and restrictive. . . . Communitarians do not want to eliminate all forms of prejudices. Instead they want to replace certain forms of prejudice . . . with prejudices more in keeping with their own goals and values.[204]

Governmental action can take a number of forms, from censorship to information campaigns, but in general in one way or another government will enhance people's true autonomy by immersing them in communitarian norms. At the extreme, it has been suggested that this immersion may take the shape of 'professionally orchestrated consciousness-raising sessions', 'a plethora of mandatory workshops' and 'arbitration seminars'.[205] The rise in popularity of the compulsory use of sensitivity training in America has been charted. For example, students or employees who are considered insensitive to race, gender or sexuality issues have been penalised by being required to take sensitivity training. While the ostensible purpose of sensitivity training is fairly innocuous, namely to make people sensitive to these issues, it has been argued that in reality the sessions encourage the ideological adoption of a particular mindset, verging on indoctrination. Even where the sessions are not formally compulsory, it has been suggested that refusal to participate damages career prospects.[206]

Although more contested within feminism, strands of feminism also hold that reflection is insufficient if it reaches a conventional answer. The common feminist association between subordination and pleasure obtained in erotic submission has been criticised on this ground, in that

---

[201] Schneider, above n 112, 1849.
[202] Sunstein, above n 197, 55.
[203] Frohnen, above n 74, 166.
[204] *Ibid*, 161.
[205] Frohnen, above n 74, 164–65.
[206] Nolan, above n 92, 293–94.

the association violates all three of the methodological principles of consciousness-raising discussed above:

> First, the judgment that women's desires for erotic submission are 'false' is typically made by reference to the *content* of those desires, not their source. The desire for eroticized submission is false because of the content of the desire itself, not because it has been discovered to constitute, in masked form, the desires of others. Second, the desire is judged false not because it is determined to be a *lie* – not truly felt to be pleasurable but only reported as such – but solely because it is a desire for sexual submission. And, finally and most revealingly, the discovery of the falsity of these desires has not typically come from the women who have them, but almost always from the women who do not. The desire is judged to be false, not because the subject herself has come to feel it as false, but because someone else has come to judge it as such. The judgment of falsehood is almost always against the will as well as the opinion of the woman who has the desire. This truly is a profound departure from feminist methodology which is also truly offensive – consciousness-raising is not about the imposition of judgments of truth or falsity on the desires of others. . . . If feminists abandon consciousness-raising as a method in favor of an authoritatively pronounced objective ideal, many women will pay by foregoing a source of sexual pleasure.[207]

An obvious question is who is able to stand outside of society sufficiently to affect social forces without becoming swept along by the existing social trends. This question will be tackled in chapter five. However, for the moment we can just recognise the inescapably élitist consequences of post-liberalism, as well as the paradox that these élitist consequences stem from the prima facie egalitarian premise that each subject must find and follow his or her own law:

> Communitarians present themselves as defenders of equality, but this claim seems untenable in light of their desire to reeducate all of society. Reeducation is by nature inegalitarian. In any program of reeducation a self-selected group of intellectuals asserts that it has the authority to decide what kind of character and beliefs everyone should have.[208]

The paradox can be resolved once we recognise that the apparently egalitarian premise holds only for the élite. Only the élite can shape character, both their own and other people's, because only they can change norms and put them into practice for the community.[209]

[207] R West, 'The Difference in Women's Hedonic Lives: A Phenomenological Critique of Feminist Legal Theory' in Fineman and Thomadsen, above n 91, 128–29.
[208] Frohnen, above n 74, 184.
[209] *Ibid*, 198.

At the end of this chapter, we begin to see an inexorable drive towards coercion. The process started with implementation of reflection as decision-making in the Family Law Act: decision-making was thinking and thinking was decision-making. However, a more coercive approach developed in two ways. First of all, because a decision could only be respected if preceded by reflection, a firm obligation to reflect quickly asserted itself. As we have seen, this development was fairly easily incorporated into the structure of the Family Law Act. However, the second development, namely that the only way that cognitive autonomy could be made internally coherent was by including an obligation to reach the right result from reflection, proved harder to absorb. We will see in later chapters, and particularly in chapter five, that the tension between reflection pure and simple and result-oriented reflection was part of the cause of the collapse of Part II of the Family Law Act.

3

Delaying Divorce

THE PREVIOUS TWO chapters present a puzzle as yet unmentioned. We saw in chapter one that the most crucial tenet of post-liberal theory is an emphasis on the social nature of the self. However, one of the implications of the cognitive approach to autonomy, explored in chapter two, is a conception of the self who struggles to understand, let alone recognise, social purposes.[1] As we saw in chapter two, self-discovery is not merely the only route to making decisions; it is also an obligation.[2] Because the source of moral obligation is no longer external, authenticity becomes the end in itself. Moreover, we each have an original way of being human, so that if we do not live authentically, we miss the point of our life. It is hard to see how duties to others, specifically one's spouse, can fit into this picture. Unsurprisingly, post-liberalism wants to retain the idea of marital obligation, and in this chapter I examine the route that it takes to enable it to do so. In essence, the argument will be that one's spouse is a part of one's self, so that obligations to one's spouse are a species of self-interest and divorce akin to losing an aspect of oneself. However, we will see that this conception of marriage leads to a deep-seated tension in the post-liberal approach to divorce, implying both that divorce must be allowed and that divorce must be delayed.

---

[1] U Beck and E Beck-Gernsheim, *The Normal Chaos of Love* (Cambridge, Polity Press, 1995) 40; M C Regan, *Family Law and the Pursuit of Intimacy* (New York, New York University Press, 1993) 45; C Schneider, 'Moral Discourse and the Transformation of American Family Law', 83 *Michigan Law Review* 1803; BD Whitehead, *The Divorce Culture: Rethinking Our Commitments to Marriage and the Family* (New York, Knopf, 1997); R N Bellah *et al*, *Habits of the Heart: Individualism and Commitment in American Life* (Berkeley, California, University of California Press, 1985); N Rosenblum, *Another Liberalism: Romanticism and the Reconstruction of Liberal Thought* (Cambridge, Massachusetts, Harvard University Press, 1987) 46; J Nolan, *The Therapeutic State: Justifying Government at Century's End* (New York, New York University Press, 1998) 165–66.

[2] See pp 69–71.

A SOCIAL SELF, BUT NO SOCIAL OBLIGATION?

Post-liberal theorists heavily dispute the contention that the search for authenticity implies rejection of duties beyond the self, and in this first section of this chapter I examine some preliminary arguments that they employ for doing so, before concluding at the end of this section that these arguments are unsuccessful. This conclusion will then necessitate devoting the rest of the chapter to an examination of a more sophisticated and successful post-liberal argument for recognising duties beyond the self, namely that others are part of the self, alongside the implications of this argument for divorce law.

In essence, post-liberalism seeks to drive a wedge between authenticity and self-fulfilment.[3] The argument is that decisions can only take on importance against a pre-existing and given horizon of significance; in other words, we can define our identity only against a background of things that matter. Authenticity cannot be defended in ways that collapse these horizons of significance. The initial horizon of significance is choosing in itself, in the sense that prioritising self-creation over for example conforming already creates a picture of what makes a human being. But choosing alone is not sufficient as a horizon, because otherwise all choices would be of equal significance, and the idea of choosing would become incoherent. So the agent who is seeking meaningful self-definition has to do so within a horizon of important questions. But to bracket out everything except that which we find in ourselves would eliminate all candidates for what is important; to shut out demands emanating beyond the self is precisely to suppress the conditions of significance. In a world in which absolutely nothing was important but self-fulfilment, nothing could actually count as self-fulfilment.[4] Therefore self-fulfilment cannot exist in opposition to demands that emanate beyond the self. Self-centred forms of self-fulfilment are shallow and trivialised, but this is not because they stem from the culture of authenticity but rather because they fly in the face of its requirements:[5]

---

[3] C Taylor, *The Ethics of Authenticity* (Cambridge, Massachusetts, Harvard University Press, 1991).

[4] See also C Taylor, *Sources of the Self: The Making of the Modern Identity* (Cambridge, Cambridge University Press, 1989) 507.

[5] See also K Struering, 'Feminist Challenges to the New Familialism: Lifestyle Experimentation and the Freedom of Intimate Association', 11 *Hypatia* 135.

Only if I exist in a world in which history, or the demands of nature, or the needs of my fellow human beings, or the duties of citizenship, or the call of God, or something else of this order *matters* crucially, can I define an identity for myself that is not trivial. Authenticity is not the enemy of demands that emanate from beyond the self; it supposes such demands.[6]

On this view, an instrumental view of relationships based on rejection of obligations to one's spouse is just one more travesty of authenticity:[7]

Two people enter marriage committed to its success and endurance, though not, as in the past, because of religious obligation or moral duty to the spouse. Rather, each person determines that individual self-fulfillment will be promoted by a substantial investment in a stable, interdependent, long-term relationship with a marital partner.[8] . . . commitment, responsibility, and mutual dependence . . . may be important in modern marriage, not as ends in themselves, but because they contribute to an exchange that promotes long-term personal fulfillment.[9]

The argument is that long-term personal fulfilment, not short-term gratification or absence of commitment, is what self-realisation really requires.[10] Concern for self-development should not be reduced to mere selfishness.[11] By failing to honour obligations to their spouses, people may be thwarting their long-term interest in authenticity for the sake of short-term self-gratification. The former is promoted by a stable rewarding relationship, and the latter by maximum individual freedom to pursue current sexual preferences.[12] If we put together the belief that authenticity must not be confused with self-gratification with the implication from the previous two chapters that people cannot be trusted not to confuse the one with the other, then one of the conclusions to this chapter is already emerging. This conclusion is that 'ready dissolution of the currently unsatisfactory relationship may not promote self-realization over time.'[13]

However, the argument that self-fulfilment is a travesty of authenticity cannot avoid the fundamental difficulty that post-liberals do

---

[6] Taylor, above n 3, 40–41.

[7] *Ibid*, 22; Bellah, above n 1, 85.

[8] E S Scott, 'Rational Decisionmaking About Marriage and Divorce', 76 *Virginia Law Review* 9 at 12.

[9] *Ibid*, 25.

[10] *Ibid*.

[11] Struering, above n 5, 143.

[12] Scott, above n 8.

[13] *Ibid*, 25.

reject any formulation of life goals that transcends personal development. Transcendental goals never justify leading a life impoverished in relation to self-discovery but rather are relevant only if and to the extent that they help the subject to develop.[14] The argument could be paraphrased as the suggestion that we should kid ourselves that things that matter are important in themselves because only in this way can they serve their instrumental purpose:

> Apparently Taylor wants us to convince ourselves that people and commitments are not tentative when in fact they are. Such a self-imposed false consciousness seems unlikely to motivate unselfish conduct for long.[15]

Arguably, commitment to goals beyond the self can be neither encouraged nor justified on the basis that the goals are only of instrumental importance, with fulfilment of our own life plan being the ultimate goal.[16] This applies to relationships, as elsewhere:

> On the more intimate level, it fosters a view of relationships in which these ought to subserve personal fulfilment. The relationship is secondary to the self-realization of the partners. On this view, unconditional ties, meant to last for life, make little sense. A relationship may last till death, if it goes on serving its purpose, but there is no point declaring a priori that it ought to.[17]

This relationship is the famous 'pure relationship', which:

> . . . refers to a situation where a social relation is entered into for its own sake, for what can be derived by each person from a sustained association with another, and which is continued only in so far as it is thought by both parties to deliver enough satisfaction for each individual to stay within it.[18]

---

[14] B Frohnen, *The New Communitarians and the Crisis of Modern Liberalism* (Lawrence, University Press of Kansas, 1996) 47; J Hewitt, *Dilemmas of the American Self* (Philadelphia, Temple University Press, 1989) 27; Beck and Beck-Gernsheim, above n 1, 40.

[15] Frohnen, above n 14, 47. See also Nolan, above n 1, 166.

[16] Frohnen, above n 14, 47.

[17] Taylor, above n 3, 43–44. See also Beck and Beck-Gernsheim, above n 1, 53; Schneider, above n 1, 1855; Whitehead, above n 1; Struering, above n 5, 141; Rosenblum, above n 1, 47; B Hafen, 'Individualism and Autonomy in Family Law: The Waning of Belonging', 1991 *Brigham Young University Law Review* 1 at 34; C Schneider, 'Marriage, Morals and the Law', 1994 *Utah Law Review* 503; Scott, above n 8; D Popenoe, 'American Family Decline, 1960–1990: A Review and Appraisal', 55 *Journal of Marriage and the Family* 527 at 537.

[18] A Giddens, *The Transformation of Intimacy: Sexuality, Love and Eroticism in Modern Societies* (Cambridge, Polity, 1992) 58. See also A Giddens, *Modernity and Self-Identity: Self and Society in the Late Modern Age* (Cambridge, Polity Press, 1991) 6; C Smart and B Neale, *Family Fragments?* (Cambridge, Polity Press, 1999) 8; C Smart, 'Wishful Thinking and Harmful Tinkering? Sociological Reflections on Family

In the pure relationship, trust can no longer be anchored in external criteria such as social duty or traditional obligation;[19] rather, the relationship is free-floating.[20] The roots of the pure relationship go back to the rise of romantic love, in that the latter was premised on the finding of a durable emotional tie on the basis of qualities intrinsic to the tie itself rather than for economic or familial reasons.[21] Although romantic love is the precursor to the pure relationship they are also in conflict,[22] because romantic love is forever while the pure relationship is contingent.[23] In essence, under the romantic love complex individuals seek the perfect partner, while with the pure relationship one seeks the perfect relationship and moves on if one's partner does not provide it.[24] If our most important obligation is to live an authentic life then our most important obligation when considering marriage or divorce is to ourselves. Remaining in or leaving a marriage becomes a personal decision, prompted by a set of needs and feelings that are not subject to external interests or claims. Divorce is re-defined as an individual experience, the locus of which is no longer the outer social world but rather the inner world of the self. It becomes a complex emotional voyage, steered by the individual's needs, desires, and feelings.[25] If the main duty when considering divorce is to one's self then there is no place for the requirement to prove fault: we can now reclaim one of the apparently liberal strands of the Family Law Act, namely the total removal of fault, for the post-liberal interpretation.[26] Another upshot of this argument is that in order to ensure that authenticity is not hampered,

---

Policy', 26 *Journal of Social Policy* 301 at 307; J Rodger, *Family Life and Social Control: A Sociological Perspective* (Basingstoke, Macmillan, 1996) 7; J Weeks *et al*, 'Everyday Experiments: Narratives of Non-Heterosexual Relationships' in E Silva and C Smart (eds), *The New Family?* (London, Sage, 1999).

[19] Giddens, *Modernity*, above n 18, 6.

[20] *Ibid*, 89.

[21] *Ibid*; Struering, above n 5, 145; D Cheal, *Family and the State of Theory* (London, Harvester Wheatsheaf, 1991) 43.

[22] Giddens, *Intimacy*, above n 18, 2.

[23] *Ibid*, 61. See also SD Sclater and C Piper, 'The Family Law Act 1996 in Context' in S D Sclater and C Piper (eds), *Undercurrents of Divorce* (Aldershot, Ashgate, 1999) 8.

[24] Smart, above n 18, 307; Whitehead, above n 1; Struering, above n 5, 143.

[25] Whitehead, above n 1; Schneider, above n 1; L Wardle, 'Divorce Violence and the No-Fault Divorce Culture', 1994 *Utah Law Review* 741 at 762; I M Ellman, 'The Misguided Movement to Revive Fault Divorce, and Why Reformers Should Look Instead to the American Law Institute', 11 *International Journal of Law, Policy and the Family* 216 at 228–29; MC Regan, *Alone Together: Law and the Meanings of Marriage* (New York, Oxford University Press, 1998) 7; Hafen, above n 17, 34.

[26] See Introduction, p 2.

indisputably in the final analysis post-liberal society must allow divorce.[27]

Whatever the connection between authenticity and self-fulfilment in strict theory, post-liberals generally accept that in practice the connection is often made. If horizons of significance fade from view, then self-fulfilment becomes increasingly attractive, because if all other sources of meaning fail then the only possibility left for conferring significance is pure choice, which can at least make our lives an exercise in freedom:

> Self-determining freedom is in part the default solution of the culture of authenticity, while at the same time it is its bane.[28]

In addition, often they both accept and lament a present trend towards making this connection, consisting of the subordination of the traditional demands of morality to the requirements of personal fulfilment.[29] This can be illustrated by examining the trend in self-help books,[30] and supported by a recent American empirical study:

> On the whole, even the most secure, happily married of our respondents had difficulty when they sought a language in which to articulate their reasons for commitments that went beyond the self. These confusions were particularly clear when they discussed problems of sacrifice and obligation. While they wanted to maintain enduring relationships, they resisted the notion that such relationships might involve obligations that went beyond the wishes of the partners.[31]

While the pure relationship is exemplified most clearly by lesbian and gay relationships, it can be seen as part of a generic restructuring of intimacy.[32] Therefore, even marriage is increasingly veering towards taking the form of the pure relationship for many sections of society,[33] becoming merely one lifestyle among many[34] and taking a flexible form.[35] Marriage is now a signifier rather than a determinant of commitment:[36]

---

[27] Schneider, above n 17, 525–526; Schneider, above n 1, 1847; Popenoe, above n 17, 537–38; Ellman, above n 25, 228–29.

[28] Taylor, above n 3, 69. See also Taylor, above n 4, 507.

[29] Taylor, above n 4, 507; Hewitt, above n 14, 6; Bellah, above n 1, 109.

[30] Beck and Beck-Gernsheim, above n 1, 54; Rodger, above n 18, 79; Nolan, above n 1, 5.

[31] Bellah, above n 1, 109.

[32] Giddens, *Intimacy*, above n 18, 58; J Weeks *et al*, 'Everyday Experiments: Narratives of Non-Heterosexual Relationships' in Silva and Smart, above n 18, 86.

[33] Giddens, *Intimacy*, above n 18, 58. For discussion, see Smart and Neale, above n 18, 11.

[34] Giddens, *Intimacy*, above n 18, 154.

[35] Schneider, above n 17, 527; H Brook, 'Stalemate: Rethinking the politics of marriage', 3 *Feminist Theory* 45.

[36] Giddens, *Intimacy*, above n 18, 192.

Marriage becomes more and more a relationship initiated for, and kept going for as long as, it delivers emotional satisfaction to be derived from close contact with another. Other traits – even such seemingly fundamental ones as having children – tend to become sources of 'inertial drag' on possible separation, rather than anchoring features of the relationship.[37]

The duty to be true to oneself above all else can be starkly illustrated by changing attitudes toward self-sacrifice in marriage. Self-sacrifice once seemed the ultimate proof of love, but now seems suspect, not noble so much as parasitic:[38]

... someone who for the sake of true love sacrifices a marriage, family ties, parenthood, perhaps ultimately even the well-being of those dependent on him/her, is not committing a sin but merely obeying the rules, answering the call of the heart and seeking fulfilment for him/herself and others. He or she is not to blame; it would be wrong to cling to an order which does not value love highly enough[39] ... Abandoning one's own children for someone else is not a breach of love but a proof of it; idealizing love means pledging to break with all false forms of it.[40]

Correspondingly, it has also been suggested that having children is increasingly influenced by the belief that parenthood will be a satisfying experience that will enhance individual growth and development, rather than by any sense of obligation.[41]

Post-liberals also generally accept that the current emphasis on self-fulfilment combined with the belief that personal fulfilment can be promoted through therapy has led to a cultural turn towards the therapeutic.[42] This cultural turn has been seen as reflected in a shift from moral discourse to therapeutic language, drawn in particular from medicine and psychology.[43] The afore-mentioned empirical study found evidence for this shift, in that most of the interviewees used a language influenced by therapy to articulate their thoughts and feelings:

Today we are likely to see not only our marriages but also our families, work, community, and society in therapeutic terms. Life's joys and deeper

[37] Giddens, *Modernity*, above n 18, 89. See also Smart and Neale, above n 18, 10–11; Whitehead, above n 1, 72.

[38] Schneider, above n 17.

[39] Beck and Beck-Gernsheim, above n 1, 173.

[40] *Ibid*, 174.

[41] Regan, above n 1, 45.

[42] Taylor, above n 4, 507; Bellah, above n 1, 113; Hewitt, above n 14, 6; A Etzioni, *The New Golden Rule: Community and Morality in a Democratic Society* (New York, Basic Books, 1998) 135. See also Nolan, above n 1.

[43] Schneider, above n 1.

meanings, and its difficulties too, are less often attributed to material conditions and interpreted in traditional moral terms than they were even a generation ago. Now the 'interpersonal' seems to be the key to much of life.[44]

The triumph of the therapeutic has been charted with respect to relationships and marriage in particular.[45] It has been argued that people have begun to see marriage as part of the domain of mental health. Accordingly, psychotherapeutic thought and practice have invaded marriage counselling, even religious marriage counselling, so that counselling has begun to take a client-centred approach in order to avoid damage to the client's selfhood. Clearly, only a few people seek professional help when their marriage is in difficulty, but a much greater number have started talking and thinking in a language influenced by the therapeutic discourse, referring to 'self-esteem and self-validation, about finding oneself and feeling good about oneself.'[46]

Cognitive autonomy leads to therapeutic culture via the emphasis on self-fulfilment. However, cognitive autonomy also leads to therapeutic culture directly: the same American study found that people's definition of the ideal therapeutic relationship was 'one in which everything is completely conscious and all parties know how they feel and what they want.'[47] Moreover, the relationship between therapeutic culture and cognitive autonomy is mutually reinforcing. Given that behaviour is increasingly interpreted on the basis of health rather than morality,[48] self-discovery becomes a more urgent imperative: because moral faults become illnesses[49] and personality traits symptoms,[50] members of society 'are called to heed the leading requirement of the sick role – to devote themselves to healing themselves.'[51] The relationship between therapeutic culture and self-fulfilment is also mutually reinforcing because therapeutic culture reinforces the idea of commitment as commitment to the self.[52]

Cognitive autonomy, self-fulfilment and therapeutic culture work symbiotically to recast divorce into a new and potentially more positive

---

[44] Bellah, above n 1, 113.

[45] Whitehead, above n 1.

[46] *Ibid*, 49. See also Schneider, above n 1; Wardle, above n 25, 762; Ellman, above n 25, 228–29; Regan, above n 25, 7; Hafen, above n 17, 34.

[47] Bellah, above n 1, 139.

[48] Nolan, above n 1, 9.

[49] Schneider, above n 1, 1854.

[50] J Purdy, 'Age of Irony', 39 *The American Prospect* 84 at 87.

[51] Schneider, above n 17, 525. See also Regan, above n 1, 44; Hewitt, above n 14, 6.

[52] Whitehead, above n 1; Etzioni, above n 42, 135.

light. If the life goal is to live authentically by discovering one's true self then divorce can offer this potential for personal growth alongside the opportunity 'to build a stronger identity and to achieve a more coherent and fully realized sense of self.'[53] Accordingly, an empirical study found that half of the divorcing women interviewed said that divorce had given them a newfound sense of freedom to acquire a stronger sense of self, or of wholeness.[54] This recasting of divorce has been charted in divorce literature from the late 1970s onwards, in which are commonly linked the culturally powerful themes of freedom and an emotional journey:

> Sometimes the journey is described in therapeutic terms: from sickness to health. Other times it is characterized in political terms: from slavery to freedom. Occasionally it is cast in spiritual terms: from darkness into the light.[55] . . . unvaryingly the narrative is that of an odyssey. At the center of virtually every book is the questing self, seeking and eventually achieving a new identity.[56] . . . In divorcing, the self is not only made new but also made whole. Marital breakup brings about a coherent and integrated identity.[57]

At the extreme, a rhetorical shift within divorce literature has turned divorce rather than marriage into the symbol of a mature identity, signifying self-knowledge and personal growth.[58]

However, this approach is problematic, if not contradictory:

> . . . the pure relationship contains internal tensions and even contradictions. By definition, it is a social relation which can be terminated at will, and is only sustained in so far as it generates sufficient psychic returns for each individual. On the one hand it demands commitment, not only to the other individual, but to the social relation itself: this is again intrinsic to the pure relationship. On the other hand, the relationship can be voluntarily broken, and is acknowledged by both parties to be only 'good until further notice'. The possibility of dissolution, perhaps willingly brought about by the individual in question, forms part of the very horizon of commitment.[59]

---

[53] Whitehead, above n 1, 54.

[54] CK Riessman, *Divorce Talk: Men and Women Make Sense of Personal Relationships* (New Brunswick, New Jersey, Rutgers University Press, 1990) 165, quoted in *ibid*, 57. See also S D Sclater, 'Narratives of Divorce', 19 *Journal of Social Welfare and Family Law* 423 at 429; L Hodgkinson, 'The Beginning of a Whole New Life Apart', *The Guardian*, 20 July 1990.

[55] Whitehead, above n 1, 59.

[56] *Ibid*, 60.

[57] *Ibid*, 61.

[58] *Ibid*.

[59] Giddens, Modernity, above n 18, 187. See also Giddens, *Intimacy*, above n 18, 63.

There is a structural contradiction within the pure relationship, cen-
tring on commitment. To generate commitment and develop a shared
history, the person must give of himself or herself to the other. That is,
he or she must provide some kind of guarantee that the relationship can
be sustained indefinitely. But it is a feature of the pure relationship that
it can be terminated more or less at will. For the relationship to stand a
chance of lasting, commitment is necessary, but given that dissolution
is possible, commitment without reservation is risky.[60]

We are beginning to see a tension in the post-liberal attitude to
divorce. On the one hand, post-liberals believe that the life goal is self-
discovery leading to authenticity, so despite the distinction that they
draw between authenticity and self-gratification, the primary duty
must be to the self. Therefore in the final analysis post-liberalism could
never outlaw divorce. On the other hand, because post-liberals stress
that authenticity is not synonymous with self-gratification and given
the implication from the previous two chapters that people cannot be
trusted not to confuse them, self-discovery would be thwarted if
divorce were too readily available. We will see that Part II of the Family
Law Act reflected this tension.

THE SPOUSE AS PART OF THE SELF

If the self is inherently social, then a concern for other persons is fundamental to the self and is not reducible to a mere variety of self-concern.[61] . . . I
care about you – indeed, I count you as a part of my expanded sense of self
– because of our shared identity, so I will address you not as a competitor for
scarce resources, but as a part of the self whose interest we jointly pursue.[62]

---

[60] Giddens, *Intimacy* above n 18, 137. See also U Beck, 'The Reinvention of Politics'
in U Beck, A Giddens and S Lash, *Reflexive Modernization: Politics, Tradition and
Aesthetics in the Modern Social Order* (Cambridge, Polity Press, 1994) 15; Whitehead,
above n 1, 76.

[61] M Friedman, *What are Friends For?: Feminist Perspectives on Personal
Relationships and Moral Theory* (Ithaca, New York, Cornell University Press, 1993) 68.
See also M Friedman, 'The Social Self and the Partiality Debates' in C Card (ed), *Feminist
Ethics* (Lawrence, Kansas, University Press of Kansas, 1991) 165.

[62] S Williams, 'A Feminist Reassessment of Civil Society', 72 *Indiana Law Journal* 417
at 419. See also P Weiss, 'Feminism and Communitarianism: Comparing Critiques of
Liberalism' in P Weiss and M Friedman (eds), *Feminism and Community* (Philadelphia,
Temple University Press, 1995) 171; C Berry, *The Idea of a Democratic Community*
(Hemel Hempstead, Harvester Wheatsheaf, 1989) 116.

The tension could perhaps be avoided if post-liberal theory gave a strong meaning to the social nature of the self, so that one's spouse could be part of oneself. In that case, divorcing one's spouse would be akin to losing an aspect of oneself, and remaining married could be regarded as a species of self-interest. Accordingly, in the next section I examine in more detail the post-liberal argument for strengthening the meaning given to the social subject, and in the subsequent section I look at how post-liberals square a strong sense of the social self with retention of autonomy.

A Stronger Sense of the Social Self

Within post-liberal theory relationships are central in constituting the self.[63] The relationship between the self and others is an essentially shared relation in which the identity of each self is partially or even wholly constituted by the relation,[64] so that it is meaningful to speak of two or more separate selves becoming one, or even of one self differentiating itself.[65] In certain moral circumstances therefore, the relevant description of the self may embrace more than a single, individual human being, such as a family or nation.[66]

[63] A Hutchinson and L Green, 'Introduction' in A Hutchinson and L Green (eds), *Law and the Community: The End of Individualism?* (Toronto, Carswell, 1989) 2; J Nedelsky, 'Reconceiving Autonomy: Sources, Thoughts and Possibilities' in A Hutchinson and L Green (eds), *Law and the Community: The End of Individualism?* (Toronto, Carswell, 1989) 222; S Benhabib and D Cornell, 'Beyond the Politics of Gender' in S Benhabib and D Cornell (eds), *Feminism as Critique: Essays on the Politics of Gender in Late-Capitalist Societies* (Cambridge, Polity, 1987) 12; R Lister, *Citizenship: Feminist Perspectives* (Basingstoke, Macmillan Press Ltd, 1997) 37; Etzioni, above n 42, 6; SL Hoagland, 'Why *Lesbian* Ethics?' in C Card (ed), *Adventures in Lesbian Philosophy* (Bloomington, Indiana University Press, 1994) 205; MC Regan, 'Market Discourse and Moral Neutrality in Divorce Law', 1994 *Utah Law Review* 605 at 668–69; J B Elshtain, 'Feminism, Family, and Community', 29 *Dissent* 442 at 445; M Griffiths, *Feminisms and the Self: The Web of Identity* (London, New York, Routledge, 1995) 78; Friedman, above n 61, 69; M Friedman, 'The Social Self and the Partiality Debates' in C Card, above n 61, 165.

[64] P Neal and D Paris, 'Liberalism and the Communitarian Critique: A Guide for the Perplexed', 23 *Canadian Journal of Political Science* 419 at 425.

[65] *Ibid*, 427.

[66] M Sandel, *Liberalism and the Limits of Justice* (Cambridge, Cambridge University Press, 1998) 63; D Greschner, 'Feminist Concerns with the New Communitarians: We Don't Need Another Hero' in Hutchinson and Green, above n 63, 134; D Phillips, *Looking Backward: A Critical Appraisal of Communitarian Thought* (Princeton, New Jersey, Princeton University Press, 1993) 179.

This has been described as the fundamentally dialogic character of human life.[67] We become full human agents through acquiring language, into which we are inducted in exchange with others who matter to us, and which no one can accomplish on his or her own. This is not just a fact about the genesis of agency: it is not that we learn language in dialogue and then go on to use it for our own purposes, although this is true to some extent, in that we develop opinions through solitary reflection. However, this is not the case for important issues, such as the definition of our identity. We always define our identity in dialogue with and sometimes in struggle against the identities that our significant others give us.[68] The ongoing validation of every subject's world, as socially defined, including crucially the validation of his or her identity and place in the world, depends upon the strength and continuity of significant relationships in which conversation about the world can be carried on. In other words, the reality of the world is sustained through conversation with significant others. This reality includes the way in which the person views himself or herself.[69]

On this view, even to attempt to minimise the influence of others by defining ourselves to the fullest degree possible is to underestimate the place of the dialogical in human life:

> It forgets how our understanding of the good things in life can be transformed by our enjoying them in common with people we love, how some goods become accessible to us only through such common enjoyment.[70]

Because of this, it would take a great deal of effort to *prevent* our identity being formed by significant others. Our identity requires recognition by others. The conclusion is that:

> . . . the making and sustaining of our identity, in the absence of a heroic effort to break out of ordinary existence, remains dialogic throughout our lives.[71]

---

[67] Taylor, above n 3.

[68] For discussion, see Frohnen, above n 14, 201.

[69] P Berger and H Kellner, 'Marriage and the Construction of Reality', 46 *Diogenes* 1 at 4–5; D Cornell, *At the Heart of Freedom: Feminism, Sex and Equality* (Princeton, New Jersey, Princeton University Press, 1998) 62; A Hutchinson, 'Talking the Good Life: From Liberal Chatter to Democratic Conversation' in Hutchinson and Green, above n 63, 168.

[70] Taylor, above n 3, 34.

[71] *Ibid*, 35. See also Struering, above n 5; DT Meyers, *Self, Society, and Personal Choice* (New York, Columbia University Press, 1989) 85.

The discovery and articulation of the dialogic nature of identity has been tied in with the development of the ideal of authenticity. Previously, social hierarchies largely fixed a person's identity: what a person regarded as important, his or her roles and activities were to a great extent determined by his or her social position. The emergence of the ideal of authenticity undermined this because it called on the subject to discover his or her own original way of being, which had to be inwardly generated not socially provided.[72] But since there is no such thing as monologic inward generation of identity, the development of an ideal of inwardly generated identity gives crucial importance to recognition by others, because identity now depends on dialogic relations with others. Of course, in the previous era identity was also dependent on society: indeed it rested on the social hierarchy; but what is different now is that identity is not taken for granted: identity is now created by others' recognition, and so it can also fail. For the first time, the need for recognition is acknowledged.[73]

A stronger interpretation is that the self is defined by the totality of its relations with other beings. Since these relations are social, they fall under the principle that applies to all social phenomena, that what something is thought to be is in part what it is. Therefore we are our relations, in that the way others see us is one of the determinants of our own selfhood. If one could imagine a situation in which no one treated or had ever treated a person as a self then that person would have no self. The self cannot be imagined apart from social relations, nor can it be extracted from the bonds of its association with others.[74]

There is a strand within feminism that characterises women's perspective on moral reasoning as recognition of the connection between self and other.[75] This recognition can be so strong that there is feminist concern that it can impede a recognition of self, evidence of which is provided by women's tendency to describe themselves in terms of a relationship such as future mother or present wife.[76] Accordingly, it has been argued that feminism does not generally see the self as defined so completely through others as communitarianism, so that feminists

---

[72] Taylor, above n 3; Nolan, above n 1, 4.

[73] Taylor, above n 3; D Cornell, *The Imaginary Domain: Abortion, Pornography and Sexual Harassment* (New York, Routledge, 1995) 156; Cornell, above n 69, 62.

[74] R Unger, *Knowledge and Politics* (New York, Free Press, 1975).

[75] Carol Gilligan, *In a Different Voice: Psychological Theory and Women's Development* (Cambridge, Massachusetts, Harvard University Press, 1982).

[76] *Ibid*; Williams, above n 62.

talk of attachment, interdependence and connection, while communitarians posit fusion.[77]

Autonomy and The Social Self

We saw in chapter one that very few post-liberals are prepared to abandon the notion of autonomy.[78] The question raised by the previous section is how such a strongly social sense of the self in which our identity is defined by our relations with others can coexist with a meaningful notion of autonomy. The post-liberal response to this question is essentially that relations with others are the fount of autonomy, rather than a barrier to autonomy.[79]

The argument is that since close social relationships are essential for the creation of self-identity, we should not resign ourselves to the need for others but rather find and create ourselves through them, knowing that others give autonomy more than they restrict it.[80] It follows that while boundary is the current metaphor in the rhetoric of freedom, the metaphor is misleading about the nature of human selfhood: we need a new conception of the tension between the collective and the individual. Moreover the metaphor is destructive because its thrust is to emphasise protection of the individual from the intrusion of the collective by drawing boundaries around him or her when in fact the collective is more important as a source of autonomy than as a threat to it.[81] If we ask what enables people to be autonomous, the answer is not isolation, but constructive relationships that provide the support and guidance necessary for the development and experience of autonomy. Dependence is not the antithesis of autonomy, but a literal precondition of autonomy, and interdependence a constant component of

---

[77] D Greschner, 'Feminist Concerns with the New Communitarians: We Don't Need Another Hero' in Hutchinson and Green, above n 63, 141–42.

[78] Pp 28–32.

[79] J Nedelsky, 'Reconceiving Autonomy: Sources, Thoughts and Possibilities' in Hutchinson and Green, above n 63, 225.

[80] Griffiths, above n 63; Friedman, above n 61; Williams, above n 62, 434; Lister, above n 63; 36; Frohnen, above n 14, 166; Struering, above n 5, 144; Etzioni, above n 42, 26–27; G Kateb, 'Democratic Individuality and the Meaning of Rights' in N Rosenblum (ed), *Liberalism and the Moral Life* (Cambridge, Massachusetts, Harvard University Press, 1989) 183; D Cornell, 'Two Lectures on the Normative Dimensions of Community in the Law', 54 *Tennessee Law Review* 327 at 336.

[81] J Nedelsky, 'Law, Boundaries, and the Bounded Self', 30 *Representations* 162; Griffiths, above n 63.

autonomy.[82] Conversely, a mature identity involves the ability to foster and preserve relationships with others.[83] The separateness implied by the metaphor of boundary distorts our understanding of autonomy by splitting off relations with others, setting separateness up in opposition to integration.[84] This approach has been taken further: Hoagland replaces the concept of autonomy with the term 'autokoenony', meaning self in community, on the basis that autonomy implies separation and that we should instead seek to articulate a self defined in terms of its relations with others.[85]

On this view, the more pertinent question is what kinds of interactions with others enrich autonomy as opposed to being oppressive,[86] although some believe that even oppressive interactions enhance autonomy more than the absence of interactions.[87] For example, Etzioni paints a gloomy picture of the effect on individuals of being severed from the stable and positive attachments that communities best provide. He argues that they tend to be 'mentally unstable, impulsive, prone to suicide, and otherwise predisposed to mental and psychosomatic illnesses.'[88] But ideally the subject needs to find interactions that satisfy his or her need for recognition without surrendering his or her distinctiveness:

> He would have to find a way in which union with the others would foster rather than diminish the sense of his own individual being. This union could be described as a circumstance in which others are complementary rather than opposing wills in the sense that to join with them in a community of understandings and purposes increases rather than diminishes one's own individuality. This hypothetical condition in which the greatest individuality is allied with the greatest sociability and realized through it, is the ideal of sympathy. . . . It is the dreamt-of circumstance in which one is both 'at one' with other selves and 'separate' from them.[89]

Feminists argue that that this dreamt-of circumstance is best achieved in communities that are constitutive of their members' identities

---

[82] J Nedelsky, 'Reconceiving Autonomy: Sources, Thoughts and Possibilities' in Hutchinson and Green, above n 63, 224–25; Griffiths, above n 63.

[83] Regan, above n 25, 12; Griffiths, above n 63.

[84] Nedelsky, above n 81.

[85] SL Hoagland, *Lesbian Ethics: Toward New Value* (Palo Alto, California, Institute of Lesbian Studies, 1988) 144. For discussion, see S Hekman, *Moral Voices, Moral Selves: Carol Gilligan and Feminist Moral Theory* (Cambridge, Polity, 1995) 66–67.

[86] Nedelsky, above n 81.

[87] Griffiths, above n 63.

[88] Etzioni, above n 42, 25.

[89] Unger, above n 74, 217. For discussion, see Frohnen, above n 14, 46.

rather than those made up of instrumental relationships. This is because constitutive communities are most likely to provide the recognition and security that allows for the development of self-esteem and self-trust, as the sense that the other person values you for yourself not your usefulness is essential to the development of self-esteem. This self-esteem then provides the foundation for the skills involved in telling one's own story, while the community itself provides the substance out of which the story is constructed. Similarly, the vulnerability necessary to search for self-knowledge and self-trust flourishes in a relationship in which one feels secure.[90] Other feminists have suggested that instrumental communities can make an additional important contribution by having constitutive effects.[91] For example, a woman may begin to view her relationship with her spouse differently when she is valued at work.[92]

Family as Community

In the last two sections, I looked at the post-liberal argument for strengthening the sense of social self while retaining autonomy. It was necessary to do so because this is the first stage in the argument that the spouse is part of the self and therefore that one's duties to one's spouse are part of one's duties to oneself. However, having determined that for the post-liberal relationships in general are integral to identity, we now need to look at their argument for holding that the spousal relationship in particular is crucial to one's sense of self. There are four steps to this argument, which I will examine in this section and the subsequent three sections. The first is that post-liberals generally regard the family as the paradigm of community. Secondly, when they object to treating the family as paradigm, they do so because the family is imposed, and they wish to prioritise communities of choice. Thirdly, this objection can be overcome by treating the relationship between husband and wife as best encapsulating the model community, since this relationship is voluntary. Finally and consequently, marriage is a profoundly identity-forming relationship.

---

[90] Williams, above n 62, 441; Struering, above n 5, 142.
[91] K Abrams, 'Redefining Women's Agency: A Response to Professor Williams', 72 *Indiana Law Journal* 459 at 462; Rosenblum, above n 1, 157.
[92] Abrams, above n 91, 462.

'The task, then, is to think of autonomy in terms of the forms of human interactions in which it will develop and flourish.'[93] For communitarians and civic republicans, as well as many feminist theorists, the family is the paradigm of a constitutive community because it is within the family that we experience the closest connection and greatest commitment to others.[94] Some take this point further to argue that the family is the only community in which we experience the complete absence of self-interest and the consequential replacement of justice by a higher good.[95] Therefore, the family is significant as an inspiration or model for community rather than just an example.[96]

Post-liberals, specifically communitarians, disagree on whether the family is a perfect or flawed model for community. Those that see it as flawed do so because the family is incapable of embracing more than a few people at once as a result of the family's reliance on particularistic commitments and face-to-face interactions.[97] On this analysis, family

[93] J Nedelsky, 'Reconceiving Autonomy: Sources, Thoughts and Possibilities' in Hutchinson and Green, above n 63, 225–26.

[94] See eg A Etzioni, *The Spirit of Community: Rights, Responsibilities and the Communitarian Agenda* (New York, Random House, 1993); Etzioni above n 42, 52 and 74; RB Fowler, *The Dance with Community: The Contemporary Debate in American Political Thought* (Kansas, Kansas University Press, 1991); Elshtain, above n 63; JB Elshtain and J Buell, 'Families in Trouble', 38 *Dissent* 262; ME Albert, 'In the Interest of the Public Good? New Questions for Feminism' in C Reynolds and R Norman (eds), *Community in America: The Challenge of Habits of the Heart* (Berkeley, California, California University Press, 1988); Wardle, above n 25, 763; Regan, above n 1, 1; D Greschner, 'Feminist Concerns with the New Communitarians: We Don't Need Another Hero' in Hutchinson and Green, above n 63, 132; Regan, above n 63, 668; B Woodhouse, ' "It All Depends on What You Mean By Home": Toward a Communitarian Theory of the "Nontraditional" Family', 1996 *Utah Law Review* 569 at 586.

[95] See eg Elshtain, above n 63, 447; M Sandel, 'Morality and the Liberal Ideal', *New Republic*, 7 May 1984, 15 at 17; Bellah, above n 1, 85; R Beiner, 'What's the Matter with Liberalism?' in Hutchinson and Green, above n 63, 38. For discussion, see Lister, above n 63, 150; Struering, above n 5; A Gutmann, 'Communitarian Critics of Liberalism', 14 *Philosophy and Public Affairs* 308 at 309; E Frazer, *The Problems of Communitarian Politics: Unity and Conflict* (Oxford, Oxford University Press, 1999) 175; SM Okin, *Justice, Gender and the Family* (New York, Basic Books, 1989); SM Okin, 'Humanist-Liberalism' in Rosenblum, above n 80, 50.

[96] See eg R Bellah *et al*, *The Good Society* (New York, Knopf, 1991) 48–49; Regan, above n 63, 669; Unger, above n 74, 264; R Chadwick, 'Moral Reasoning in Family Law – A Response to Katherine O'Donovan' in D Morgan and G Douglas (eds), *Constituting Families: A Study in Governance* (Stuttgart, Germany, Steiner (Franz) Verlag Wiesbaden GmbH, 1994) 59. For discussion, see Frazer, above n 95, 175–77; Gutmann, above n 95, 309; D Greschner, 'Feminist Concerns with the New Communitarians: We Don't Need Another Hero' in Hutchinson and Green, above n 63, 133; ME Albert, 'In the Interest of the Public Good? New Questions for Feminism' in Reynolds and Norman, above n 94, 88; Fowler, above n 94, 95; Hewitt, above n 14; Rosenblum, above n 1, 156.

[97] Unger, above n 74, 264. For discussion, see Frazer, above n 95, 176.

relations are insufficient for civic virtue,[98] so that 'communitarian politics must treat the family as both a source of inspiration and a foe to be
contained and transformed.'[99] However, the predominant communitarian view is to see the family more positively as the building block of
community,[100] or as a mini-community.[101] The family works here as a
stepping stone towards participation in the wider community,[102] but only
if we heed its moral lessons and do not value the family purely in its own
terms.[103] The family assists the wider community by contributing to the
creation of the right kind of citizens.[104] Within communitarianism, the
strength of families and the strength of wider communities are seen as
mutually reinforcing,[105] and their meanings as mutually constitutive:[106]

> Families *are*, ideally at least, communities, and conversely the idea of com-
> munity is analysed *as* 'family writ large'. In some communitarian analyses,
> wider communities are conceptualized as 'communities of communities' –
> communities of families and other institutions like firms and schools and
> neighbourhoods.[107]

This approach explains how communitarians manage to see the family
as both a defence against individualism and a bulwark against the state.
Unsurprisingly, the approach leads to a conception of 'the communitarian family' in which all members of the family are active in the
wider community and the parents understand that their moral responsibility to bring their children up well is a responsibility to the
community.[108] At this point, it would be difficult not to see the adoption of a communitarian agenda by the Labour Party; Tony Blair has
proclaimed: 'It is in the family that a sense of community is born.'[109]

---

[98] See Frazer, above n 95, 176.
[99] Unger, above n 74, 264. For discussion, see Rosenblum, above n 1, 184; Hewitt,
above n 14, 143.
[100] See Frazer, above n 95, 176.
[101] A Etzioni, 'Introduction' in A Etzioni (ed), *The Essential Communitarian Reader*
(Lanham, Rowman & Littlefield, 1998) xiii. For discussion, see M Phillips, 'Father of
Tony Blair's Big Idea', *The Observer*, 24 July 1994.
[102] See Hewitt, above n 14, 130.
[103] See Frohnen, above n 14.
[104] W Galston, 'A Liberal-Democratic Case for the Two-Parent Family' in Etzioni,
above n 101; Hewitt, above n 14, 120.
[105] See Frazer, above n 95, 37.
[106] See *Ibid*, 174.
[107] *Ibid*, 173–4.
[108] Etzioni, above n 42, 74. For discussion, see Frazer, above n 95, 176.
[109] S Boseley and P Wintour, 'Blair Backs "Stable" Two-Parent Families', *The
Guardian*, 30 March 1995.

While feminists generally agree that the earliest and most fundamental way that our selves are constituted is within the family,[110]
clearly, many feminists do not regard this as a reason to endorse the
family.[111] They believe that the family harbours social roles and structures that have been highly oppressive to women and have sustained
gender hierarchies,[112] so that it is regrettable that we are formed within
it.[113] From this perspective, the flaw in the communitarian approach is
to treat the family as the smallest unit of political analysis rather than
seeing the people and power relations within it.[114] It has been argued
that once we peer inside the family, justice becomes a crucial virtue: it
is only when the family is idealised or even mythologised that justice
seems unnecessary.[115] Despite communitarian complacency about the
moral authority of the family,[116] from a feminist standpoint there is no
legitimacy in norms and claims of communities that sustain gender
hierarchies.[117]

Most post-liberal feminists are not so hostile to the family however,
although they generally feel the need to argue rather than assume support
for the family, given women's range of negative experiences within families.[118] It has been suggested that initially feminist theorising identified

[110] SM Okin, 'Humanist-Liberalism' in Rosenblum, above n 80, 48–50; Okin, above
n 95.

[111] ES Scott, 'Rehabilitating Liberals in Modern Divorce Law', 1994 *Utah Law
Review* 687 at 735; R Bellah, 'The Idea of Practices in *Habits*: A Response' in Reynolds
and Norman, above n 94, 283.

[112] See eg M Friedman, 'Feminism and Modern Friendship: Dislocating the
Community', 99 *Ethics* 275; Williams, above n 62; Scott, above n 111, 735; E Frazer and
N Lacey, *The Politics of Community: A Feminist Critique of the Liberal-Communitarian
Debate* (Buffalo, New York, University of Toronto Press, 1994) 139; Rosenblum, above
n 1, 156. For discussion, see M E Albert, 'In the Interest of the Public Good? New
Questions for Feminism' in Reynolds and Norman, above n 94, 89.

[113] S M Okin, 'Humanist-Liberalism' in Rosenblum, above n 80, 48–50; Okin, above
n 95.

[114] D Greschner, 'Feminist Concerns with the New Communitarians: We Don't Need
Another Hero' in Hutchinson and Green, above n 63; P Weiss, 'Feminism And
Communitarianism: Comparing Critiques of Liberalism' in Weiss and Friedman, above
n 62, 173–74.

[115] SM Okin, 'Humanist-Liberalism' in Rosenblum, above n 80, 48–50; Okin, above
n 95.

[116] Friedman, above n 112; Scott, above n 111, 737–38; P Weiss, 'Feminism And
Communitarianism: Comparing Critiques of Liberalism' in Weiss and Friedman, above
n 62, 161.

[117] Friedman, above n 112.

[118] D Greschner, 'Feminist Concerns with the New Communitarians: We Don't Need
Another Hero' in Hutchinson and Green, above n 63, 133.

the family as the core site of women's oppression,[119] but it was the development of post-liberal theory that led feminism to be less hostile. This was because post-liberal feminism rejected the notion of any core site of oppression, along with the idea that the family could have the same significance for all women.[120] Because post-liberal feminism placed more importance on relationships, it criticised liberalism for ignoring rather than for supporting the family.[121] Even when post-liberal feminism is hostile towards the family, this hostility tends to be based on the failure of the family as community, with the ideal still being supported.[122]

Of course, feminists who support the model of family as community emphasise that they are not advocating the traditional patriarchal family premised on the subordination of women but are rather supporting a critical view of the family,[123] which recognises the need for change in family practices that show gender differentiation.[124] But once feminism has come this far, it begins to blend with the communitarian approach to the family, since most communitarians also support a critical view of the family. For example, Etzioni makes clear that he does not favour a return to the traditional family but rather 'a peer marriage in which father and mother have the same rights and responsibilities and both are more dedicated to their children.'[125] The ideal communitarian family has been described as involving a cooperative and egalitarian relationship, with both marital partners deeply and actively involved in their children's upbringing.[126] It is right to recognise however that, unlike most feminists, most communitarians are clear that while they

[119] Smart and Neale, above n 18, 3; Elshtain, above n 63, 444; D Greschner, 'Feminist Concerns with the New Communitarians: We Don't Need Another Hero' in Hutchinson and Green, above n 63, 131.

[120] Smart and Neale, above n 18, 3; Brook, above n 35, 50.

[121] P Weiss, 'Feminism And Communitarianism: Comparing Critiques of Liberalism' in Weiss and Friedman, above n 62, 174; Okin, above n 95, 45.

[122] See eg J Stacey, 'Families against "The Family": The transatlantic passage of the politics of family values', 89 *Radical Philosophy* 2. For discussion, see Fowler, above n 94, 100; Okin, above n 95, 125.

[123] See eg ME Albert, 'In the Interest of the Public Good? New Questions for Feminism' in Reynolds and Norman, above n 94; Elshtain, above n 63, 446; D Greschner, 'Feminist Concerns with the New Communitarians: We Don't Need Another Hero' in Hutchinson and Green, above n 63, 133; P Weiss, 'Feminism And Communitarianism: Comparing Critiques of Liberalism' in Weiss and Friedman, above n 62, 174; Okin, above n 95. For discussion, see Fowler, above n 94, 98.

[124] Friedman, above n 112; Williams, above n 62.

[125] Etzioni, above n 42, 74.

[126] Bellah, above n 96, 49; R Bellah, 'The Idea of Practices in *Habits*: A Response' in Reynolds and Norman, above n 17, 283; Popenoe, above n 17, 535. For discussion, see Frazer, above n 95, 176; Fowler, above n 94, 98; Struering, above n 5, 145.

are prepared to accept or even welcome some change in the family, they still favour a two parent heterosexual family.[127]

Communities of Choice

An examination of residual feminist opposition to the family as the model for community shows that the chief objection is that the family is imposed. This point highlights a bifurcation between the feminist and communitarian approaches to community: feminists regard chosen communities as crucial to the formation of a positive identity[128] while communitarians are relatively untroubled about giving pride of place to discovered communities.[129] Communitarians concentrate on substantive examples of community that fall into one of two groups: either governmental communities that constitute civic and national identities, principally nation states, or local communities centred around family, church or neighbourhood. Both groups are in the first instance found rather than chosen.[130] In response, feminists emphasise friendships, urban relationships, and political groups. This is because these are more likely than the family-neighbourhood-nation complex to be 'grounded in and sustained by shared interests and values, mutual affection, and possibilities for generating mutual respect and esteem',[131] thereby providing models of alternative social relationships and standpoints for critical reflection on self and community:[132]

> Feminist networks and lesbian communities, for example, have often provided women with the strength, support, and sense of self-worth

[127] See eg Etzioni, above n 42, 74. For discussion, see J Demaine, 'Beyond Communitarianism: Citizenship, Politics and Education' in J Demaine and H Entwistle (eds), *Beyond Communitarianism: Citizenship, Politics and Education* (Basingstoke, Macmillan, 1996) 8–9; Frazer, above n 95, 176; A Skolnick and S Rosencrantz, 'The New Crusade for the Old Family', 18 *The American Prospect* 59 at 59; Struering, above n 5, 145; P Weiss, 'Feminism And Communitarianism: Comparing Critiques of Liberalism' in Weiss and Friedman, above n 62, 174.
[128] See eg Friedman, above n 112, 283–84; Rosenblum, above n 1, 156; T Simon, 'The Theoretical Marginalization of the Disadvantaged: A Liberal/Communitarian Failing' in C F Delaney (ed), *The Liberalism-Communitarianism Debate: Liberty and Community Values* (Lanham, Rowman & Littlefield, 1994), 114.
[129] See eg Taylor, above n 4, 508; Bellah, above n 1, 85; Beiner, 'What's the Matter with Liberalism?' in Hutchinson and Green, above n 63, 38.
[130] Bellah, above n 1, 85; Beiner, 'What's the Matter with Liberalism?' in Hutchinson and Green, above n 63, 38. For discussion, see P Weiss, 'Feminism and Community' in Weiss and Friedman, above n 62, 4; Friedman, above n 112, 283.
[131] Friedman, above n 112, 286.
[132] *Ibid*; P Weiss, 'Feminism and Community' in Weiss and Friedman, above n 62, 3.

that allowed them to live lives less constrained by sexism. These communities have frequently offered a robust sense of shared identity to their members.[133]

Many feminists accord only a supplementary role to communities of choice, accepting that communities of choice and communities of place can be equally constitutive of identity and nourishing of autonomy.[134] For example, families may offer the personal recognition necessary for self-esteem and self-respect, while a religious community may allow an individual to acquire the moral competency necessary for self-definition.[135] Particularly for the child maturing to self-consciousness the community is uncontroversially found not created, and communities of place also constitute the identity that the adult self discovers when he or she first embarks on self-reflection, so that most people are probably ineradicably constituted to some extent by communities of place.[136] But among an adult's communities of mature self-identification may be many communities of choice.[137] These chosen communities attract us in the first place because they appeal to features of ourselves which, while found, were inadequately catered for by our communities of place. Voluntary communities therefore form an important check on discovered communities. Having attained a critically reflective stance toward communities of origin, we would probably simultaneously have begun to distance ourselves from particular aspects of our identity and to have embarked on the path of personal redefinition.[138] Therefore we can concede the influence of those communities without having unreflectively to endorse it.[139]

Other feminists regard the relationship between communities of choice and communities of place as antagonistic not complementary,

---

[133] Williams, above n 62, 423. See also Struering, above n 5, 145; J Weeks *et al*, 'Everyday Experiments: Narratives of Non-Heterosexual Relationships' in Silva and Smart, above n 18, 89; P Weiss, 'Feminism and Communitarianism: Comparing Critiques of Liberalism' in Weiss and Friedman, above n 62, 169; Rosenblum, above n 1, 157.

[134] See eg Friedman, above n 112; MC Regan, 'Getting Our Stories Straight: Narrative Autonomy and Feminist Commitments', 72 *Indiana Law Journal* 449 at 454. For discussion, see Williams, above n 62.

[135] Williams, above n 62.

[136] Friedman, above n 112.

[137] *Ibid*, 289.

[138] *Ibid*; J Weeks *et al*, 'Everyday Experiments: Narratives of Non-Heterosexual Relationships' in Silva and Smart, above n 18, 88.

[139] Friedman, above n 112; P Weiss, 'Feminism and Community' in Weiss and Friedman, above n 62, 4.

because the latter are destructive of autonomy.[140] This is because they replicate the in-built social hierarchies, imprisoning women within oppressive gender politics.[141] On this view, communities of choice are absolutely crucial. In relation to lesbian communities in particular, it has been argued that in their absence, lesbians would have only heterosexual communities as a backdrop to understanding the meaning of their lives and even their innermost feelings:

> Without lesbian focus there is no lesbian context, and without lesbian context, there is no means to understand and develop the meanings of our lesbian lives. This is what I think about when I think of lesbian community.[142]

A final feminist approach is to suggest that the dichotomy between chosen and found communities is a false one, since membership is 'simultaneously found and chosen in a complex, ambiguous, and often changing mix.'[143] On a negative view, this is interpreted as meaning that oppressive forces pervade and structure all communities.[144] More positively, it can mean that we can advocate new configurations of traditional communities.[145] This is because there are always oppositional values alongside the dominant values in a community so that resistance to community values is invariably possible since one does not become constituted by only one set of values, a point that feminists argue is obscured by communitarian theory.[146] Moreover, even the oppressive aspects of communities of place are connected to communities of choice, in that they are responsible for creating the need for communities of choice.[147]

---

[140] See eg SL Hoagland, 'Why *Lesbian* Ethics?' in Card, above n 63, 201. For discussion, see Williams, above n 62.

[141] Friedman, above n 112; P Weiss, 'Feminism and Communitarianism: Comparing Critiques of Liberalism' in Weiss and Friedman, above n 62, 161; Rosenblum, above n 1, 159; T Simon, 'The Theoretical Marginalization of the Disadvantaged: A Liberal/Communitarian Failing' in Delaney, above n 128, 114.

[142] SL Hoagland, 'Why *Lesbian* Ethics?' in Card, above n 63, 204. See also Struering, above n 5, 145.

[143] Williams, above n 62, 443.

[144] P Weiss, 'Feminism and Communitarianism: Comparing Critiques of Liberalism' in Weiss and Friedman, above n 62, 166.

[145] Abrams, above n 91, 462.

[146] L Tessman, 'Who Are My People? Communitarianism and the Interlocking of Oppressions', 27 *International Studies in Philosophy* 105; I M Young, 'The Ideal of Community and the Politics of Difference' in L Nicholson (ed), *Feminism/Postmodernism* (London, Routledge, 1989); Rosenblum, above n 1, 159.

[147] P Weiss, 'Feminism and Communitarianism: Comparing Critiques of Liberalism' in Weiss and Friedman, above n 62, 166.

Marriage as Community

To recap the last two sections, post-liberalism generally regards the family as the paradigm of a constitutive community, the caveat being that feminists to differing degrees place primary emphasis on constitutive communities of choice. However, in this section an investigation of which relationship within the family best encapsulates the ideal community will dispose of the caveat.

One strong contender has been the mother-child dyad.[148] Two main arguments for this relationship have been put forward. The first is that it encapsulates the emergence of autonomy through others,[149] and so teaches us not to mistake interdependence or dependence as antithetical to autonomy.[150] On this view, childrearing can provide fruitful images and insights into the nature of relationships that foster rather than undermine autonomy.[151] The second argument is that placing the mother-child dyad rather than the sexual unit at the centre of the family would de-emphasise some of the traditional configurations that have exposed women to systematic oppressive treatment.[152]

However, the predominant post-liberal approach is to hold up marriage as the ideal community.[153] The first and most pertinent reason is that marriage is 'our most personal experience of committing to another person . . . an obligation we must assume; to be married, we can no longer be absolutely "freely choosing." '[154] Marriage is a rela-

---

[148] Nedelsky, above n 81, 169; Abrams, above n 91, 462. For discussion, see ME Albert, 'In the interest of the public good? New questions for feminism' in Reynolds and Norman, above n 94, 94; Lister, above n 63, 150; D Greschner, 'Feminist Concerns with the New Communitarians: We Don't Need Another Hero' in Hutchinson and Green, above n 63, 132.

[149] Nedelsky, 'Reconceiving Autonomy: Sources, Thoughts and Possibilities' in Hutchinson and Green, above n 63, 225; Abrams, above n 91, 462. For discussion, see Fowler, above n 94, 98; D Greschner, 'Feminist Concerns with the New Communitarians: We Don't Need Another Hero' in Hutchinson and Green, above n 63, 132.

[150] Abrams, above n 91, 462.

[151] *Ibid*, 462.

[152] *Ibid*, 462.

[153] See eg A Buchanan, 'Assessing the Communitarian Critique of Liberalism', 99 *Ethics* 852 at 868; ME Albert, 'In the interest of the public good? New questions for feminism' in Reynolds and Norman, above n 94, 94; Bellah, above n 1, 85; Regan, above n 25, 7; Etzioni, above n 94, 86–87. For discussion, see Brook, above n 35.

[154] ME Albert, 'In the interest of the public good? New questions for feminism' in Reynolds and Norman, above n 94, 94. See also Regan, above n 25, 7; Bellah, above n 1, 85. For discussion, see Struering, above n 5, 145; Ellman, above n 25, 236.

tionship formed by individual choice that nonetheless generates a commitment that is not fully captured by the idea of consent.[155]

The second reason is the empirical importance of marriage as community. If Etzioni regards people who are severed from communities as less healthy and happy than those who belong, then he sees the comparison between single and married people as no less stark. Although he accepts that people can have a variety of relationships with friends, family and pets, he sees these as either supplements to or inadequate substitutes for the stable and institutionalised bonds provided by marriage,[156] which is the primary example of a sustained relationship.[157] Accordingly, he reports that the unmarried are more likely to be unhappy, or physically or mentally ill, and have higher mortality rates.[158]

Thirdly, it is argued that the increasing importance placed on a close relationship is correlated with the dilution of the other traditional communities.[159] When life seems to be falling apart, people no longer seek protection from the church or their neighbours but from someone who literally shares their world and so can offer support and understanding:[160]

> Everything that one has lost is sought in the other.[161] . . . The direction in which modern developments are taking us is reflected in the way we idealize love. Glorifying it in the way we do acts as a counterbalance to the losses we feel in the way we live. If not God, or priests, or class, or neighbours, then at least there is still You. And the size of the 'You' is inversely proportional to the emotional void which otherwise seems to prevail.[162]

The implication is that it is less material security or affection than the fear of being alone that keeps marriages together.[163] The argument is that as society becomes more prosperous and people's lives are less restricted, people turn their attention increasingly to the search for

[155] Regan, above n 25, viii.
[156] Etzioni, above n 94, 87.
[157] *Ibid*, 87.
[158] *Ibid*, 86.
[159] Beck and Beck-Gernsheim, above n 1, 32; Whitehead, above n 1, 192; Hewitt, above n 14, 120; D Morgan, 'Risk and Family Practices: Accounting for Change and Fluidity in Family Life' in Silva and Smart, above n 18, 26.
[160] Beck and Beck-Gernsheim, above n 1, 182.
[161] *Ibid*, 32. See also U Beck, *Risk Society: Towards a New Modernity* (London, Sage Publications, 1992) 114.
[162] Beck and Beck-Gernsheim, above n 1, 33.
[163] *Ibid*, 33; Hafen, above n 17, 32.

emotional satisfaction. The conviction that love alone gives life purpose and meaning is seen as the logical outcome of modern social changes.[164] On this view, a large proportion of people are content for their public involvements to have little subjective importance, for work to be just a necessity and for politics to be at best a spectator sport. Therefore they turn to their relationship to experience self-realisation:

> It is here that the individual will seek power, intelligibility and, quite literally, a name – the apparent power to fashion a world, however Lilliputian, that will reflect his own being . . .[165]

The final argument is that marriage has all the characteristics that a community of choice needs in order to be able to enhance autonomy and create identity. It has been argued that a community must be personal, in that the parties must focus on the whole person not a narrow aspect of the other person. A consequence of this is that there will be an element of emotional attachment. This is necessary for the same reasons that it is necessary for the community to be constitutive, that is, to enable the person to acquire the skills necessary to tell his or her story.[166] The community must occur in face-to-face situations and be credited with primary significance by the subject.[167] Membership of the community must be consistent with membership of other communities because many people experience themselves as having many different aspects, from wife to teacher to neighbour.[168] In addition, the tensions among these different communities allow us and sometimes force us to criticise our communities, challenging the assumptions on which they are based.[169] These challenges can themselves be the basis for forming new communities of resistance.[170] Marriage meets these criteria. It has also been argued that it is the primacy of internal goods that distinguishes communities from mere associations and that the following are just some examples of the internal goods of marriage:

> Deserved mutual trust, openness, a stable sense of accomplishment in building together a relationship of deep mutual affection, and the recognition that

---

[164] Beck and Beck-Gernsheim, above n 1, 182; Beck, above n 161.
[165] Berger and Kellner, above n 69, 7.
[166] Williams, above n 62, 442.
[167] Berger and Kellner, above n 69, 5.
[168] Williams, above n 62; Rosenblum, above n 1.
[169] Williams, above n 62, 446; Griffiths, above n 63, 142–43.
[170] Abrams, above n 91, 462.

you are profoundly understood by a person whom you profoundly understand . . .[171]

Marriage as Identity Forming

So the predominant view within post-liberalism is that marriage is the paradigm of an autonomy-enhancing constitutive community. If this is the case then post-liberal theory must also maintain that marriage is a primary identity-creating relationship.[172] This section will investigate this claim, substantiation of which will enable post-liberalism to dodge the difficulty of recognising obligations to one's spouse by proclaiming instead that divorcing one's spouse is akin to losing a part of one's self.

Post-liberals do indeed claim as a minimum that one's sense of self is crucially influenced by marriage.[173] They suggest that it is not simply one of many communities but a relationship that most people believe should engage our being more fully than any other attachment.[174] More strongly put and at its best, marriage is seen as offering a distinctive kind of good, namely the possibility of bridging the distance between separate selves.[175] Indeed, examples of the essentially shared relations postulated by post-liberalism are usually drawn from the sphere of familial and interpersonal relations, especially the relationship between a husband and wife. Post-liberals suggest that although it is possible for spouses to see their relationship as analogous to a contract, there is another and older description of marriage as a union, which expresses the idea that one shared self can take the place of the two prior separate selves.[176] This conception of marriage has recently been described as the internal stance, in which marriage appears as a universe of shared meaning which makes it possible for the spouses to live in intimate concert, rather than mere parallel association.[177] The internal stance blurs the boundary between oneself and one's spouse, so that operating from within the internal perspective involves suspending the capacity to differentiate between the interests of oneself

---

[171] Buchanan, above n 153, 869. See also Unger, above n 74, 218; Okin, above n 95, 45.
[172] Buchanan, above n 153.
[173] Taylor, above n 3; Regan, above n 63, 669.
[174] Regan, above n 25, 205.
[175] *Ibid*, 11; Unger, above n 74, 218; Rosenblum, above n 1, 47; Scott, above n 8, 62.
[176] See Neal and Paris, above n 64, 427.
[177] Regan, above n 25; MC Regan, 'Spousal Privilege and the Meanings of Marriage', 81 *Virginia Law Review* 2045.

and one's spouse. This means that the relationship is not reducible to separate interacting individuals who use it to pursue their own distinct interests. Rather, there is a larger relational unit that represents a shared way of life the viability of which is a collective concern.[178] Accordingly, the reason that Etzioni believes that the married are healthier and happier is that 'people are born as halves and gravitate toward one another to find their completion.'[179]

The dilution of traditional communities referred to above is also viewed as playing a role in rendering marriage identity-forming. The argument here is that rapid social change, the erosion of traditional ties, and social and geographic mobility give us a huge number of complex and contradictory options to choose from,[180] making it more difficult for us to establish a sense of identity.[181] Therefore those in the immediate vicinity become indispensable in helping us to find our place in the world.[182] It has been argued that this represents the exacerbation of a longstanding trend that places the centre of gravity not in some higher sphere but in ordinary life, that is, the life of, among other things, the family and love.[183] As a result, our love lives gain enormous significance, with our view of reality and sense of self-esteem largely depending on them:

> The more other reference points have slipped away, the more we direct our craving to give our lives meaning and security towards those we love. More and more we tend to pin our hopes on another person, this man or that woman. He or she is supposed to hold us upright and steady in a world whirling round faster and faster.[184]

If our emotional and mental stability depends on the close support of those nearest to us, then 'love acquires a new significance at the very

---

[178] Regan, above n 25; Regan, above n 177.

[179] Etzioni, above n 94, 87.

[180] U Beck, 'The Reinvention of Politics: Towards a Theory of Reflexive Modernization' in Beck, Giddens and Lash, above n 60, 14.

[181] Beck and Beck-Gernsheim, above n 1, 181; Smart and Neale, above n 18, 15; Smart, above n 18, 308; Schneider, above n 17, 525; Regan, above n 1, 57; D Morgan, 'Risk and Family Practices: Accounting for Change and Fluidity in Family Life' in Silva and Smart, above n 18.

[182] Beck and Beck-Gernsheim, above n 1, 181; Smart and Neale, above n 18, 15; Smart, above n 18, 308; Schneider, above n 17, 525; Regan, above n 1, 57; D Morgan, 'Risk and Family Practices: Accounting for Change and Fluidity in Family Life' in Silva and Smart, above n 18.

[183] Taylor, above n 3. For discussion, see Struering, above n 5, 145.

[184] Beck and Beck-Gernsheim, above n 1, 50.

heart of our lives.'[185] On this view, while we may develop a variety of relationships to make up for the lack elsewhere, this is 'no substitute for a stable primary bond which gives one a sense of identity.'[186] Marriage has become of central importance in the social design of reality.[187]

If marriage has become increasingly important to identity, then identity has also become increasingly important to marriage. The fundamental theme behind marriage is no longer seen as just the social structure of our lives, but also as a matter of identity. The argument is that marriage is becoming an institution specialised in the development and maintenance of the individual self.[188] Today's pursuit of intimacy is regarded as an individual quest for authentic self-definition.[189] The pure relationship is a key environment for self-discovery because it both allows for and demands continuous self-understanding as the means of creating a durable tie to the other person.[190] Therefore engagement with the project of the self is a prerequisite for having a pure relationship.[191] The symbiotic relationship between the pure relationship and self-understanding is another factor in explaining the triumph of therapeutic discourse. This is because the more pure relationships become dominant, the more crucial becomes an in-depth understanding of oneself which allows one to feel positive about oneself: 'self-mastery is the condition of that opening-out process through which hope (commitment) and trust are generated in the pure relationship.'[192]

> In living together a man and a woman build up a universe of shared attitudes, opinions and expectations covering everything from trivial

---

[185] *Ibid*, 49. See also Giddens, *Modernity*, above n 18, 79; Rodger, above n 18, 85; E Silva and C Smart, 'The New Practices and Politics of Family Life' in Silva and Smart, above n 18, 6.

[186] Beck and Beck-Gernsheim, above n 1, 33. See also J Weeks *et al*, 'Everyday Experiments: Narratives of Non-Heterosexual Relationships' in Silva and Smart, above n 18, 85.

[187] Beck and Beck-Gernsheim, above n 1.

[188] *Ibid*, 50.

[189] Regan, above n 1, 53; J Weeks *et al*, 'Everyday Experiments: Narratives of Non-Heterosexual Relationships' in Silva and Smart, above n 18, 85; Cheal, above n 21, 43.

[190] Giddens, *Modernity*, above n 18; Smart and Neale, above n 18, 3; Rodger, above n 18, 87; Bellah, above n 1, 85; J Weeks *et al*, 'Everyday Experiments: Narratives of Non-Heterosexual Relationships' in Silva and Smart, above n 18, 85.

[191] Giddens, *Modernity*, above n 18; Smart and Neale, above n 18, 139; Beck and Beck-Gernsheim, above n 1, 44.

[192] Giddens, *Modernity*, above n 18, 186; Giddens, *Intimacy*, above n 18; Scott, above n 8.

day-to-day matters to the great events in world politics. This develops in verbal or non-verbal dialogue, in shared habits and experiences, in a continuous interplay between one's other half and oneself. The shared image of the world is continuously being negotiated, shifted, replaced, questioned and reaffirmed.[193]

Let us look in a little more detail at how this is supposed to work. A key source here is the classic text by Berger and Kellner, Marriage and the Construction of Reality, in which marriage is conceived of as a social arrangement that creates the order for the person in which he or she can experience his or her life as making sense.[194] They argue that marriage occupies a privileged status among the significant validating relationships for adults in this society. They see it as a dramatic act in which two people re-define themselves, internally anticipated and socially legitimated long before it takes place in the person's biography.[195] However, the marital relationship is vulnerable for two reasons: first, because in contemporary society each marriage constitutes its own segregated community with a closed conversation; secondly, because the partners are virtual strangers who do not share a common past. This vulnerability necessitates greater effort on the part of the spouses: marriage has to make up for its vulnerability in intensity.[196]

Therefore from the marriage onwards, the majority of the spouses' actions and their very definition of reality must be carried out jointly with the other spouse, so that the other spouse is present in nearly all horizons of everyday conduct, and is seen by the outside world as being conjoined. All other significant relationships have to be re-perceived in accordance with the shift that marriage brings about, and every problem is experienced in a new way, within a new and ever-changing reality. To give a concrete example:

> . . . the husband's image of his friend is transformed as he keeps talking about this friend with his wife. Even if no actual talking goes on, the mere presence of the wife forces him to see his friend differently. This need not mean that he adopts a negative image held by the wife. Regardless of what image she holds or is believed by him to hold, it will be different from that

[193] Beck and Beck-Gernsheim, above n 1, 50.
[194] Berger and Kellner, above n 69, 1. For discussion, see Smart and Neale, above n 18, 141.
[195] Berger and Kellner, above n 69, 5.
[196] *Ibid*, 9; J Brown and SD Sclater, 'Divorce: A Psychodynamic Perspective' in Sclater and Piper, above n 23, 148; Rodger, above n 18, 86.

held by the husband. This difference will enter into the joint image that now must needs be fabricated in the course of the ongoing conversation between the marriage partners – and, in due course, must act powerfully on the image previously held by the husband.[197]

The dominance of this marital conversation over all others is one of its most important identity-forming characteristics.[198] Unsurprisingly, the couple generally perceive their changed reality and identity as discovered rather than constructed, so that they 'discover who they really are' and 'what they have always really believed'.[199]

Marriage thus posits a new reality, but because the reality is vulnerable, the groups with which the couple mix are called upon to assist in defining this reality. Therefore the couple are pushed towards groups that strengthen their new definition of themselves and away from those that weaken it. The forces of group association again act on the definitions of reality, so that the new reality goes on being re-defined not just through the interaction between the couple but also in the group relationships into which the couple enter:

> In the individual's biography marriage then, brings about a decisive phase of socialization that can be compared with the phases of childhood and adolescence.[200]

This shared reality operates backwards and forwards: 'Reconstructed present and re-interpreted past are perceived as a continuum, extending forwards into a commonly projected future.'[201]

THE IMPLICATIONS FOR DIVORCE LAW

Allowing Divorce

In order that obligations to the spouse could be recognised within post-liberalism, they have been effectively re-defined as a species of self-interest. But there is a snag: the flip-side is that it would be impossible for any post-liberal to maintain that divorce should be outlawed:[202]

---

[197] Berger and Kellner, above n 69, 11–12. See also Hewitt, above n 14, 166.

[198] Berger and Kellner, above n 69, 12.

[199] *Ibid*, 16.

[200] *Ibid*, 13. See also J Brown and SD Sclater, 'Divorce: A Psychodynamic Perspective' in Sclater and Piper, above n 23, 148.

[201] Berger and Kellner, above n 69, 16. See also Smart and Neale, above n 18, 69.

[202] Whitehead, above n 1, 188; Struering, above n 5; Frohnen, above n 14, 47; Scott, above n 8, 58.

because the spousal relationship is constitutive of the self's identity, if divorce is denied then the self is denied. As Sandel has argued, for the government to burden practices central to the self-definition of its citizens is to frustrate them more profoundly than if they were deprived of interests less central to the projects that give meaning to their lives.[203] An essentially shared relation may be positive or negative, so that while spouses may share a relation of love and devotion, they may also share a relation of dependence and debasement,[204] and while the effect on self-identity may be good or bad, it is always crucial. Accordingly, it is equally crucial that the spouse is able to escape the effect. It is unsurprising that recent research found that one of the main difficulties that women encountered on divorce was the recognition that they had lost sight of their true selves and that they needed to find and become themselves again.[205] Since the life goal is still, and inescapably, authenticity through self-discovery, where there is a conflict between the project of the self and the relationship, the relationship has to give way.[206]

Conversely, it has been argued that the marriages that work are the ones where there is no conflict between self-identity and the relationship, in that the spouse understands who we really are and helps us to become the person who we really want to be.[207] Founded purely on authenticity, pure relationships offer the possibility of the development of trust based on voluntary commitments and intensified intimacy.[208] They offer the chance of a 'bond of fellow spirits', or at least a close partnership.[209] But since the project of self-discovery is inevitably open-ended, it will not necessarily reach the conclusion of continued commitment.[210] Every decision must be revocable in the course of the marriage: the constant search for self assumes that everyone can update and optimise their decisions.[211] The consequential monitoring of the extent to which the marriage is providing personal satisfaction makes it impossible for spouses to 'coast along'. Trust in the pure relationship is circumscribed, tentative and fragile, perpetually subject to disrup-

---

[203]   Sandel, above n 66, xiii.
[204]   Neal and Paris, above n 64, 428.
[205]   Smart and Neale, above n 18, 195.
[206]   *Ibid*, 136–37; Schneider, above n 17, 527; Regan, above n 1, 45; Rosenblum, above n 1, 47; Beck and Beck-Gernsheim, above n 1, 53.
[207]   Regan, above n 1, 45.
[208]   Giddens, *Modernity*, above n 18, 186–87.
[209]   Beck and Beck-Gernsheim, above n 1, 61.
[210]   Cheal, above n 21, 43.
[211]   Beck and Beck-Gernsheim, above n 1.

tion as both spouses continually reassess the desirability of involvement in the relationship:[212]

> In other words, psychological man cannot come to rest in any relationship, or any community, or any creed; he must keep asking whether they are working for him.[213]

So far we have seen that on a post-liberal analysis divorce must be permitted because marriage is crucial to self-identity. The importance of permitting divorce is enhanced once we recognise that during the course of self-discovery one or both of the spouses may discover that he or she is a different self from the self who married. This will be avoided only if people find spouses with whom they can grow over a lifetime,[214] and there are factors that pull in this direction: since the couple share future horizons, this leads both to stabilisation and more dramatically to an inevitable narrowing of each spouse's future projections:

> Before marriage the individual typically plays with quite discrepant daydreams in which his future self is projected. Having now considerably stabilized his self-image, the married individual will have to project the future in accordance with this maritally defined identity. This narrowing of future horizons begins with the obvious external limitations that marriage entails, as, for example, with regard to vocational and career plans. However, it extends also to the more general possibilities of the individual's biography. . . . At least until further notice she has decided upon who she [the wife] is – and, by the same token, on who she will be. The stabilization brought about by marriage thus affects the total reality in which the partners exist. In the most far-reaching sense of the word, the married individual 'settles down' . . .[215]

But there are also factors that pull in the opposite direction. In particular, the links that once joined biography to family are slackening:

> A lifelong nuclear family which blends together the biographies of a man and a woman as parents is becoming the exception, whereas alternating between various family and non-family settings, depending on what phase of biography one has reached, is becoming the rule. The family roots behind our biographies are gradually being severed as we move from one phase to

---

[212] Regan, above n 177; Regan, above n 25, 11; Rodger, above n 18, 83; Whitehead, above n 1, 76; J Weeks *et al*, 'Everyday Experiments: Narratives of Non-Heterosexual Relationships' in Silva and Smart, above n 18, 93; Berger and Kellner, above n 69, 16.

[213] Schneider, above n 1, 1848.

[214] Schneider, above n 17, 527–28.

[215] Berger and Kellner, above n 69, 15.

the next, and are losing their influence. Everybody takes part in several family and non-family phases . . .[216]

Where the spouses do not grow and change in tandem, they may be different selves from the ones who married in a very fundamental sense. One view of personal identity allows for intrasubjective conceptions of the self, in which the appropriate description of the moral subject is a plurality of selves within a single human being, and holds that this description is not merely of metaphorical importance, but sometimes of genuine moral and practical importance.[217] On another view, a person's identity as a separate person over time is grounded in psychological connections such as memory, character traits, and plans. The extent to which these connections exist between different parts of a person's life is a matter of degree, and totally separate selves, while rare, do exist. Therefore:

> If a person's character changes, memory fades, and intentions and goals shift significantly over time, then the person is a 'self' different today from the 'self' that existed at an earlier time.[218]

Moreover, the determination of whether one or both spouses will experience significant personal change is probably impossible at the time of marriage. Just because an autonomous person feels that he or she has taken an unsatisfactory course, this does not show that the earlier decision was not the best exercise of autonomy competency possible at the time:[219]

> Even a marriage that was entered after careful consideration may later fail to offer personal fulfillment. Based on all information available at the time of the marriage, a commitment to a future with the partner may have been a thoughtful, reflective choice. Ten years later, the couple may no longer share the same values, plans and interests that supported the earlier commitment.[220]

---

[216] Beck and Beck-Gernsheim, above n 1, 33. See also Beck, above n 161, 114; D Morgan, 'Risk and Family Practices: Accounting for Change and Fluidity in Family Life' in Silva and Smart, above n 18; Whitehead, above n 1, 77; Cheal, above n 21, 51; Giddens, *Intimacy*, above n 18, 140; Smart and Neale, above n 18; Purdy, above n 50, 87.

[217] Sandel, above n 66, 63; Rosenblum, above n 1, 52; Meyers, above n 71, 90; Griffiths, above n 63, 175–76. For discussion, see W Kymlicka, 'Liberalism and Communitarianism', 18 *Canadian Journal of Philosophy* 181.

[218] Scott, above n 8, 59.

[219] Meyers, above n 71, 90.

[220] Scott, above n 8, 58.

This view of identity clearly has implications for lasting commitment:

> If the person binds himself to perform certain acts in the future, he may be binding a different person without that person's agreement. If psychological connections are very weak over time, a commitment that seriously restricts one's own behavior in later life is no more supportable than a commitment that would bind a different individual without that person's consent. . . . the individual is not free to commit his later selves and is not responsible for behavior of earlier selves.[221]

One or both spouses may have grown and changed so significantly that continuation in the marriage would represent self-denial.[222] Just as someone may be absolved from responsibility for heretical beliefs that he or she held before his or her religious conversion,[223] a spouse may be absolved from responsibility for a marriage that a previous self contracted.[224]

To return to the conception of marriage as constitutive community, post-liberals invariably regard being allowed to leave communities and join others as an inextricable part of autonomous living.[225] What makes any identity or affinity voluntary is the availability of alternative identities or affinities, so that what makes marriage voluntary is the permanent possibility of divorce: voluntariness is the right to withdraw.[226] Taking this further, it has been argued that the possibility of divorce acts to affirm the *community* of marriage even as it dissolves the individual marriage. Divorce:

> . . . becomes not merely an act of 'personal fulfillment,' but rather a statement that the jointly created community has failed. Divorce under the new morality is thus grounded in notions of community as well as autonomy and seeks to resolve the tensions inherent in those concepts.[227]

---

[221] *Ibid*, 60.

[222] *Ibid*, 58.

[223] Sandel, above n 66, 63; Griffiths, above n 63, 175–76; Rosenblum, above n 1, 52.

[224] Meyers, above n 71, 90; Rosenblum, above n 1, 52.

[225] Unger, above n 74, 279–80; R Bauman, 'The Communitarian Vision of Critical Legal Studies' in Hutchinson and Green, above n 63, 22; W Galston, *Liberal Purposes: Goods, Virtues, and Diversity in the Liberal State* (New York, Cambridge University Press, 1991) 57. For discussion, see Schneider, above n 1, 1855.

[226] M Walzer, 'The Communitarian Critique of Liberalism', 18 *Political Theory* 6 at 21.

[227] NR Cahn, 'The Moral Complexities of Family Law', 50 *Stanford Law Review* 225 at 262.

One suggested escape route from the necessity to allow divorce is for
spouses to avoid giving up too much of their individual identities. The
argument is that there is a 'we-zone' and an 'I-zone', and that boundaries need to be worked out between the zones. The 'I-zone', which has
also been conceptualised as the adoption of an external stance towards
marriage, is insufficient to ensure full enjoyment of the distinctive good
of marriage, because a continuous posture of critical distance, acutely
sensitive to costs and benefits, is inimical to the sense of shared experience.[228] However, sustaining marriage requires only that the 'we-zone'
be significant, not that the 'I-zone' be suppressed.[229] Clearly, this solution leads straight back to the problem posed at the beginning of
the chapter: post-liberals must hold on to the notion of marriage as
identity-forming in order to be able to recognise duties to the spouse.

Restricting Divorce

> Divorce, from a communitarian perspective, is sometimes necessary when
> great harm would be caused by staying in the marriage. Particularly in the
> presence of minor children, the decision to divorce would be akin to ampu-
> tating a limb: to be avoided if at all possible by sustained, alternative treat-
> ments, but pursued if necessary to save the person's life.[230]

The conception of marriage as identity-forming implies that divorce
must be permitted, and permitted for no other reason than a change in
at least one of the spouses. To reiterate, this means that we are now
able to reclaim the apparently liberal dimension of the Family Law Act
as consistent with a full-blown post-liberal interpretation. The absence
of necessity to prove fault, or any other substantive criteria, alongside
the practical inevitability of eventual divorce in the face of one spouse's
settled wish, is a required feature of post-liberal divorce law. However,
in no sense does it follow that post-liberal law would *readily* allow
divorce. At the end of the first section of this chapter, I presented a rudi-
mentary sketch of the reason for this tension: since self-fulfilment is
not equivalent to authenticity and since people may confuse the two,
ready divorce does not enhance authenticity. We have just seen that the

---

[228]   Regan, above n 177; Regan, above n 25, 11; Etzioni, above n 42, 26; Regan, above
n 63, 671; M Dan-Cohen, 'Responsibility and the Boundaries of the Self', 105 *Harvard
Law Review* 959 at 966.
[229]   Etzioni, above n 94, 87–88; Regan, above n 25, vii–viii; Whitehead, above n 1, 193.
[230]   W Doherty, 'How Therapists Threaten Marriages' in Etzioni, above n 101, 164.

identity-forming nature of marriage means that divorce must be allowed. In this section, I return to the repressive side of the post-liberal approach to divorce to show that the identity-forming nature of marriage implies equally that divorce must be restricted.

In the first section of this chapter, we saw that while post-liberals disputed the connection between authenticity and an instrumental view of marriage, their reasons were at that point unconvincing. Drawing on the identity-forming nature of marriage however strengthens the argument: it is because intimate relationships are identity-forming that we cannot treat them instrumentally, and therefore that we cannot approach them tentatively, even though they may break up. This is because although our identities change, when we explore and form them, we try to make sense of our whole lives. Rather than defining an identity for ourselves at that moment, we try to give meaning to our lives as they have been and how we think they will be. Therefore identity-defining relationships have to fall into line with this, because if our self-exploration takes the form of deliberately temporary relationships then we are not exploring our identity but some modality of enjoyment.[231] Purely instrumental relationships develop only a limited range of our capacities and powers; in particular relations based on self-interest cannot meet our need for mutual understanding, trust, and intimacy.[232] Since we develop our characters by interacting with others, using other people results in a shallow, unfulfilled identity.[233] More prosaically, it has been argued that it is because loyalty is a virtue essential to our sense of a genuine self that we need to feel obliged, even though we are not.[234] In other words, although we can, and often should, end our marriage, we can develop ourselves only if we act as if we cannot.[235]

The argument becomes still stronger when post-liberals add the following dimension. Although it is crucial that we are able to question any of our commitments by adopting an external stance towards them, we can never secure a point from which we can take an external stance toward all of our commitments. In order to gain a critical distance from

---

[231] Taylor, above n 3, 52–53; Hewitt, above n 14, 160; R Beiner, 'Revising the Self', 8 *Critical Review* 247 at 248.

[232] Struering, above n 5, 144.

[233] Frohnen, above n 14, 47; Whitehead, above n 1, 193.

[234] Bellah, above n 96, 48; ME Albert, 'In the Interest of the Public Good? New Questions for Feminism' in Reynolds and Norman, above n 94, 94.

[235] Regan, above n 177, 2086–88; Regan, above n 25, 12; Regan, above n 1, 34; Etzioni, above n 42, xv; Frohnen, above n 14, 47.

one set of commitments we need to be embedded in other commitments that for the moment are taken for granted.[236] By identifying with one subset of the self's characteristics at a time while incrementally revising others, the self can eventually transform itself in its entirety. The presupposition is however that at any given stage, a subject exists that is not undergoing a transformation. This implies that a pre-existing subject must launch the series of transformations–even though eventually the process may come full circle and replace the characteristics of the launching self itself.[237] It is the presence of an unchanging core of existing beliefs that makes scrutiny and revision of non-core existing beliefs possible, in that revision can only take place by reference to unquestioned beliefs.[238] Therefore the external stance is not a moment in which a radically disengaged self can evaluate all of its commitments, but rather is one in which a person weighs the claims of one self-in-relationship against another self-in-relationship.[239] It follows that while all beliefs are in principle subject to revision, not all can be questioned or revised simultaneously *or in the space of a short period of time*.[240] If we can too easily cast off any of our commitments, marriage included, then our identities will become unstable.[241]

Moreover, because the self is constructed through time, spontaneous action, rooted in the present, gives only a snapshot of the authentic self. Although there can be no unchanging authentic self, sentiments such as 'this is really me' or 'I am being true to myself' demand more than a snapshot.[242] The self may be experienced as acting authentically in the present, but there is no present that does not result from the past and the expected future,[243] and memory and anticipation may disrupt the sense of integration and continuity that we achieve from living in the moment.[244] We saw in chapter two that intellectual reflection on spon-

---

[236] Regan, above n 177; Regan, above n 25, 15; Dan–Cohen, above n 228, 976; Beiner, above n 231, 249; Friedman, above n 61, 77; M Friedman, 'The Social Self and the Partiality Debates' in Card, above n 61, 172; Hewitt, above n 14, 156; Berry, above n 62, 104; Griffiths, above n 63, 184.

[237] Dan-Cohen, above n 228, 976; Berry, above n 62, 104.

[238] M Galston, 'Taking Aristotle Seriously: Republican-Oriented Legal Theory and the Moral Foundation of Deliberative Democracy', 82 *California Law Review* 331 at 361.

[239] Regan, above n 177; Friedman, above n 112, 282.

[240] Galston, above n 238, 361.

[241] Walzer, above n 226, 21. For discussion, see Kymlicka, above n 217; W Kymlicka, *Contemporary Political Philosophy: An Introduction* (Oxford, Oxford University Press, 1990) 207.

[242] Griffiths, above n 63, 175–76.

[243] *Ibid*, 175–6.

[244] Hewitt, above n 14, 164.

taneous action may change the spontaneous feelings that arise in the future.[245] Therefore each action requires understanding if authenticity is to be maintained.[246] The momentary self must be distinguished from the total self, the latter being a single composite picture that incorporates all the momentary selves. The relative salience of each characteristic in the composite picture depends both on their importance within any given momentary self and the frequency with which they appear in the momentary selves.[247] A spontaneous desire to divorce is therefore inauthentic.

Finally, unrestricted divorce burdens the conception of marriage as an identity-forming constitutive community, because it handicaps the traditional marriage involving a high degree of mutual dependence and obligation.[248] Rejecting lifelong obligations recasts the institution of marriage in the image of the unencumbered self.[249]

So ready divorce does not promote authenticity because uncommitted relationships do not allow us to explore our whole selves but only to experience pleasure. On this view, the state respects our self-determination not by enabling us to stand back from our relationships and commitments but by encouraging a deeper immersion in and understanding of them.[250]

Delaying Divorce

The remaining question is what restrictions on divorce would best allow us to discover our true selves. The optimal solution for the post-liberal is the one that was adopted in Part II of the Family Law Act of a mandatory extensive waiting period.[251] Having to delay divorce gives us a secure vantage point from which we can question other commitments,

---

[245] P 64.

[246] Griffiths, above n 63, 179.

[247] Meir Dan-Cohen, above n 228, 966.

[248] M Sandel, *Democracy's Discontent: America in Search of a Public Philosophy* (Cambridge, Massachusetts, Belknap Press, 1996); U Beck, 'The Reinvention of Politics: Towards a Theory of Reflexive Modernization' in Beck, Giddens and Lash, above n 60, 15; Wardle, above n 25, 766; Hafen, above n 17, 34.

[249] Sandel, above n 248; Scott, above n 8; Galston, above n 225, 63; J Weeks *et al*, 'Everyday Experiments: Narratives of Non-Heterosexual Relationships' in Silva and Smart, above n 18, 93.

[250] For discussion, see Kymlicka, above n 241, 208.

[251] Etzioni, above n 94, 81. For discussion, see J Eekelaar, 'Family Law: The Communitarian Message', 21 *Oxford Journal of Legal Studies* 181 at 182.

preventing our identity from becoming unstable. Being required to wait before divorcing recognises that the spontaneous self is only a snapshot of the authentic self. A mandatory period of reflection gives spouses the security to allow themselves to depend on their spouse, thus enabling marriage to function as a constitutive community.[252] It is noteworthy that none of these considerations has any necessary connection with *preventing* divorce, a point that will be explored in the next chapter.

There is one more reason that the waiting period is the optimal post-liberal restriction on divorce. If marriage is profoundly identity-forming then it follows that divorce is dramatically identity-*changing*. A waiting period before divorce avoids too great a rupture to the continuity of the spouse's experience of identity.

> If marriage is central to the construction of both a shared reality and a personal identity, then divorce represents a process in which the old certainties are dismantled, and the subject is confronted with a mammoth task of rebuilding the world and the self. When a marriage breaks down, important anchors break loose and we are cast adrift; continuity is lost, of the world and of the biographical self. Who and what we are, and what the world is like, are all called into question. We can no longer unproblematically look to the past, to our memories, to feel safe in the knowledge that things are as they always have been; the past has irrevocably changed and has to be read in new ways. Established biographical patterns are dislocated, and we are faced with the task of reconstructing new meanings for the past, a new sense of self and a new vision for the future. These tasks have to be faced against the backdrop of the deep emotional and psychological investments we have made in our intimate relationships . . .[253]

Divorce constitutes a process over time rather than a discrete event.[254] Part of the process is the development of an independent identity that is tied neither to the status of being a spouse nor to one's ex-spouse: relationship breakdown means that both spouses have to give up the intimate world that they have constructed.[255] Since marriage creates a joint reality and is critical to a sense of self, when a marriage breaks down, there is not only search for new meaning but also a fundamental loss of self.[256] Therefore, divorce is inevitably a process of recon-

[252] Scott, above n 8.

[253] SD Sclater, *Divorce: A Psychosocial Study* (Aldershot, Ashgate, 1999) 175.

[254] *Ibid*; Hodgkinson, above n 54.

[255] Smart and Neale, above n 18.

[256] Sclater, above n 253; SD Sclater and C Piper, 'The Family Law Act in Context' in Sclater and Piper, above n 23, 6; Sclater, above n 54, 424; Wardle, above n 25, 764; Hewitt, above n 14, 164.

structing the self and the past, in which people interpret their experiences in order to make sense of them. The spouse seeks to resolve ambivalences and construct a new life and a new sense of self, with feelings of distress co-existing with creative and constructive striving to create a better future. This makes divorce simultaneously traumatic and positive. Attachments persist, but they do so in tension with a need to rebuild an independent self, separate from the self that was bound to the spouse during marriage.[257] Because divorce is traumatic, it represents an acute version of the process of finding oneself that is constantly demanded by post-liberalism.[258]

However, if this new and separate identity can be successfully established then divorce can be a transformative experience:[259]

> Coming through divorce is about overcoming our sense of failure to pursue new developmental pathways, it is about meeting challenges and finding new strengths to cope with adversity, it is about creating new hopes to carry us through the pain towards a better future. Coming through divorce involves creating new meanings to replace the old.[260]

A personal transition such as divorce is an occasion on which the person is momentarily acutely conscious of who he or she is: it can even give rise to an enhanced sense of self.[261] 'Divorce can therefore be said to be a kind of threshold to a self-conscious project of the self.'[262]

Divorce can only be transformative however if time is allowed for a new post-divorce identity to emerge. Marriage breakdown involves destruction of the shared reality of the marriage, the shattering of one's self-image and disintegration of one's image of one's spouse;[263] divorce involves 'the reconstruction of self, and these psychological processes take place in a context, over time'.[264] Recovery from marriage breakdown involves fundamentally reinterpreting the history of the marriage from the standpoint of the present; making sense of the past is a necessary part of negotiating a new reality to replace the shared reality of the

---

[257] Sclater, above n 253. For discussion, see Whitehead, above n 1, 75.

[258] Giddens, *Modernity*, above n 18, 12.

[259] Sclater, above n 54, 436.

[260] Sclater, above n 253, 175.

[261] Hewitt, above n 14.

[262] Smart and Neale, above n 18, 121. For discussion, see Whitehead, above n 1, 5.

[263] See J Brown and S D Sclater, 'Divorce: A Psychodynamic Perspective' in Sclater and Piper, above n 23, 149.

[264] Sclater, above n 253, 161. See also J Brown and SD Sclater, 'Divorce: A Psychodynamic Perspective' in Sclater and Piper, above n 23, 149.

marriage.[265] So, one researcher found that a consistent theme among
the divorcees whom she interviewed was that of looking back over
the marriage, of trying to make sense of what had gone wrong, and
trying to piece together a coherent and plausible account. Her conclusion was that these divorce narratives showed the profound emotional
significance of revisiting and reinterpreting the past.[266] This also takes
time.

Accordingly, Part II of the Family Law Act imposed a mandatory
waiting period. After the spouse had made a statement that his or her
marriage had broken down he or she had to wait a period of at least
nine and a half months.[267] At any time during this period, the court had
a general power to adjourn.[268] The period was to have been automatically extended by another six months[269] at the request of the other
spouse[270] or where there was a child of the family under the age of
16,[271] unless one of two conditions was met. These conditions were
that the delay would be significantly harmful to the welfare of a child
of the family,[272] or that there was an occupation order or non-molesta-
tion order in force in favour of the individual or a child of the family
against the other spouse.[273] According to Lord Habgood during the
Family Law Act debates:

> Surely the Bill strikes at the right point by giving legal significance to the pas-
> sage of time. It says, 'Slow down. What is wrong is precisely that you do
> want everything immediately.'[274] . . . The Bill gives a couple the gift of time,
> and the help to use it.[275]

[265] J Brown and SD Sclater, 'Divorce: A Psychodynamic Perspective' in Sclater and
Piper, above n 23.
[266] SD Sclater, 'Experiences of Divorce' in Sclater and Piper, above n 23; Sclater, above
n 54, 424.
[267] S 7(3) Family Law Act 1996.
[268] S 14(1) Family Law Act 1996. For discussion of this provision, see Lord Irvine,
Hansard, House of Lords, 4 March 1996, Col 42.
[269] S 7(13) Family Law Act 1996.
[270] S 7(10)(a) Family Law Act 1996.
[271] S 7(11) Family Law Act 1996.
[272] S 7(12)(b) Family Law Act 1996.
[273] S 7(12)(a) Family Law Act 1996.
[274] Lord Habgood, Hansard, House of Lords, 29 February 1996, Col 1645.
[275] *Ibid*, Col 1646. For similar sentiments, see Lord Irvine, Hansard, House of Lords,
11 January 1996, Col 286; Lord Stoddart, Hansard, House of Lords, 29 February 1996,
Col 1705; Baroness Strange, Hansard, House of Lords, 11 March 1996, Col 639; Lord
Jakobovits, Hansard, House of Lords, 11 March 1996, Col 640; Viscount Cranbourne,
Hansard, House of Lords, 5 July 1996, Col 1774.

CONCLUSION

This chapter has explored a tension deep within the post-liberal approach to divorce. At the same time as we are placing more and more store in relationships as the route to self-discovery and authenticity, self-discovery and authenticity themselves demand that when love fades, we move on.[276] It has been argued that since marriage engages us more fully than any other attachment, it is to be expected that marriage evokes profound ambivalence: a desire both to transcend and to protect the boundaries of the self.[277] It is also unsurprising that married couples, when interviewed, found it hard to accept a tension between attachment and self-sacrifice, believing instead that love might require hard work but could never create real costs to the self since therapeutic work could turn apparent sacrifices into freely chosen benefits.[278] As we have seen, this tension when translated into legal form implies both that divorce must be permitted even in the absence of substantive justification and that divorce must be restricted. By both allowing eventual divorce on unilateral request and imposing an extensive mandatory waiting period, Part II of the Family Law Act was the ideal legal expression of post-liberal ambivalence towards divorce.

---

[276] J Dewar, 'The Normal Chaos of Family Law' 61 *Modern Law Review* 467 at 484; Etzioni, above n 42, 26–27; W Doherty, 'How Therapists Threaten Marriages', in Etzioni, above n 101, 164.

[277] Regan, above n 25, 205; Hafen, above n 17, 34; Hewitt, above n 14, 161; Whitehead, above n 1; Bellah above n 1, 89.

[278] Bellah, above n 1, 109–10. See also Hafen, above n 17, 34.

4

Learning from Divorce

INTRODUCTION

IN THE LAST chapter, we discovered that post-liberalism adopts an ambivalent attitude to divorce: we should remain married only if the marriage is consistent with our primary duty to live authentically. I suggested further that there is at least a strand of post-liberal thought that adopts a positive attitude to divorce, in that divorce rather than marriage embodies a mature self-identity. This chapter takes this theme further, focusing on a broader influence on the self than the previous two chapters. While chapter two examined the constitution of the self from his or her ends and chapter three looked at the contribution that the spousal relationship makes to identity, this chapter concentrates on the impact of the wider community on the self.

Looking at the impact of the wider community allows the positive attitude to divorce to emerge even more strongly. In this chapter, I suggest that the moral divide is no longer between those who have divorced and those who have stayed married but rather between those who divorce well and those who divorce badly. I conclude that those who divorce well may exit their marriage with enhanced moral standing. In order to reach this conclusion, I begin in the first two sections of this chapter by examining a number of interconnected themes within post-liberalism, principally civic-republicanism. Taken together, these themes imply the conclusion that post-liberal society must inculcate virtue into adults, primarily through civic education, and crucially that the virtue is procedural not substantive while the civic education is an end not a means. In the rest of the chapter, I argue that this conclusion was brought over into divorce law. Part II of the Family Law Act set out to inculcate procedural virtues into divorcing adults through educating them, and the education that was provided was for the sake of the education itself.

THE COMMON GOOD

Post-liberals differ as to how the self is identified with his or her community. While some emphasise the primacy of the collective, ascribing supreme value to the community itself rather than individual members,[1] others suggest that the two are intertwined.[2] On this view, instead of a problematic relationship of part to whole where both threaten to subsume the other, personal identity is maintained simultaneously with communal identity. There is no self to understand apart from the community, just as there is no community apart from the members, and neither the individual nor the community has any priority.[3] We create the community at the same time as the community creates us; like intimate relationships, the community constrains but also enables our capacity to develop ourselves,[4] so that at least ideally, we feel a heightened sense of both community and individuality.[5]

Whatever the precise relationship, if we are at least partly constituted by our community then it is impossible to separate our own interests from those of the community.[6] Collective values such as solidarity and reciprocity cannot be enjoyed by individuals, but only realised communally.[7] Arguably, the very idea of community is to seek the good of others at the same time as, but sometimes in neglect of, one's own good.[8] To

---

[1] See D Phillips, *Looking Backward: A Critical Appraisal of Communitarian Thought* (Princeton, New Jersey, Princeton University Press, 1993) 175.

[2] See P Kahn, 'Community in Contemporary Constitutional Theory', 99 *Yale Law Journal* 1 at 5.

[3] *Ibid*, 5.

[4] R Bellah *et al*, *The Good Society* (New York, Knopf, 1991).

[5] R Unger, *Knowledge and Politics* (New York, Free Press, 1975) 233.

[6] M Sandel, 'Morality and the Liberal Ideal', *New Republic*, 7 May 1984, 15 at 17; Phillips, above n 1, 176; C Berry, *The Idea of a Democratic Community* (Hemel Hempstead, Harvester Wheatsheaf, 1989) 116; R Eckstein, 'Towards a Communitarian Theory of Responsibility: Bearing the Burden for the Unintended', 45 *University of Miami Law Review* 843 at 845–46; Unger, above n 5, 233.

[7] E Frazer and N Lacey, *The Politics of Community: A Feminist Critique of the Liberal-Communitarian Debate* (Buffalo, New York, University of Toronto Press, 1994) 111; K Abrams, 'Kitsch and Community', 84 *Michigan Law Review* 941 at 951; A Oldfield, *Citizenship and Community: Civic Republicanism and the Modern World* (London, Routledge, 1990) 145.

[8] Oldfield, above n 7, 173. For discussion, see S Gey, 'The Unfortunate Revival of Civic Republicanism', 141 *University of Pennsylvania Law Review* 801 at 825; J Nolan, *The Therapeutic State: Justifying Government at Century's End* (New York, London, New York University Press, 1998) 29.

serve the public interest is to do no more than to serve enlightened self-interest.[9]

Although this approach is most pronounced within the civic republican strand of communitarianism, it is shared with versions of feminism.[10] In relation to lesbian feminism in particular, Hoagland explains that she sees little distinction between her own interests and those of the (lesbian) community:

> I thought about myself and my friends. We did not consider our political work a sacrifice (even though one could note many sacrifices); it was how we made our lives meaningful. We did not consider our work away from our centers; and on nights like those, as well as others, we were taking the reality we were creating in our homes, collectives, bars, consciousness raising groups, and other meeting places, and extending it to the streets. In considering actual lesbian lives, I found that our actions were not sacrificial but creative.[11]

To grasp the connection between self and community, post-liberals conceptualise relationships within the community as not those of membership but as those of friendship, or something even closer than friendship.[12] We saw in chapter three that post-liberals generally regard the intimacy between spouses as making marriage the model community relationship, but that some regard marriage as a flawed model because of its particularity.[13] Therefore, in relation to wider community relations, it is necessary to seek a substitute.[14] One suggestion has been the cultivation of qualities of civic friendship and solidarity, which mediate between the standpoints of the generalised and concrete other by teaching us to reason, understand and appreciate the standpoint of collective concrete others.[15] A more general formulation

[9] B Barber, 'A Mandate for Liberty: Requiring Education-Based Community Service' in A Etzioni (ed), *The Essential Communitarian Reader* (Lanham, Rowman & Littlefield, 1998) 241; Unger, above n 5, 233. For discussion, see Gey, above n 8, 818.

[10] See EF Kittay and DT Meyers, 'Introduction' in EF Kittay and DT Meyers (eds), *Women and Moral Theory* (Totowa, New Jersey, Rowman & Littlefield, 1987) 10; A Hutchinson, 'Talking the Good Life: From Liberal Chatter to Democratic Conversation' in A Hutchinson and L Green (eds), *Law and the Community: The End of Individualism?* (Toronto, Carswell, 1989) 153; Berry, above n 6, 110.

[11] SL Hoagland, 'Why *Lesbian* Ethics?' in C Card (ed), *Adventures in Lesbian Philosophy* (Bloomington, Indiana University Press, 1994) 201.

[12] N Rosenblum, *Another Liberalism: Romanticism and the Reconstruction of Liberal Thought* (Cambridge, Massachusetts, Harvard University Press, 1987) 180.

[13] Pp 99 and 106–109.

[14] Unger, above n 5.

[15] S Benhabib, 'Introduction' in S Benhabib, *Situating the Self: Gender, Community and Postmodernism in Contemporary Ethics* (Cambridge, Polity, 1992) 11–12.

is that people need to experience strong sentiments of attachment: since impersonal relations are the problem, the correctives are friendship, sympathy, empathy and solidarity.[16] If these personal relations are achieved then there is no discrepancy between the selflessness hoped for in the setting of the family and the self-interest generally experienced in wider community relationships.[17]

Acceptance of the interconnection between the interests of self and community allows post-liberals to imagine community relationships as at least as close as those of friendship. However, imagining the relationships in this way also necessitates accepting the interconnection between the interests of self and community. This is because the conditions of love and community are still different. While love is strong enough to withstand lovers' opposing values, because relationships within community are inevitably weaker, they need to be held together by an allegiance to common purposes.[18]

The interconnection between the interests of the self and community, strengthened by community relationships conceptualised as close, leads post-liberals to downplay if not abandon the traditional liberal emphasis on that which people have the right to do, as opposed to that which it is good for people to do. If human identity is constructed out of particular community traditions and ways of life so that the good for individuals is intrinsically linked to that of the collective then a rigid separation of right from good does not make sense.[19] If community relationships are those of friendship then such separation makes even less sense. Indeed, it has been argued that it is not a question of whether rights should be respected but rather whether rights can be justified or even identified in a way that does not presuppose any particular conception of the good.[20] One answer is that they cannot be, because rights and the good are linked through intrinsic good, so that the good is inevitably prior to rights.[21] This answer has been illustrated with the example of religious freedom, the argument being that the right to religious freedom is not best understood as a particular case of a more

---

[16] Rosenblum, above n 12, 180–82.

[17] *Ibid*, 184; Unger, above n 5, 233.

[18] Unger, above n 5, 233.

[19] Eckstein, above n 6, 845. For discussion, see Frazer and Lacey, above n 7, 113; Gey, above n 8, 842.

[20] M Sandel, *Liberalism and the Limits of Justice* (Cambridge, Cambridge University Press, 1998) 186; R Beiner, *What's the Matter with Liberalism?* (Berkeley, California, University of California Press, 1992) 84.

[21] Sandel, above n 20, xii.

general right to individual freedom. Accordingly, it is wrong to equate the right to time off work to attend worship with, for example, the right to time off to attend a football match because what makes a religious belief worthy of respect is:

> . . . its place in a good life, or the qualities of character it promotes, or (from a political point of view) its tendency to cultivate the habits and dispositions that makes good citizens.[22]

Just like the interconnection between self and community, the priority of the good over rights is perhaps most pronounced within civic republicanism.[23] However, there are strong connections between the civic republican emphasis on a politics of the common good and the feminist emphasis on an ethic of care and responsibility.[24] Nevertheless, as we saw in chapter one, feminists are more wary of the appeal to notions of universalism and impartiality and the downgrading of difference inherent in the concept of the common good, since this clashes with the relativism of post-liberal feminism. In passing, we can note that just as we reclaimed the removal of fault from the liberal for the post-liberal interpretation of the Family Law Act, we can reclaim the other main strand in the liberal interpretation of the Family Law Act, that of the de-legalisation of divorce. One aspect of law is to advance people's rights, whereas administrative processes are primarily designed to appeal to individuals' duties to the community.[25]

---

[22] *Ibid*, xii. See also Beiner, above n 20, 82.

[23] See eg M Galston, 'Taking Aristotle Seriously: Republican-Oriented Legal Theory and the Moral Foundation of Deliberative Democracy', 82 *California Law Review* 331 at 335; M Sandel, *Democracy's Discontent: America in Search of a Public Philosophy* (Cambridge, Massachusetts, Belknap Press, 1996) 25. For discussion, see Frazer and Lacey, above n 7; S Avineri and A de-Shalit, 'Introduction' in S Avineri and A de-Shalit (eds), *Communitarianism and Individualism* (Oxford, New York, Oxford University Press, 1992) 7; W Kymlicka, *Liberalism, Community, and Culture* (Oxford, New York, Clarendon Press, 1991) 2; A Hutchinson, 'Talking the Good Life: From Liberal Chatter to Democratic Conversation' in Hutchinson and Green, above n 10, 153.

[24] For the connection, see Berry, above n 6, 110. On the ethic of care, see EF Kittay and DT Meyers, 'Introduction' in Kittay and Meyers, above n 10, 10. On the common good, see A Hutchinson, 'Talking the Good Life: From Liberal Chatter to Democratic Conversation' in Hutchinson and Green, above n 10, 153.

[25] J Eekelaar, 'Family law: keeping us "on message"', 11 *Child and Family Law Quarterly* 387 at 394; J Eekelaar, 'Family Law: The Communitarian Message', 21 *Oxford Journal of Legal Studies* 181 at 189; K O'Donovan, 'Love's Law: Moral Reasoning in Family Law' in D Morgan and G Douglas, *Constituting Families: A Study in Governance* (Stuttgart, Germany, Steiner (Franz) Verlag Wiesbaden GmbH, 1994) 45; MDA Freeman, 'Questioning the Delegalization Movement in Family Law: Do We Really Want a Family Court?' in J Eekelaar and SN Katz (eds), *The Resolution of Family*

ADULT EDUCATION

The two themes explored so far, namely the interconnection between self and community and the priority of the good over rights, have implications for the post-liberal conception of freedom. If the self cannot be imagined apart from social relations then the traditional liberal conception of freedom as the absence of external interference with one's capability to do what one wants is fatally imprecise, because other people's conduct impedes, facilitates and encourages one's own in countless ways.[26] So instead we have to distinguish between legitimate and illegitimate interference, but doing so relies on developing a view on what is good.[27] A partial view is developed out of our first theme, the interconnection between self and community, in that a community with common values and in which each member regards these common values as his or her own is a good in itself.[28]

Crucially, it follows that people are free only when their duty and interest coincide.[29] The traditional protection of individual civil liberties has to be abandoned because liberty is a collective enterprise.[30] Moreover, to broaden out a point made in chapter three in relation to spousal obligations specifically, it follows from our constitutive identity that our duties are not limited to chosen duties. We are sometimes obliged to fulfil ends given by our membership of the community because these ends are part of what constitutes us.[31] Whether or not freedom is regarded as also belonging to individuals, freedom should

---

Conflict: Comparative Legal Perspectives (Toronto, Butterworths, 1984) 16; MDA Freeman, 'Down with informalism: Law and lawyers in family dispute resolutions', 2 *Family Law Journal* 67 at 71.

[26] Unger, above n 5, 278; MC Regan, 'Getting Our Stories Straight: Narrative Autonomy and Feminist Commitments', 72 *Indiana Law Journal* 449 at 452; P Weiss, 'Feminism and Communitarianism: Comparing Critiques of Liberalism' in P Weiss and M Friedman (eds), *Feminism and Community* (Philadelphia, Temple University Press, 1995) 164.

[27] Unger, above n 5, 278.

[28] Oldfield, above n 7, 164. For discussion, see S Avineri and A de-Shalit, 'Introduction' in Avineri and de-Shalit, above n 23, 6–7; Berry, above n 6, 57.

[29] Oldfield, above n 7, 153.

[30] For discussion, see Gey, above n 8, 803.

[31] Sandel, above n 20, 186–88. For discussion, see S Avineri and A de-Shalit, 'Introduction' in Avineri and de-Shalit, above n 23, 6; Phillips, above n 1, 176; Berry, above n 6, 101.

be thought of primarily as the property of collectives and, as such, requires dedication:[32]

> We can now redefine freedom as the measure of an individual's capacity to achieve the good. One is free according to the perfection of this power.[33]

Post-liberals do not recognise automatic ascription of autonomy. They do not believe that humans possess full capacity for choice simply by virtue of being alive; rather, they believe autonomy is a potential to be developed that can on occasions fail to be developed. Freedom to choose is seen as an identity and a way of understanding ourselves rather than a birth-right, autonomy not as a given but as an achievement.[34] Therefore, giving any support at all to freedom of choice within the post-liberal conception of freedom depends on nurturing the capacity to choose. The capacity to choose involves being able to conceive alternatives, defining what we really want and discerning what commands our allegiance:

> This kind of freedom is unavailable to one whose sympathies and horizons are so narrow that he can conceive only one way of life, for whom indeed the very notion of a way of life which is his as against everyone's has no sense. Nor is it available to one who is riveted by fear of the unknown to one familiar life-form, or who has been so formed in suspicion and hate of outsiders that he can never put himself in their place.[35]

Support for freedom of choice demands that we become beings capable of choice, rising to a sufficient level of self-consciousness and autonomy, and ridding ourselves of 'fear, sloth, ignorance, or superstition in some code imposed by tradition, society or fate'.[36] Rendering ourselves worthy of choice leads back to the obligation, investigated in chapter two, to achieve authenticity through self-discovery: the condition for the full development of our capacities is that we require a certain conception of ourselves.[37]

The strenuous task of becoming worthy of choice leads post-liberals, specifically civic republicans, to reject one of:

[32] For discussion, see W Kymlicka, 'Communitarianism, Liberalism, and Superliberalism', 8 *Critical Review* 262 at 274; Gey, above n 8, 819–20.

[33] Unger, above n 5, 278. See also C Taylor, 'Atomism' in C Taylor, *Philosophy and the Human Sciences: Philosophical Papers 2* (Cambridge, Cambridge University Press, 1985).

[34] R Beiner, 'What's the Matter with Liberalism?' in Hutchinson and Green, above n 10, 47.

[35] C Taylor, 'Atomism' in C Taylor, above n 33, 204.

[36] *Ibid*, 197.

[37] *Ibid*; R Fallon, 'Two Senses of Autonomy', 46 *Stanford Law Review* 875 at 883–885. For discussion, see J Friedman, 'The Politics of Communitarianism', 8 *Critical Review* 297 at 299.

... the central tenets of the liberal-individualist tradition of political thinking ... that once children reach and pass the threshold of adulthood, the courtesy is paid of regarding them as fully responsible moral agents.[38]

This is not only on the basis that capability cannot be assumed to accompany adulthood;[39] willingness cannot be assumed either,[40] because as we saw in chapter 1 civic virtue requires self-sacrifice, so that the motivational obstacles to responsible citizenship also need to be addressed.[41] To overcome these obstacles, it is necessary for citizens to have internalised the demands of virtue.[42]

We have seen that the priority of the good over rights implies that freedom of choice can exist only alongside the capacity to choose, but the latter also implies the former. For example, it has been argued that Ronald Dworkin's conception of the right to equal concern and respect is really an embryonic theory of human good because it is an empirical question whether we all do in fact form reflective life plans that warrant respect. Likewise, if it is our capacity for choice that yields rights then we have rights only if we choose with seriousness and intelligence.[43]

It follows that if this capacity can only develop in society or a specific form of society then we have a duty to sustain that society.[44] It has been argued that this is the case, in that the capacity for autonomy does not exist in every society and does not fully exist in our own.[45] This creates

[38] Oldfield, above n 7, 152.

[39] *Ibid*, 152.

[40] *Ibid*.

[41] Galston, above n 23, 354.

[42] *Ibid*, 365. For discussion, see also Rosenblum, above n 12, 173.

[43] Beiner, above n 20.

[44] Oldfield, above n 7, 164; Sandel, above n 23, 26; Regan, above n 26, 452. For discussion, see R Lister, *Citizenship: Feminist Perspectives* (Basingstoke, Macmillan Press Ltd, 1997) 23; S Holmes, *The Anatomy of Antiliberalism* (Cambridge, Massachusetts, Harvard University Press, 1993) 88; Kymlicka, above n 23, 78; A Gutmann, 'Communitarian Critics of Liberalism', 14 *Philosophy and Public Affairs* 308 at 308; G Kateb, 'Democratic Individuality and the Meaning of Rights' in N Rosenblum (ed), *Liberalism and the Moral Life* (Cambridge, Massachusetts, Harvard University Press, 1989) 183; Phillips, above n 1, 175; A Hutchinson, 'Talking the Good Life: From Liberal Chatter to Democratic Conversation' in Hutchinson and Green, above n 10, 153; P Simpson, 'Liberalism, State, and Community', 8 *Critical Review* 159 at 159; J Tomasi, 'Community in the Minimal State', 8 *Critical Review* 285 at 285.

[45] C Taylor, 'Atomism' in C Taylor, above n 33, 205; J Shotter, 'Psychology and Citizenship: Identity and Belonging' in B Turner (ed), *Citizenship and Social Theory* (London, Sage, 1993) 129. For discussion, see Kymlicka, above n 23, 2; E Frazer, *The Problems of Communitarian Politics: Unity and Conflict* (Oxford, Oxford University Press, 1999) 212; Abrams, above n 7, 951–52.

a significant obligation to belong. Since the free subject can only maintain his or her freedom within a certain type of society, he or she has to be concerned about the shape of this society as a whole. He or she cannot be concerned purely with his or her individual choices to the neglect of the matrix in which such choices take their form. It is important to him or her that certain activities and institutions flourish:

> It is even of importance to him what the moral tone of the whole society is – shocking as it may be to libertarians to raise this issue – because freedom and individual diversity can only flourish in a society where there is a general recognition of their worth.[46]

The crucial modes of self-understanding for freedom of choice are always created and sustained by the common expression and recognition that they receive in social life. The conclusion is inevitable:

> . . . the free individual who affirms himself as such *already* has an obligation to complete, restore, or sustain the society within which this identity is possible.[47] . . . even the extreme libertarians acquire their uncompromising passion for individual autonomy by virtue of participating in a civilization that has learned, over the course of many centuries, to put a premium upon such aspirations. Abstracted from such a global social-historical context, the very desire for command of one's individual destiny would be inaccessible, void of meaning. Therefore, precisely those aspirations that define the atomist perspective are the expression of a debt to one's society, and in turn the source of social obligations, that the libertarians themselves overlook.[48]

Two main points have emerged from this section so far. The first is that we are free only if we have developed the capacity to choose; the second is that because this capacity can only exist in a certain form of society we have an obligation to sustain society. The implication is that people *become* free by taking their civic duties seriously:[49]

> We think of ourselves as 'born free,' but we are, in truth, born weak and dependent and acquire equality as a concomitant of our citizenship. Liberty is learned: it is a product rather than the cause of our civic work as citizens.[50]

---

[46] C Taylor, 'Atomism' in C Taylor, above n 33, 207. See also Regan, above n 26, 452.
[47] C Taylor, 'Atomism' in C Taylor, above n 33, 209. For discussion, see J Shotter, 'Psychology and Citizenship: Identity and Belonging' in Turner, above n 45, 129; Friedman, above n 37, 299.
[48] R Beiner, 'What's the Matter with Liberalism?' in Hutchinson and Green, above n 10, 39. See also Eckstein, above n 6, 845.
[49] Oldfield, above n 7, 159, emphasis added.
[50] B Barber, 'A Mandate for Liberty: Requiring Education-Based Community Service' in Etzioni, above n 9, 238.

Regarding political participation as the essence of both liberty and citizenship is central to contemporary civic republicanism.[51] If realising our freedom depends partly on the society in which we live, then we exercise a fuller freedom if we help determine the shape of this society by having a voice in deliberation about public action:[52]

> . . . given our nature as political beings, we are free only insofar as we exercise our capacity to deliberate about the common good, and participate in the public life of a free city or republic.[53]

This means that freedom cannot extend to allowing individuals to absent themselves from participation in governing structures or the public discussion that shapes the community's rules.[54] Since freedom is fragile and easily lost,[55] we have no right to freedom from the obligations attendant on belonging to or sustaining our community.[56] In any case, since autonomy depends on the collective, freedom from political interference would reduce rather than strengthen our autonomy.[57] It has been suggested that recognising this is the way to avoid losing the self in the community: what is needed is a notion of involvement in communal practices out of which the self grows.[58] In addition, since participation is in part a process of understanding ourselves, nobody can participate on our behalf.[59]

[51] Sandel, above n 23. For discussion, see Lister, above n 44, 24; U Vogel and M Moran, 'Introduction', in U Vogel and M Moran (eds), *The Frontiers of Citizenship* (Basingstoke, Macmillan, 1991) xv; S Avineri and A de-Shalit, 'Introduction' in Avineri and de-Shalit, above n 23, 9; Frazer and Lacey, above n 7, 113; Frazer, above n 45, 37; Abrams, above n 7, 952; G Kateb, 'Democratic Individuality and the Meaning of Rights' in Rosenblum, above n 44, 183; Nolan, above n 8, 29; S Benhabib, 'Autonomy, Modernity and Community: Communitarianism and Critical Social Theory in Dialogue' in Benhabib, above n 15, 82.
[52] C Taylor, 'Atomism' in C Taylor, above n 33, 208–9.
[53] Sandel, above n 23, 26.
[54] *Ibid*, 5. For discussion, see Kymlicka, above n 32, 274; Gey, above n 8, 819–20; Gardbaum, 'Law, Politics and the Claims of Community', 90 *Michigan Law Review* 685 at 749.
[55] See Frazer, above n 45, 211–12.
[56] See Friedman, above n 37, 299.
[57] B Barber, *Strong Democracy: Participatory Politics for a New Age* (Berkeley, University of California Press, 1984) 153; Berry, above n 6. For discussion, see Kymlicka, above n 32, 274; Gey, above n 8, 878; Lister, above n 44, 24; G Kateb, 'Democratic Individuality and the Meaning of Rights' in Rosenblum, above n 44, 183; Friedman, above n 37, 299; Fallon, above n 37, 883.
[58] S Lash, 'Reflexivity and its Doubles: Structure, Aesthetics, Community' in U Beck, A Giddens and S Lash, *Reflexive Modernization: Politics, Tradition and Aesthetics in the Modern Social Order* (Cambridge, Polity Press, 1994) 164; Berry, above n 6, 116.
[59] Berry, above n 6, 58–59.

Community grows out of participation and at the same time makes participation possible.[60] Participation, as well as an acceptance of duty, is a precondition of citizenship: to be a citizen *is* to participate; citizenship is something that follows from participation, so that citizenship is not a condition of participation but one of participation's richest fruits:[61]

> To participate *is* to create a community that governs itself, and to create a self-governing community *is* to participate. Indeed, from the perspective of strong democracy, the two terms *participation* and *community* are aspects of one single mode of social being: citizenship.[62]

A virtuous circle of participation breeding participation results because 'the more one participates, the more one develops the attitudes appropriate to a citizen:'[63]

> Politics becomes its own university, citizenship its own training ground and participation its own tutor. Freedom is what comes out of this process, not what goes into it.[64]

However, participation per se is insufficient; participation has an intrinsically normative dimension, in that participation is what citizens do:

> Masses make noise, citizens deliberate; masses behave, citizens act, masses collide and intersect, citizens engage, share, and contribute. At the moment when 'masses' start deliberating, acting, sharing, and contributing, they cease to be masses and become citizens. Only then do they 'participate.'[65]

Citizenship is participation in a specific mode, that is participation with public responsibility, with attention to the common good.[66] To be a citizen is to participate in a certain conscious fashion that presumes awareness of and engagement with the activities of others.[67]

Crucially, participation is an end rather than a means, with moral rather than merely instrumental value.[68] Values such as justice or

---

[60] Barber, above n 57, 152.
[61] Oldfield, above n 7, 160.
[62] Barber, above n 57, 155. See also Galston, above n 23, 335.
[63] Oldfield, above n 7, 155. See also Berry, above n 6.
[64] Barber, above n 57, 152.
[65] *Ibid*, 154.
[66] Oldfield, above n 7, 160. For discussion, see Abrams, above n 7, 952.
[67] Barber, above n 57, 155.
[68] Berry, above n 6, 56; Galston, above n 23, 365. For discussion, see Lister, above n 44, 24.

equality do not have substantive content, according to which future enactments can be measured, but are subordinated to self-government, participation and procedure.[69] The community's decisions are granted ethical validity and political legitimacy if and only if the decisions are made collectively. This is because the community is regarded as something more than the sum of its members. It becomes an organic entity, possessing an ethical and political legitimacy entirely distinct from its components.[70] Here again therefore, we have a virtuous circle because participation elevates the moral character of individual action:[71]

> ... new communitarians seek to construct a civil religion proclaiming democratic participation ... the key virtue. ... So long as we decide in common what we shall deem good, communitarians argue, we have done our duty and should be satisfied that we have done justice.[72]

So there is an obligation to participate, and to participate in a particular mode. However, civic republicanism demands much, much more than this. Although participation helps to develop the attitudes appropriate to a citizen, participation also requires the systematic and direct inculcation of civic virtue.[73] This is because, although participation is an end in itself, civic republicanism does want to have this both ways. The common good that civic republicanism affirms does not correspond to the utilitarian notion of aggregating individual preferences: as we saw in chapter one, civic republicanism does not take people's existing preferences and try to satisfy them.[74] The common good is rather a standard by which people's preferences are evaluated, and the weight given to an individual's preferences depends on how much that individual conforms and contributes to the common good.[75] Therefore the republican community seeks to cultivate in citizens the qualities of character necessary for the common good:[76]

> It requires a knowledge of public affairs and also a sense of belonging, a concern for the whole, a moral bond with the community whose fate is at stake.

---

[69] See Abrams, above n 7, 955–56.

[70] For discussion, see Gey, above n 8, 814.

[71] For discussion, see Abrams, above n 7, 956.

[72] B Frohnen, *The New Communitarians and the Crisis of Modern Liberalism* (Lawrence, University Press of Kansas, 1996) 12.

[73] Galston, above n 23, 365. For discussion, see Rosenblum, above n 12, 173; Gey, above n 8; *ibid*, 163; Nolan, above n 8, 29; S Gardbaum, 'Why the Liberal State can Promote Moral Ideals After All', 104 *Harvard Law Review* 1350 at 1352.

[74] See pp 32–39.

[75] See Kymlicka, above n 23, 77.

[76] Sandel, above n 23, 25. For discussion, see Frazer and Lacey, above n 7, 106.

To share in self-rule therefore requires that citizens possess, or come to acquire, certain qualities of character, or civic virtues. But this means that republican politics cannot be neutral toward the values and ends its citizens espouse. The republican conception of freedom, unlike the liberal conception, requires a formative politics, a politics that cultivates in citizens the qualities of character self-government requires.[77] . . . Insofar as certain dispositions, attachments, and commitments are essential to the realization of self-government, republican politics regards moral character as a public, not merely private, concern. In this sense, it attends to the identity, not just the interests, of its citizens.[78]

Civic republicans are quite clear that in the process of performing the duties of citizenship, citizens will find their interests changing.[79]

So how is civic virtue to be inculcated? It might be thought that the demise of religious belief, which used to generate an understanding and acceptance of duty, makes this task nigh on impossible.[80] But undaunted, civic republicans respond that the demise of religion merely:

. . . suggests that one must build on whatever religion is available, and that a different social institution must be brought into focus: education.[81] . . . Even if religion is not necessary to provide the motivation, some form of moral or civic education is.[82]

Education is the new civil religion,[83] and it must continue into, and throughout, adult life:[84]

Freedom in this sense . . . involves apprenticeship and . . . periodic retraining. . . . Human beings not only have to be taught what moral autonomy means as a practice, but, being weak and shortsighted, they also have to be reminded of what it is that they have been taught . . . The practice of citizenship, which is what moral autonomy means within civic republicanism, is an unnatural practice for human beings, and Rousseau was correct to say that their 'natural' character has to be 'mutilated' before they will engage in it. This is the cost of the practice of citizenship. It is not surprising that

---

[77] Sandel, above n 23, 5–6.
[78] *Ibid*, 25.
[79] Oldfield, above n 7, 164.
[80] *Ibid*, 153.
[81] *Ibid*, 154.
[82] *Ibid*, 164. For discussion, see Frazer, above n 45, 212; J Rodger, *Family Life and Social Control: A Sociological Perspective* (Basingstoke, Macmillan, 1996) 80.
[83] Frohnen, above n 72, 12.
[84] A Etzioni, *The New Golden Rule: Community and Morality in a Democratic Society* (New York, Basic Books, 1998) 172. For discussion, see M D'Antonio, 'The Next Big Idea', *The Guardian*, 23 June 1994.

liberal individualists will not pay it: it is an unwelcome entrance fee to social living. Liberal individualists object to having their characters systematically mutilated (as if this did not already take place); civic republicans know that it is worth paying the price.[85] . . . The moral character which is appropriate for genuine citizenship does not generate itself; it has to be authoritatively inculcated. This means that minds have to be manipulated. People, starting with children, have to be taught what citizenship means for them . . .[86]

There are strong similarities between civic education and consciousness-raising, discussed in chapter two. Although consciousness-raising is originally internal, both are seen as educative processes within communitarianism, that is, discovery procedures that operate as ways of uncovering previously unperceived oppression.[87] For example, both compulsory re-education classes and consciousness-raising sessions have been proposed for people who express racist or sexist opinions.[88]

As we have already seen, theory and practice must go hand in hand: active participation in citizenship has to be accompanied by overt education in one's duty. Civic activity educates people how to think publicly as citizens, at the same time as their understanding of citizenship informs their civic activity.[89] Neither education nor participation is adequate on its own to generate commitment to the practice of citizenship, however:

. . . what is required is a much broader educative effort to inculcate both knowledge of the duties of citizenship and willingness to perform them.[90]

Civic republicans have recognised that from a liberal standpoint, the republican claim that freedom depends on civic virtue gives the state a stake in the character of its citizens that could open the way to coercion and oppression.[91] Ironically, as the tendency to exclude people from the community recedes, the danger of coercion increases, because given the demands of republican citizenship, the more expansive the bounds of membership, the more demanding the task of cultivating virtue. In Aristotle's polis, the formative task was to cultivate virtue among a small group of people who shared a common life:

[85] Oldfield, above n 7, 153–54. See also Barber, above n 57, 235.
[86] Oldfield, above n 7, 164.
[87] Berry, above n 6.
[88] Frohnen, above n 72, 141 and 164; Nolan, above n 8, 293–94.
[89] Barber, above n 57, 152; Berry, above n 6.
[90] Oldfield, above n 7, 156.
[91] Sandel, above n 23, 27; Galston, above n 23, 379–80. For discussion, see Simpson, above n 44, 159–160; Rosenblum, above n 12, 173

When republican thought turns democratic, however, and when the natural bent of persons to be citizens can no longer be assumed, the formative project becomes more daunting. The task of forging a common citizenship among a vast and disparate people invites more strenuous forms of soulcraft. This raises the stakes for republican politics and heightens the risk of coercion.[92]

However, it has been argued that there is a distinction between coercion, which imposes beliefs, and pedagogy, which aims at empowerment and the cultivation of autonomy. Those who are most in need of training in citizenship are the least likely to volunteer for such training, because an inability to see the relationship between self-interest and broader community interests is not only the target of civic education but also an attitude that disposes people against civic education. People who have neither any sense of the meaning of citizenship nor any conception of civic responsibilities are going to remain untouched by volunteer programmes. Education is the exercise of legitimate coercion in the name of freedom, because forced participation in education makes the participants responsible, autonomous and empowered.[93] That education has this effect also means that in the final analysis, while good character is dependent on the formation of habits and so to some extent involuntary, citizens will nevertheless be able to reflect on their education and confirm or repudiate it.[94] Moreover, given that virtue is neither innate nor comfortable, it is argued that compulsory education in civic virtue is essential if communitarianism is be anything more than a theoretical concept:[95]

> There are certain things a democracy simply must teach, employing its full authority to do so: citizenship is first among them.[96]

As in chapter two, we can note the inescapably élitist consequences of a focus on civic education.

So childhood is no longer the exclusive province of education: adults must continue their education. However, even children's education serves a different purpose for the communitarian than for the liberal:

---

[92] Sandel, above n 23, 319.
[93] B Barber, 'A Mandate for Liberty: Requiring Education-Based Community Service' in Etzioni, above n 9, 238.
[94] Galston, above n 23, 385.
[95] *Ibid*, 379–80; Oldfield, above n 7, 164–65. For discussion, see Rosenblum, above n 12, 173; Gey, above n 8, 842.
[96] B Barber, 'A Mandate for Liberty: Requiring Education-Based Community Service' in Etzioni, above n 9, 241.

On some issues, the two theories may produce different arguments for similar policies. For example, . . . where liberals might support public education in hopes of equipping students to become autonomous individuals, capable of choosing their own ends and pursuing them effectively, communitarians might support public education in hopes of equipping students to become good citizens, capable of contributing meaningfully to public deliberations and pursuits.[97]

Accordingly, the curriculum may need adapting, and it is worth noting that from August 2002 citizenship has been introduced as a compulsory subject for all children between the ages of 11 and 16.[98] From a communitarian perspective, schools and universities currently teach many subjects that are less important than the skills necessary to preserve freedom:[99]

The school, particularly the university, is the 'church' of our secular society, and we shall consider how well it fulfills that function. In particular we ask if our schools and universities can become democratic learning communities, whether they can help us deal with the moral as well as the technical problems of a complex society.[100]

For children as for adults, education and participation march hand in hand:

If you want children to come out of them (schools) understanding good and bad you don't teach them morals as if they were chemical equations: you encourage them to learn through working with others.[101]

According to civic-republicanism, education-based community service programmes should be part of the mandatory curriculum because these empower students at the same time as teaching them, bringing the lessons of the community into the classroom and vice versa. When students use experience in the community as a basis for critical reflection in the classroom and turn classroom reflection into a tool to examine the nature of communities, this provides an opportunity to teach liberty and to expose the interdependence of self and other:

[97] Sandel, above n 6, 15.
[98] www.dfes.gov.uk/a–z/CURRICULUM.html.
[99] B Barber, 'A Mandate for Liberty: Requiring Education-Based Community Service' in Etzioni, above n 9, 239. For discussion, see also Frohnen, above n 9, 162.
[100] Bellah, above n 4, 16.
[101] G Mulgan, 'Our Built-in Moral Sense is the Basic We Should Go Back To', *The Guardian*, 4 August 1994.

... to teach the art of citizenship and responsibility is to practice it: so that teaching in this domain must be about acting and doing as well as about listening and learning, but must also afford an opportunity for reflecting on and discussing what is being done. In practical terms, this means that community service can only be an instrument of education when it is connected to an academic learning experience in a classroom setting. But the corollary is also true, that civic education can only be effective when it encompasses experiential learning of the kind offered by community service or other similar forms of group activity.[102]

What is the virtue that the community is trying to teach? We have seen that one answer to this question is that participation and education are ends in themselves. It is difficult for education to be aimless however: there needs to be something to teach. This question will be addressed in the concrete context of divorce later in this chapter, but one preliminary suggestion, which our investigation of divorce law will confirm, is that the state should inculcate as a minimum those values, virtues and character traits that enable citizens to be deliberative.[103]

(DIVORCE) LAW AS EDUCATION

Traditionally, one fundamental distinction between morality and law was that while morality could concern itself with our thoughts and feelings, law aimed only at controlling our behaviour. Recently, this distinction has been challenged. It has been argued that no one has ever considered the possibility that the parties might need information about anything during the course of the trial:

> The philosophical record contains no discussion of situations in which the parties engage in unlawful behaviour because of a lack of interpersonal skills or knowledge.[104]

The argument has been made that while current court procedures are designed to inform only the judge, the parties may be in just as much need of information. Focusing on cases of domestic violence, the suggestion is that legal proceedings would be much more powerful if the

---

[102] B Barber, 'A Mandate for Liberty: Requiring Education-Based Community Service' in Etzioni, above n 9, 240.

[103] Galston, above n 23, 384.

[104] N Rourke, 'Domestic Violence: The Challenge to Law's Theory of the Self' in DT Meyers *et al* (eds), *Kindred Matters: Rethinking the Philosophy of the Family* (Ithaca, New York, Cornell University Press, 1993) 278.

court lent its legitimacy to a process designed to help the batterer to understand the harm that he or she is causing. Where the parties need to be informed, the court is in a unique position to help them to obtain the necessary information. This requires a structure in which lack of understanding can be exposed and addressed.[105]

Stephen Cretney has expressed sheer bewilderment at the fact that this was in essence the approach recently attempted in divorce law. As far as he was concerned, as early as the Law Commission report, policy makers confused the legal process of divorce, which could only be concerned with the legal consequences of marriage breakdown, with the psychological process of adjusting to change. He maintained that while the law should not do anything to hinder couples from reflecting, reaching agreement and otherwise acting responsibly, these were not legal questions.[106] It has been argued that it was perhaps because the information meeting most starkly embodied the fusion of the legal process and social welfare provision that the information meeting proved the downfall of Part II of the Family Law Act, as we will explore in the next chapter.[107]

However, the interpretation of the Family Law Act provided in this book practically necessitates a focus on feelings rather than behaviour. As we saw in chapter three, one consequence of our primary obligation being to live authentically was that the Family Law Act abandoned any attempt to pass judgement on marital behaviour.[108] The resulting frustration of policy makers in this field was understandable. Traditionally, the main task of the law is precisely to pass judgement on

---

[105] N Rourke, 'Domestic Violence: The Challenge to Law's Theory of the Self' in Meyers, above n 104, 276–78.

[106] S Cretney, *Elements of Family Law* 2nd edn (London, Sweet & Maxwell, 1992) 68. For similar views, see P Brown, 'Divorce—The Fault Fiction', 138 *New Law Journal* 377; J Walker, 'Whither the Family Law Act, Part II?' in M Thorpe and E Clarke (eds), *No Fault or Flaw: The Future of the Family Law Act 1996* (Bristol, Jordan Publishing, 2000) 6.

[107] J Walker, 'Whither the Family Law Act, Part II?' in Thorpe and Clarke, above n 106, 6.

[108] Cretney, above n 106, 67–68; Sandel, above n 23, 111; Law Commission, *The Ground for Divorce* (London, HMSO, 1990) 10–11; Lord Chancellor's Department, *Looking to the Future: Mediation and the Ground for Divorce* (London, HMSO, 1995) 17; MC Regan, 'Market Discourse and Moral Neutrality in Divorce Law', 1994 *Utah Law Review* 605 at 606; M Phillips, 'Death blow to marriage', *The Observer*, 7 May 1995; K O'Donovan, *Family Law Matters* (London, Pluto Press, 1993) 112–13; K O'Donovan, 'Love's Law: Moral Reasoning in Family Law' in Morgan and Douglas, above n 20, 43–45; J Dewar, 'The Normal Chaos of Family Law' 61 *Modern Law Review* 467 at 484.

behaviour, and faced with the redundancy of the traditional task, it was almost inevitable that the law would struggle to regain relevance by finding a new role. Some commentators have suggested that the approach that Part II of the Family Law Act adopted was to keep the same end but to change the means, that is to turn to persuasion rather than regulation as a way of passing judgement on marital behaviour.[109] We will see in the next chapter that this did become an important element in the later stages of the reform process, particularly post-1997. But if our life-goal is authenticity through self-discovery then finding fault by any means is equally problematic. Therefore, the original solution when Part II of the Family Law Act was conceived was for policy makers to turn instead to persuasion *as an end in itself*. Divorce law was replaced by, or perhaps *became*, moral suasion, and just as for civic republicans civic education is principally an end not a means,[110] so the principal aim of morally educating divorcing couples was the moral education itself.

Other commentators have gone further to argue that the search for authenticity implies not only the redundancy of fault-finding but also of legal or social regulation of divorce in its entirety. If individuals are entitled to seek divorce for their own reasons then there is no point placing any impediments in their way.[111] This goes too far. It is true that the law is, and realises itself to be, increasingly irrelevant to the fundamental traditional legal question in the divorce process, that is, whether or not the couple actually divorces.[112] But there is a way for the law to regain relevance within the parameters identified, a way which we have already explored to some extent in chapter two, and that is for the law to insist that a prospective divorcee must seek authenticity. The law can consistently demand that a divorcee discover himself or herself more deeply through his or her divorce, so that he or she emerges from divorce enriched and more fully developed. If society now views marital breakup as a vehicle for self-improvement,[113] then

---

[109] Eekelaar, 'on message', above n 25, 393; J Eekelaar, *Regulating Divorce* (Oxford, Clarendon Press, 1991) 154; A Etzioni, 'Introduction' in Etzioni, above n 9, xiii; Dewar, above n 108, 477; J Dewar, 'Family Law and Its Discontents', 14 *International Journal of Law, Policy and the Family* 59 at 79; A Skolnick and S Rosencrantz, 'The New Crusade for the Old Family', 18 *The American Prospect* 59 at 60; JH DiFonzo, *Beneath the Fault Line: The Popular and Legal Culture of Divorce in Twentieth-Century America* (Charlottesville, University Press of Virginia, 1997) 2.

[110] See p 143.

[111] B D Whitehead, *The Divorce Culture: Rethinking Our Commitments to Marriage and the Family* (New York, Knopf, 1997) 67–68; Phillips, above n 108.

[112] O'Donovan, above n 108, 111.

[113] Whitehead, above n 111, 76.

the law can mirror this view and remould regulation of divorce accordingly. Faced with irrelevance at the point of divorce, law struggles to regain relevance, and to some extent succeeds by concentrating on and fetishising the divorce *process*.

A puzzle can now be solved. Given that the Family Law Act dispensed with any criteria for granting or refusing divorce, it is at first glance difficult to make sense of the claim in the White Paper that 'the Government's proposals will result in a harder divorce process for everyone'.[114] The claim can now be endorsed, so long as we emphasise the word, 'process'. Indeed, the Government went on to explain that it did not mean 'harder' in the sense that people would be less likely to be granted a divorce, but rather in the sense that:

> ... they will be required to spend time reflecting on whether their marriage can be saved and, if not, to face up to the consequences of their actions and make arrangements to meet their responsibilities before a divorce is granted.[115]

Although it goes too far to suggest that legal regulation of divorce is obsolete, the profundity of the change in regulation should not be underestimated. Essentially, divorce law was no longer primarily about preventing divorce. Divorce regulation shifted from *preventing* marriage breakdown to *managing* the end of relationships.[116] It has been argued that this shift was in part a result simply of the prevalence of divorce. When divorce was rare, there would have been few expectations about the proper thing to do when a marriage ended. Now that divorce is more likely to be conjectured upon, if not anticipated, family policy has begun to develop normative frameworks to guide divorcing couples towards a preferred or proper method of divorcing.[117] The means become the end, as the aim of divorce law switches from prevention or control of divorce to ensuring that divorce is an educative experience.[118] Law's struggle for relevance in relation to divorce,

---

[114] Lord Chancellor's Department, above n 108, 26.

[115] *Ibid*, 26.

[116] C Piper and SD Sclater, 'Changing Divorce' in SD Sclater and C Piper (eds), *Undercurrents of Divorce* (Aldershot, Ashgate, 1999) 233; Regan, above n 108, 607; C Dyer, 'Law and Church Welcome End to Quickie Divorces', *The Guardian*, 28 April 1995.

[117] C Smart and B Neale, 'Good Enough Morality? Divorce and Postmodernity', 17 *Critical Social Policy* 3 at 8; O'Donovan, *Family Law*, above n 108, 111.

[118] J Dewar and S Parker, 'English Family Law since World War II: From Status to Chaos' in S Katz et al (eds), *Cross Currents: Family Law and Policy in the United States and England* (New York, Oxford University Press, 2000) 139. See also Dewar, above n 109, 68–69.

combined with the civic republican emphasis on moral education as a precondition of citizenship, leads to divorce re-imagined as education.

As we saw above, education cannot be completely reflexive however: it does need an object. Just as one of the questions that civic republicans have to address is the goal of civic education, so divorce law needed a lesson to teach divorcees, or a message to impart to them. We can investigate the content of the message in relation to three distinct aspects of the Family Law Act: the period of reflection and consideration, the information meetings and mediation.

I have already made two observations about the period of reflection and consideration. In chapter three I observed that this was the main means of delaying divorce.[119] In chapter two I noted that during the reform process there was a shift in the purpose of the period from being to provide an opportunity to reflect to being to create an obligation to reflect.[120] However, now we are about to see that even providing an opportunity to reflect was not the original purpose of the period; the period was initially intended merely to provide conclusive evidence that the marriage had broken down. It has been argued that when the Law Commission originally developed the reform, the Commission expressed scepticism over the extent to which the law could promote marriage.[121] The primary purpose that the Commission envisaged for the period of reflection was accordingly evidentiary, although their report did add that the period should also give the parties time to resolve practical questions and decide whether they wished to reconcile.[122] The ideology underlying this approach has been described as regularisation, which comes close to acknowledging the redundancy of regulating divorce.[123] The ideology of regularisation accepted that separation and divorce would occur whatever the legal process did and, apart from ensuring that the legal process did not do additional harm, largely left the people involved to settle the consequences of divorce. Accordingly, the legal process was at this stage mainly confined to ensuring that cases were processed efficiently and formalities properly attended to.[124] However, the primary purpose was reversed in the 1993 Governmental Consultation Paper in that the Paper identified *the*

---

[119] See p 124.
[120] See pp 71–73.
[121] Eekelaar, above n 109, 142.
[122] *Ibid*, 142; Law Commission, above n 108, 31; Brown, above n 106.
[123] Eekelaar, above n 109.
[124] *Ibid*.

purpose as being to enable the parties to reflect and consider, with the evidentiary function being the adjunct.[125] When the Family Law Act itself was reached, the proposals had moved from regularisation to a stronger element of regulation, and the evidential purpose of the period had disappeared entirely. The two statutory aims were first, for the parties to reflect on whether the marriage can be saved and to have the opportunity to effect a reconciliation, and secondly to consider what arrangements should be made for the future.[126] This shift has been read in the following manner:

> The statute might have proclaimed, as the Law Commission did, that the main purpose of the waiting period was to make sure the marriage had completely failed. But that would have signalled a willingness for the state to stand by and accept the situation as it had worked itself out between the parties. Such was not the message the Government sought to convey. The structure is now avowedly viewed primarily as giving the parties an opportunity to explore the possibility of holding back from divorce, and making them aware that they are expected to use it in this way.[127]

It is clearly accurate that the aim of the period shifted from being to provide evidence that the marriage is over to being to provide a time to 'explore the possibility of holding back from divorce'.[128] But crucially and paradoxically, at the point at which the Family Law Act became law the latter aim was not to *prevent* divorce by persuading couples to 'explore the possibility of holding back'.[129] The subtly different message was that divorce is respectable only if preceded by exploration of this possibility. We were to be 'kept on message'[130] but the message was not that we should stay married but rather that we should divorce well, and divorcing well meant learning from our divorce. The message was about how to divorce not whether to divorce, as is evident in the following description of the divorce process in the 1995 White Paper:

> The divorce process . . . should enable couples to consider their future in an environment that allows them to address together what went wrong with their marriage.[131]

---

[125] Lord Chancellor's Department, *Looking to the Future: Mediation and the Ground for Divorce* (London, HMSO, 1993); *ibid.*

[126] S 7(1) Family Law Act 1996; Eekelaar, above n 109.

[127] Eekelaar, 'on message', above n 25, 389.

[128] *Ibid*, 389.

[129] *Ibid*, 389.

[130] *Ibid.*

[131] Lord Chancellor's Department, above n 108, 9–10.

A similar picture emerges with the information meetings. It has been rightly suggested that the intention of the meetings was to bring home to people that they had to act responsibly, which meant conforming with received ideas about the desirability of marriage and undesirability of divorce.[132] But crucially, we need to add that acting responsibly *is* agreeing that divorce is undesirable. Paradoxically, so long as we have absorbed the message about the undesirability of divorce, the divorce itself is (at least) morally neutral.[133]

Finally, mediation as envisaged by the Family Law Act has been interpreted as not being primarily a method of bringing parties to agreement; instead it is one more way of informing people how they should have behaved and should behave.[134] This interpretation is supported by the following description of mediation from the White Paper:

> Mediation requires each party to accept that the marriage is over before proceeding to address the future of a life apart. In this way, the couple have to deal with issues of fault, acknowledge that the marriage has broken down irretrievably, and take responsibility for the consequences.[135]

It has been regarded as contradictory that at the same time as moral concern about the divorce itself was receding, specific proposals to alleviate harm such as mediation took on additional importance.[136] Far from being contradictory, this trend is consistent with a shift from moral acting as not divorcing towards moral acting as knowing how to divorce and knowing what message to take away from the divorce.

The hypothesis that the aim of divorce law became purely and simply to educate the couple is supported by the remarkable and unprecedented emphasis during the Family Law Act debates on making sure that the couple *understood*. What the couple needed to understand was given much less prominence. The White Paper set the tone in this respect:

> . . . there is a serious need for better information about marriage breakdown, separation and divorce to be made more widely available and to be better understood.[137]

---

[132] Eekelaar, 'on message', above n 25, 390; G Brown, 'A View from the Temple', 128 *Law and Justice* 35.
[133] R Collier, 'The Dashing of a "Liberal Dream"?—The Information Meeting, The "New Family" and the Limits of Law', 11 *Child and Family Law Quarterly* 257 at 261.
[134] Eekelaar, 'on message', above n 25, 391.
[135] Lord Chancellor's Department, above n 108, 10.
[136] Whitehead, above n 111, 9.
[137] Lord Chancellor's Department, above n 108, 56.

Lord Mackay continued this theme in relation to the information meetings in particular:

> I wish . . . to try to ensure that people do not just obtain the information but that they obtain it in such a way that they understand it . . . It is important . . . that they have taken that information on board. There is a limit to what anyone can do about that matter, but that is why I have suggested an information session. The first point is to try to obtain some method by which people do not merely have pieces of paper presented to them, but that some effort is made on behalf of the state to ensure that they have assimilated the information as it affects them.[138] If the information has been given effectively, I would hope that the parties would not forget it[139] . . . I believe it is extremely important that these matters should be effectively communicated and that people are not left with an ineffectual communication of information. We are all familiar with the situation of receiving pieces of paper, sometimes in fairly large quantities, where perhaps we do not always study them as fully as the importance of the information they contain would require.[140]

Similarly, Baroness David wanted the Government's assurance:

> . . . that this information will be given in such a way that those receiving it will be helped to envisage and fully understand the divorce process before they are caught up in it. It is important that the Government make clear that they intend that information given under the provisions of the Bill will be in a form that continues to be perceived as helpful to those receiving it so that they will feel safe, comfortable, unstigmatised and treated with dignity; and that the information will be imparted in ways which ensure that they understand it.[141]

Lord Bishop of Oxford felt that it was vital that people who attended the information sessions were 'ready to hear' the information.[142]

Lord Stallard even went so far as to propose that one of the objectives of divorce law in section 1 of the Family Law Act should be to ensure that the parties understood.[143] Although the specific proposal was rejected, the sentiment was expressed by including a power in the

---

[138] Lord Mackay, Hansard, House of Lords, 22 January 1996, Col 836. For similar sentiments, see Lord Mackay, Hansard, House of Lords, 22 January 1996, Col 837; Baroness David, Hansard, House of Lords, 22 January 1996, Col 832.

[139] Lord Mackay, Hansard, House of Lords, 22 January 1996, Col 837.

[140] Lord Mackay, Hansard, House of Lords, 22 February 1996, Col 1184.

[141] Baroness David, Hansard, House of Lords, 22 January 1996, Col 832.

[142] Lord Bishop of Oxford, Hansard, House of Lords, 22 January 1996, Col 834.

[143] Lord Stallard, Hansard, House of Lords, 11 January 1996, Col 280. For a similar sentiment, see Lord Chancellor's Department, above n 108, 56 and 66.

Family Law Act to require attendance at a supplementary meeting. In the White Paper the Government had expressed concern that in some cases parties would not appreciate what family mediation could offer them despite the information session.[144] To remedy this, section 13(1) of the Family Law Act provided that:

> . . . after the court has received a statement, it may give a direction requiring each party to attend a meeting arranged in accordance with the direction for the purpose . . . of enabling an explanation to be given of the facilities available to the parties for mediation in relation to disputes between them; and . . . of providing an opportunity for each party to agree to take advantage of those facilities.

Lord Mackay expanded on the purpose of the supplementary meeting:

> [T]he court may realise, once the matter comes before it, that the parties have not really understood what mediation can do for them in the particular circumstances . . . if the court feels that the parties, notwithstanding our efforts to inform them do not really appreciate or have understood the efforts that have been made . . . the court should invite them to attend a meeting at which that would be clearly explained to them. In a sense it is just reinforcing the message they have already got . . . I think the courts should be given discretion . . . to try to ensure that where mediation is appropriate the parties will understand what benefits it holds for them[145] . . . I think it is extremely important that in this area any refusal is an informed refusal. I do not want people just to say, 'I do not like the sound of mediation'. We want them to understand precisely what is involved . . . It is important that parties are put in a position of fully understanding mediation . . .[146] the best that I can do is to ensure that people get all the information available about the services on offer. You cannot compel them to take any particular service – that must be a matter for them – just as you cannot compel them to do other things that you might think was in their interest. They have to see to that themselves . . . The emphasis should be that we provide them with all the information that they need, as effectively as we can, and then leave them to use it . . . I do not think that compulsion is likely to be useful at that stage. Of course, there is power in the court to direct that people should attend and be told about mediation if, for example, in the course of the process the court feels that they are trying to litigate things before they have had a proper opportunity of considering, or have not considered fully, the advantages of doing it by mediation.[147] . . . it seems from experience that in

[144] Lord Chancellor's Department, above n 108, 66.
[145] Lord Mackay, Hansard, House of Lords, 23 January 1996, Col 1023.
[146] Lord Mackay, Hansard, House of Lords, 4 March 1996, Cols 95–96.
[147] Lord Mackay, Hansard, House of Lords, 23 January 1996, Col 997. For similar sentiments, see Lord Mackay, Hansard, House of Lords, 23 January 1996, Col 1019.

practice it is not uncommon for parties to say no to mediation if asked in very general terms . . . However once parties have met with a mediator and had the opportunity to discuss what is involved and its benefits, they often change their minds and become willing at least to try one or two sessions.[148]

In order to check the couple's understanding, after the meeting the mediator had to produce a report on the couple's educational progress:[149] In the words of Lord Coleraine:

[The Family Law Act] does not impose on any party a liability to mediate. It enables the court to send parties away, once they have started to litigate, to be told the advantages of mediation. At the end of that process, the person who gives the explanation has to produce to the court a report stating that they have done so and stating whether or not the parties have complied with the direction and, if they have, whether they have agreed to take part in any mediation. [The Family Law Act] does not contain any threat, inducement, incentive or compulsion on the parties to mediate. The final part of the clause is merely for the purposes of giving information to the court which would want to know the situation when the parties went away to be told about mediation.[150]

During the debates, Lord Mackay accepted an additional requirement that the couple should learn a lesson about reconciliation as well:

I believe that a requirement of this kind would be a valuable addition to the Bill as it will draw the attention of parties making a statement to the issue of reconciliation and perhaps make them question their own efforts in this regard. I have drafted the amendment to enable rules made by the Lord Chancellor to require parties to state whether or not they have attempted reconciliation since they attended an information meeting.[151]

Once reconciliation was included in the curriculum, it became even clearer that the primary purpose of the scheme was to educate not influence. Attempts at reconciliation would obviously have been absurd for a large proportion of divorcing couples; indeed, as we will see in the next chapter, it was when reconciliation became an actual aim of the scheme post-1997 that Part II of the Family Law Act began to crumble. However, every divorcee could absorb the message that a good divorce is preceded by consideration of reconciliation.

---

[148] Lord Mackay, Hansard, House of Lords, 4 March 1996, Col 96.
[149] S 13(5)(b) Family Law Act 1996.
[150] Lord Coleraine, Hansard, House of Lords, 25 January 1996, Col 1211.
[151] Lord Mackay, Hansard, House of Lords, 11 March 1996, Col 693; s 12(1)(b) Family Law Act 1996.

Just as with general civic education, under the Family Law Act it was insufficient for divorcees simply to learn the lesson: the divorce process was designed to encourage divorcees to experience moral lessons through participation.[152] This is consistent with the post-liberal conception of participation as an inclusive concept that is not only possible within a narrowly defined political realm but rather that can also be realised in the cultural sphere.[153] The emphasis on participation was apparent in the Law Commission Report, which promised that the period of reflection and consideration would ensure that 'the parties will have to consider the consequences of a separation or divorce order before it actually happens.'[154] This promise was reinforced in the Government Papers, which both stated that one of the Government's objectives for a better divorce process was 'to ensure that the parties understand the practical consequences of divorce before taking any irreversible decision'.[155] More concretely, it was evident in the recommendation contained in the Law Commission report that the statement of marital breakdown should be accompanied by detailed information about ancillary matters, including proposals for the future.[156] Where one spouse had made the statement, the Law Commission recommended further that the other spouse should have the opportunity to reply immediately in order to:

> . . . encourage couples to start thinking seriously about the future and emphasize exactly what will be involved if the separation or divorce is to proceed.[157]

The purpose of these recommendations has accordingly been interpreted as being 'to force the parties to face the harsh realities of their position sooner rather than later'.[158] This was also another objective of mediation, which Lord Irvine believed would 'bring home to the

---

[152] See pp 136–40.

[153] S Benhabib, 'Autonomy, Modernity and Community: Communitarianism and Critical Social Theory in Dialogue' in Benhabib, above n 15, 74; P Brest, 'Further Beyond the Republican Revival: Toward Radical Republicanism', 97 *Yale Law Journal* 1623. For discussion, see K Abrams, 'Law's Republicanism', 97 *Yale Law Journal* 1591.

[154] Law Commission, above n 108, 31.

[155] Lord Chancellor's Department, above n 108, 18; Lord Chancellor's Department, above n 125, 14. For similar sentiments, see Lord Chancellor's Department, above n 108, 22; Lord Chancellor's Department, above n 108, 56.

[156] Law Commission, above n 108, 30; s 12(1)(a) Family Law Act 1996.

[157] Law Commission, above n 108, 30.

[158] J Dewar, *Law and the Family* 2nd edn (London, Butterworths, 1992) 263. See also Dewar, above n 109, 79; Eekelaar, above n 109, 143.

parties what divorce will mean for them.'[159] The Family Law Bill as a whole would, according to Lord Mackay, encourage divorcees:

> . . . to look to the future, and to think hard about what the real implications of a divorce would be for themselves and their children. For the first time, couples that are considering divorce will be given full information about what divorce involves.[160]

Lord Coleraine summed this up with the hope that the proposals in general would:

> . . . give couples the chance to experience before the divorce takes place the sadness and sense of failure which so many decent divorced couples have been shown to feel after it is all over.[161]

Now that we have recognised that divorcing well meant learning moral lessons from the divorce, we can identify why the following criticism of the Family Law Act misses the point. Following interviews with divorcees, two researchers concluded that the interviewees were 'competent moral philosophers'.[162] People going through divorce were good enough moral actors, who did not abandon moral values but went through a process of balancing different needs and obligations, negotiating a route through competing value judgements. Not only were divorcees morally competent, but it was politically imperative to depict them as such, because measures such as compulsory marriage guidance or even compulsory mediation only make sense if the population of divorcing people has been successfully redefined as morally inadequate. The researchers finished with a plea for divorcees to be recognised as moral agents rather than dismissed as moral defectives in future debates around family policy: divorcees perceived divorce as a moral dilemma without instruction and did not need lessons in how to approach these dilemmas.[163] While this sentiment is to be welcomed, it side-steps the central problem that the definition of a moral agent has become *someone who accepts that he or she does need lessons in how*

---

[159] Lord Irvine, Hansard, House of Lords, 11 January 1996, Col 284.

[160] Lord Mackay, 'Champions of Marriage Should Back Me', *The Independent*, 26 April 1996.

[161] Lord Coleraine, Hansard, House of Lords, 30 November 1995, Col 723. For a similar sentiment, see Lord Chancellor's Department, above n 108, 18.

[162] Smart and Neale, above n 117, 23.

[163] *Ibid*, 23–24. For similar sentiments, see Lord Marsh, Hansard, House of Lords, 30 November 1995, Col 756; D Cornell, *The Imaginary Domain: Abortion, Pornography and Sexual Harassment* (New York, Routledge, 1995) 54 and 66 in relation to abortion.

to approach moral dilemmas. A competent moral philosopher who believes that he or she does not need moral instruction has become a contradiction in terms. Asking for advice is being moral.

Shortly after the Family Law Act received Royal Assent, divorce was memorably described as:

> . . . an assault course of obligatory meetings and immovable time periods – hurdles that will have to be cleared before a divorce can be obtained.[164]

This description was accurate in its reference to hurdles rather than barriers. This obstacle course only made sense if the object of divorce law and procedure had shifted from preventing, controlling or limiting divorce to educating the couple so as to make sure that they left the divorce process better citizens.

Of course leaving the process better citizens was also seen as of practical importance, the argument being that if divorcees had learnt their lesson well, any future marriage would stand a better chance of lasting.[165] So the Government believed that:

> It is important for the success of re-marriage that there is some understanding of what has gone wrong in the past. Rates of marriage breakdown are higher among second and subsequent marriages than among first marriages. This may well be connected with parties re-marrying without first having resolved the problems which led to the breakdown of the first marriage.[166]

Similarly, the Law Commission reported:

> It is thought that one reason why so many re-marriages fail is the unresolved legal and emotional legacy of the first.[167]

GOOD DIVORCE

Accompanying the publication of the 1990 Law Commission report was a press statement from the Law Commissioner responsible, Brenda Hoggett (now Lady Justice Hale), that the recommendations would make divorce 'not harder or easier, but in our view a great deal

---

[164] Nigel Shepherd, then Chairman of the Solicitors' Family Law Association, quoted in R Smithers, 'Divorce: A Law Nobody Wants,' *The Guardian*, 18 June 1996.

[165] Lord Mackay, Hansard, House of Lords, 25 January 1996, Col 1177.

[166] Lord Chancellor's Department, above n 125, 17. See also Lord Chancellor's Department, above n 108, 33.

[167] Law Commission, above n 108, 17.

better.'[168] In any previous era, better divorce would have been an oxy-moron;[169] in this era, better divorce is common sense.[170] It is no sur-prise that a recent empirical study found that when people expressed attitudes about the morality of family obligations publicly, they treated divorce and marriage as morally neutral events.[171]

The rehabilitation of divorce has been interpreted as a response to a perceived crisis of the family.[172] Faced with multiple family forms, the Family Law Act broadened out the concept of the family to incorporate families divided by divorce in an attempt to contain or even deny fam-ily breakdown and the anxieties that it engenders by reconstructing divorce in a new non-threatening form.[173] In this way, divorce could be seen not as a social or personal disaster, but as a means of saving the family.[174] Responding to crisis in the family is certainly a factor in the reinterpretation of divorce, but rather than the main objective, it is at most a by-product and perhaps only a pretext. Paradoxically, the motivation behind the Family Law Act did not primarily concern divorce: if anything, concern about divorce as a social problem in itself has diminished alongside recognition of its inevitability.[175] Instead, the contemporary approach to divorce has been rightly regarded as signi-fying broader concerns and anxieties about the good society.[176] Divorce is important not in its own terms but because it provides a use-ful point of contact between individuals and the authorities.[177] In other words, divorce is a golden opportunity for intervention.[178] Divorce

---

[168] Brenda Hoggett, quoted in C Dyer, ' "Quickie" Divorces Face Axe as Law Commission Urges 12-month Cooling Off Period for Couples', *The Guardian*, 2 November 1990. See also Lord Chancellor's Department, above n 125, 42.

[169] See Lord Bishop of Birmingham, Hansard, House of Lords, 30 November 1995, Col 752.

[170] R Chadwick, 'Moral Reasoning in Family Law—A Response to Katherine O'Donovan' in Morgan and Douglas, above n 25, 54. For discussion, see Whitehead, above n 111, 75. For the contrary view, see Smart and Neale, above n 117, 23–24.

[171] Janet Finch and Jennifer Mason, 'Divorce, Remarriage and Family Obligations', 38 *The Sociological Review* 219 at 227.

[172] SD Sclater, *Divorce: A Psychosocial Study* (Aldershot, Ashgate, 1999) 13–15. See also J Dewar, 'Reducing Discretion in Family Law', 11 *Australian Journal of Family Law* 309 at 310.

[173] Sclater, above n 172, 13–15; SD Sclater and C Piper, 'The Family Law Act 1996 In Context' in Sclater and Piper, above n 116, 11–13; J Dewar and S Parker, 'English Family Law since World War II: From Status to Chaos' in Katz, above n 118, 139.

[174] SD Sclater and C Piper, 'Re-moralising the Family?—Family Policy, Family Law and Youth Justice', 12 *Child and Family Law Quarterly* 135 at 144.

[175] Whitehead, above n 111, 6.

[176] Collier, above n 133, 267.

[177] Sclater, above n 172, 17.

[178] Collier, above n 133, 259–260.

presents an ideal and rare occasion to educate vast swathes of adults about how they should be behaving. Conflict over the Family Law Act was about the regulation of the family, not family morality.[179]

> ... the sooner help can be asked for the better. . . . People need to come for help and we are investigating the spread of that help, the extent to which it is known about and what can be done to make it better known.[180]

It has rightly been suggested that the most important result of the Family Law Act debates around, say, extending the period of reflection or making mediation compulsory was increasing acceptance of the idea that people could not be left alone to get on with their divorces.[181] Accordingly, even where concrete proposals failed, they succeeded in shifting the goal posts, by further legitimating intervention on divorce. For example, the proposal to establish compulsory reconciliation counselling failed, but served to consolidate and valorise mediation counselling. The debate can be conceptualised as a continuum running from law at one end to reconciliation at the other with mediation in the middle. Ironically, given that the pro-family lobby was not particularly supportive of mediation,[182] the net effect that they exerted on the final version of the Family Law Act was to have dragged the debate as far as the mid-point of the continuum, namely the acceptance of mediation. The debate was no longer between lawyers and mediators but between mediators and marriage guidance counsellors. The inevitable result was that mediation emerged unscathed, with the idea that divorcees could be left alone to come to their own decisions lost entirely, not least to divorcees themselves. Convinced that they could not manage to make their own decisions without the help of experts, they became disempowered in the management of their everyday lives.[183]

A similar stance has been taken in relation to abortion. It has been argued that even where the state is encouraging responsibility rather than coercing, the relevant question is not only who makes the ultimate decision to have an abortion but also how that decision may be made.

[179] C Smart, 'Divorce in England 1950–2000: A Moral Tale?' in Katz, above n 118, 377.

[180] Lord Mackay, Hansard, House of Lords, 22 January 1996, Col 884.

[181] Smart and Neale, above n 117.

[182] On this point, see also C Sarler, 'Let's Hear It For Divorce', *The Observer*, 21 January 2001.

[183] Smart and Neale, above n 117. On this point more generally see Nolan, above n 8, 298. For an example, see M Freely, 'Mediation Isn't Always the Right Message', *The Guardian*, 28 April 1995.

Protecting women's independence in making that decision is essential
so that they can determine the meaning of their decision themselves and
develop their own understanding of what it means to end a pregnancy.
Showing films, imposing waiting periods and providing other information designed to convince women that having an abortion is a serious
decision make it difficult for women to integrate their decision into
their own lives by developing their own accounts of their action.[184]

Given that divorce has been re-interpreted as a moral lesson, it follows that the moral divide is no longer between divorce and marriage
but is now between good and bad divorce. This moral divide allows
society to exhibit its ambivalence towards divorce, by in turn normalising and pathologising divorcing couples.[185] Alongside traditional dis-
couragement of divorce there now exists an idealised image of divorce,
constructed in discourses of welfare and harmony and representing
only a variation on the theme of the 'happy ever after' of fairy tales:

> The 'bad' divorce is conflict-ridden, accusatory, adversarial, costly (in both
> financial and emotional terms) and associated with the legal process.
> Families are torn asunder by it, children suffer at the hands of selfish and
> irresponsible parents who pursue their rights, linked to their retributive
> agendas. Fathers disappear out of children's lives and fail to keep up pay-
> ments. People are intent on dwelling on past wrongs and on obtaining just-
> ice at all costs. The 'good' divorce is the opposite. It is harmonious and
> characterised by rational appraisal and behaviour which plans properly for
> the future. Responsible parents put their own feelings to one side for the
> sake of the children, and build constructive relationships with each other, of
> a sort they were unable to do whilst married. The 'good' divorce keeps fam-
> ilies together, and is associated with mediation. This polarisation is clearly
> reflected in the Government Green and White Papers, in the Parliamentary
> debates which led to the Family Law Act 1996, and in the Act itself. Not all
> divorces are 'bad' any longer; where marriages really are incapable of being
> saved, divorce can be a solution, but we are exhorted to choose the 'civilised'
> kind. The 'good' divorce, constructed within discourses of harmony and
> welfare, has become the ideal to strive for.[186] . . . the discourses of the 'good'
> divorce represents the 'idealised' pole of a binary divide, with the shadow of
> the 'bad' divorce continually present.[187]

---

[184] Cornell, above n 163, 54 and 66.

[185] Collier, above n 133, 267.

[186] Sclater, above n 172, 176–77. See also SD Sclater and C Piper, 'The Family Law Act
1996 In Context' in Sclater and Piper, above n 116, 12–13; Sclater and Piper, above
n 174, 146.

[187] Sclater, above n 172, 178.

Similarly:

> The 'good' divorce will be characterised by civilised behaviour, reasonable-
> ness, a willingness to 'give and take' in trying to find a solution to persisting
> differences and an inclination to use the services of mediators in the process.
> The 'bad' divorce will be conflict-ridden, messy and blaming, with the
> parties attempting to engage professionals in adversarial approaches to
> resolving their problems.[188]

Importantly, the contemporary moral split may be at least as coercive
as the traditional one, if not more so: a recent empirical study of divorcing couples found that some experienced exhortations to cooperation
as persecution.[189]

It has been suggested that acceptance of good divorce by the Family
Law Act points to an interpretation of the Act as one that treats divorce
as simply a transition in the life-cycle of the family.[190] Rather than signifying the breakdown or decline of the family, divorce is an opportunity for the reorganisation of the family and paradoxically an indicator
of the continuing importance of marriage and the family.[191] Divorced
couples are divorced to each other not divorced from each other;
divorce is not the destruction of the nuclear family but the creation of
the bi-nuclear family, and so a potential growth experience for the
extended family.[192] While this approach was arguably taken the furthest in the United States during the 1980s,[193] it is becoming increasingly influential in the United Kingdom.[194] An example is the
following, taken from an article in the Guardian arguing that marriage
breakdown is akin to a partnership that has run its natural span and
must continue in another way, since partners never really divorce:

> It is not always appreciated that divorce can actually make couples far bet-
> ter friends with each other than they were before. When you remove all the
> aspects which formerly caused problems . . . you can proceed on a new, and
> better, basis. Many divorced couples . . . maintain that their relationship has

---

[188] C Clulow, 'Supporting Marriage in the Theatre of Divorce' in Thorpe and Clarke,
above n 106, 22. See also Dewar, above n 109, 68.

[189] Sclater, above n 172, 183. For the contrary view, see Eekelaar, above n 109, 144.

[190] Sclater, above n 172; SD Sclater and C Piper, 'The Family Law Act 1996 In
Context' in Sclater and Piper, above n 116; Sclater and Piper, above n 174, 144.

[191] Sclater, above n 172; Sclater and Piper, above n 174, 144.

[192] Sclater and Piper, above n 174, 144.

[193] On this point see also Regan, above n 108, 606.

[194] Sclater and Piper, above n 174, 144.

improved beyond all recognition since they split up. They find they retain a bond, without wanting to be glued together.[195]

Although this theme is beyond the scope of this book, it is noteworthy that the post-divorce family has also emerged as an extremely fertile site for intervention and regulation.[196]

BAD MARRIAGE

The corollary of the view that divorce is no longer unequivocally bad is that marriage is no longer unequivocally good. Marriage is now also a moral staging post, a lesson that needs to be learnt in order to be beneficial. The contemporary moral split is between good marriages or divorces and bad marriages or divorces.[197] The good marriage or divorce is the one from which the spouse has imbibed the message.

We have witnessed the emphasis on pre-divorce education in the Family Law Act debates: the ambivalent approach to marriage is evidenced by the near equal emphasis on pre-marital education. Lord Northbourne felt that there was:

> . . . a need to encourage young couples who are contemplating marriage to consider carefully the nature of the engagement they are entering into.[198]

The Duke of Norfolk wanted:

> . . . marriage counselling to start with advice being given by the social welfare people and, of course, by the Churches, to try to assist the very young before they become engaged.[199]

According to Lord Jakobovits:

> . . . the first line of defence against marriage breakdown is the way in which we train our brides and grooms before they enter marriage . . .[200]

---

[195] L Hodgkinson, 'The Beginning of a Whole New Life Apart', *The Guardian*, 20 July 1990.

[196] C Smart, 'Divorce in England 1950–2000: A Moral Tale' in Katz, above n 118, 384; C Smart and B Neale, *Family Fragments?* (Cambridge, Polity Press, 1999). Dewar, above n 109, 68.

[197] C Clulow, 'Supporting Marriage in the Theatre of Divorce' in Thorpe and Clarke, above n 106, 22.

[198] Lord Northbourne, Hansard, House of Lords, 2 July 1996, Col 1426.

[199] Duke of Norfolk, Hansard, House of Lords, 22 January 1996, Cols 833–44.

[200] Lord Jakobovits, Hansard, House of Lords, 23 January 1996, Col 988.

so he favoured short courses given by marriage guidance education counsellors before marriage.[201] Viscount Brentford felt that we needed more government funding for marriage preparation and more adult education on marriage in order to strengthen marriage because good marriages were needed.[202] Lord Elton believed that the priority was to teach people what marriage is about,[203] while Lord Gisborough favoured a range of services offered by the Government to help prepare young people for the responsibilities of marriage.[204]

The 1998 Home Office Consultation Document, Supporting Families, supported the tenor of the Family Law Act debates with several proposals designed to ensure that the educative potential of the point of entry into marriage was fully exploited.[205] In essence, the recommendation was to improve arrangements to help people prepare for marriage in order to:

> . . . ensure that couples planning to marry have considered, and reached an understanding on, the major issues that affect married life. Couples may consider how their finances should be organised; where they will live; whether they will have children; and what arrangements they might make, for example, for one or other parent to reduce or stop work when the children are born.[206]

To further this end, Supporting Families suggested that Registrars of Marriage should provide couples contemplating marriage with information about marriage designed to give people a clear idea of the rights and responsibilities that marriage entails, perhaps in the form of a marriage preparation pack, because:

> Marriage is a serious business, and it is important that people who plan to marry have a clear idea of the rights and responsibilities they are taking on. This could be done through a simple and clear guide to the implications of getting married . . . made available through register offices, churches and other places of worship, and other bodies providing advice to married people.[207]

---

[201] Lord Jakobovits, Hansard, House of Lords, 6 July 1999, Col 788.
[202] Viscount Brentford, Hansard, House of Lords, 6 July 1999, Col 788.
[203] Lord Elton, Hansard, House of Lords, 23 January 1996, Col 991.
[204] Lord Gisborough, Hansard, House of Lords, 30 November 1995, Col 755.
[205] Home Office, *Supporting Families: A Consultation Document* (London, HMSO, 1998).
[206] *Ibid*, 32.
[207] *Ibid*, 32. See also K Ahmed, 'U-turn Over No-fault Divorce Law', *The Observer*, 14 January 2001. For discussion, see Eekelaar, 'on message', above n 25, 390.

The suggestion was that this would allow the couple time for thought and discussion before the ceremony took place.[208] More generally, Supporting Families proposed a wider role for registrars in giving support to couples about to marry,[209] for example by informing them about pre-marriage support services.[210]

Following the model of pre-divorce information meetings, Supporting Families recommended a requirement that both partners attend the register office to make the first arrangements before marriage, in order to give an opportunity for the Registrar to provide them with support and information.[211] However, the new equivocal attitude towards marriage is most graphically illustrated by the ushering of the bride and groom into a mini period of reflection and consideration of 15 days' notice of intention to marry. Supporting Families suggested this on the basis that it:

> . . . would allow couples more time to reflect on the nature of the commitment they are entering into and to take up marriage preparation, if they wished to do so.[212]

This suggestion has now been implemented by section 160 of the Immigration and Asylum Act 1999.[213] Marriage, just like divorce, can no longer be accomplished unaided, and is becoming another fruitful opportunity for regulation and intervention.

Education as an end in itself extends beyond the sphere of marriage and divorce, both inside and outside family life. To take just one related example, also from Supporting Families, a good parent is being re-defined as one who is prepared to learn, so that good parenting is now an attitude rather than an approach:

> We want to change the culture so that seeking advice and help when it is needed is seen not as failure but the action of concerned and responsible parents.[214]

---

[208] Home Office, above n 205, 34.

[209] *Ibid*, 31. See also F Gibb, 'Irvine Will Scrap "No Fault" Divorce', *The Times*, 18 December 2000; C Dyer, 'Blow To No-Fault Divorce Hopes', *The Guardian*, 18 December 2000.

[210] Home Office, above n 205, 34.

[211] *Ibid*, 34. See also Gibb, above n 209.

[212] Home Office, above n 205, 34–35.

[213] See C Barton, 'Matrimonial Bliss or a Contract for Life?', *The Times*, 23 January 2001; Gibb, above n 209.

[214] Home Office, above n 205, 7.

CHILDREN'S EDUCATION

We have already seen the purpose that communitarians envisage for children's education.[215] In the light of this purpose, it is unsurprising that increasing emphasis is being placed on educating children about marriage and relationships.[216] Like the emphasis on pre-marital and divorce education, this emphasis was clearly in evidence during the Family Law Act debates. Lord Stallard asked:

> . . . how much are we spending on teaching children how to communicate with each other and how to handle parenting and marriage and how to discuss all the problems that they will definitely experience?[217] . . . children should learn at school about the sanctity of marriage and how to prevent breakups[218] . . . Even in schools we ought to be looking at preparation for what is a serious contract.[219]

Edward Leigh welcomed the suggestion that children should be educated about their future responsibilities,[220] and Lord Jakobovits felt that '[s]ome teaching in the responsibilities of marriage should also be included as an essential subject in school instructions'[221] because:

> . . . the first line of defence against marriage breakdown is the way in which we train our children, our students . . . before they enter marriage.[222]

He cited his experience of having invited marriage guidance education counsellors into schools as a useful model.[223] Viscount Brentford felt that more education on both marriage and parenting was needed in schools.[224] According to Lord Elton:

> The first thing that we have to do is to teach people what marriage is about. Even that has an element of the classroom in it because marriage is about human relationships . . . we discussed the fact that children were entering reception and nursery classes insufficiently educated within the family to be able to have conversations or to play with their contemporaries. That is a

---

[215] See pp 141–43.
[216] See A Etzioni, 'Introduction' in Etzioni, above n 9, xiii.
[217] Lord Stallard, Hansard, House of Lords, 11 January 1996, Col 280.
[218] Lord Stallard, Hansard, House of Lords, 30 November 1995, Col 744.
[219] Lord Stallard, Hansard, House of Lords, 22 January 1996, Col 820.
[220] Edward Leigh, Hansard, House of Commons, 19 December 1997, Col 579.
[221] Lord Jakobovits, Hansard, House of Lords, 30 November 1995, Col 722.
[222] Lord Jakobovits, Hansard, House of Lords, 23 January 1996, Col 988.
[223] Lord Jakobovits, Hansard, House of Lords, 6 July 1999, Col 788.
[224] Viscount Brentford, Hansard, House of Lords, 6 July 1999, Col 788.

disaster and it must be tackled. Those children will eventually become young married couples, so the problem has to be tackled in the school . . .[225]

In the debate that followed the Lord Chancellor's announcement that Part II of the Family Law Act would not be implemented in 2000, Lord Jakobovits took education for marriage even further back than the nursery:

We believe that the education for marriage starts long before birth, and is never finished. We are bidden to go into marriage preparation, which is so widely neglected today, by making sure that we do not allow children to be born and raised without some form of preparation and training in the most delicate art of human relations.[226]

Just as with divorcees, it was also important that children experienced the lessons of marriage, rather than merely learning them:

So many noble Lords have referred to education for marriage. I should like to end by saying something really positive, so here is a suggestion. It arises out of the question: how can young people learn of the benefits of marriage when a growing number of them have never seen marriage at work? With this problem in mind, an initiative has been taken to introduce married couples to volunteering sixth formers who wished to have the opportunity to discuss the institution of marriage . . . there is a hunger to learn about marriage.[227]

In 1998 Supporting Families proclaimed that '[e]ducation about parental and personal responsibility can help prepare children for entering adult relationships'[228] and promised 'greater emphasis in the curriculum on the responsibilities of parenthood at the first opportunity.'[229] The recent Learning and Skills Act 2000 provided an opportunity: section 148 mandates guidance designed to secure that, when sex education is provided, children 'learn the nature of marriage and its importance for family life and the bringing up of children'. While controversy raged up until the last minute over whether the Act would explicitly rank marriage above other stable relationships, there was almost no opposition to the central plank of section 148, that children should be educated about marriage at school.[230]

[225] Lord Elton, Hansard, House of Lords, 23 January 1996, Col 991.
[226] Lord Jakobovits, Hansard, House of Lords, 6 July 1999, Col 788.
[227] Lord Craigmyle, Hansard, House of Lords, 24 March 1999, Col 1322.
[228] Home Office, above n 205, 17.
[229] *Ibid*, 17.
[230] See M Kallenbach and A Sparrow, 'Peers Back Guidelines on Sex Education in Schools', *The Daily Telegraph*, 19 July 2000.

GRADUATING IN DIVORCE

During the passage of the Family Law Bill through Parliament, the Times columnist Libby Purves drew attention to the fact that she had ventured no opinion on divorce. She explained that this reticence was not caused by a lack of opinions:

> No: this silence in fact has had a curiously shamefaced quality about it. Nobody, in writing about divorce, is without a personal hinterland, and mine hinders me.[231]

A pervading atmosphere, she continued, had gone beyond normalising divorce to treating marital breakdown as 'an unmissable life-experience, a personal test, a 'learning curve' or stimulus for creativity':[232]

> How many celebrities, authors, actors, wear their failed marriages like campaign medals? How many murmur modestly that they have 'made mistakes', expecting and getting a pat of sympathetic approbation in the next paragraph? Only yesterday in these pages, Sir Andrew Lloyd Webber was clapped on the back for being on good terms with both of his ex-wives, as if that were somehow a better achievement than if he had managed to stay married to one of them. . . . Who are the two modern goddesses of family life, patronesses of babies and children, fêted for their compassionate wisdom? Why, Esther Rantzen and Anne Diamond: yet both are married to men who – during their courtship – were already married with children and living at home.[233]

A good example of this attitude is Carol Sarler writing in the Observer in early 2001:

> It seems not to occur to [the anti-divorce lobby] that . . . divorce might be the bravest, most liberating, exhilarating thing that someone has ever done, for themselves and their families, and they should be fulsomely congratulated.[234]

Purves' conclusion was that we should return not to ruin and disgrace but to acknowledging that divorce is an event without merit:

> . . . more like a pointless road accident than an act of heroism, more like tripping on a kerbstone while drunk than leaping a challenging hurdle.[235]

[231] L Purves, 'Divorce is About Remorse', *The Times*, 18 June 1996.
[232] *Ibid.*
[233] *Ibid.*
[234] Sarler, above n 182. See also Hodgkinson, above n 195; Sclater, above n 172.
[235] Purves, above n 231. See also J Hewitt, *Dilemmas of the American Self* (Philadelphia, Temple University Press, 1989) 159.

Libby Purves correctly identifies that if divorcees learn their lesson well then they may exit divorce with positively enhanced moral standing. If divorce is treated as a voyage of self-discovery then divorce can be a moral growth experience, and if divorce is to be a moral growth experience then it must be a voyage of self-discovery.

5

Informing Divorce

THE MAIN ARGUMENT of this book is that the divorce reform in the Family Law Act was a post-liberal reform. The main question that has not yet been fully explored is why, then, given the demise of liberalism, the reform was not implemented. Of course, the starting point must be to examine the reasons that the Government gave for not implementing Part II of the Family Law Act. Their decision was presented as an evidence-based response to the failure of the pilot projects that tested the information meetings. In simple terms, the results of the pilot projects were disappointing therefore it made sense to abandon them; the divorce reform would not work without the information meetings, so it made sense to jettison Part II of the Family Law Act in its entirety.[1]

However, as soon as we look in more detail at the results of the pilots and the reasons that the Government considered these results disappointing, the evidence-based explanation becomes untenable. Whether or not the results are considered disappointing depends on the purpose of providing information. The obvious purpose of providing information is to inform. If this needs any expansion, this would mean that after the information had been provided, people would know or understand more than they did before. If the success of providing information were to be measured on this model, it would be measured by the amount of information that people had absorbed, for example by

---

[1] Lord Chancellor's Department, 'Divorce Law Reform—Government Proposes to Repeal Part II of the Family Law Act 1996', 16 January 2001; Lord Irvine, Hansard, House of Lords, 17 June 1999, Col WA 39; Baroness Hollis, Hansard, House of Lords, 6 July 1999, Col 781; Lord Chancellor's Department, *Information Meetings and Associated Provisions within the Family Law Act 1996: Summary of Research in Progress* (London, Lord Chancellor's Department, 1999) vii; F Gibb, 'Irvine Forced to Drop "No-Fault" Divorces', *The Times*, 17 January 2001; F Gibb, 'Irvine Will Scrap "No Fault" Divorce', *The Times*, 18 December 2000; C Dyer, 'Blow To No-Fault Divorce Hopes', *The Guardian*, 18 December 2000; *BBC News*, 'Divorce Reforms Hit the Rocks', www.bbc.co.uk/news, 17 June 1999.

administering a test. As well as being the obvious purpose of providing information, this is also the liberal understanding. If this liberal purpose for information provision had been applied to the pilot projects then the pilots would not have been disappointing but would on the contrary have been a resounding success. Dramatically, over 90 per cent of attendees stated that they found the meetings useful.[2] Moreover, according to the final Report produced by the researchers responsible for conducting the pilot projects, the majority of attendees found the meetings not only useful but even invaluable, 'since it informed them about what they needed to know.'[3] When the Lord Chancellor announced in 1999 that implementation was to be postponed pending the final results of the pilot projects,[4] the Chief Executive of Relate responded:

> The feedback we have been having of the meetings with a marriage counsellor project, which was associated with all this, was that the people who came found them extremely helpful and came in much larger numbers than we would have expected.[5]

The conclusion that the results of the pilot projects were disappointing also runs counter to the conclusion reached by the researchers, who saw the information meetings as a qualified success.[6] Their view was that the research revealed tensions in all the models of information meeting tested that would need to be resolved, but that could be resolved, before Part II of the Family Law Act was implemented. The principal tension was that attendees needed very diverse information, from information about marriage guidance to information about very specific topics, such as the tax implications of a financial settlement. This meant that a standardised approach to the provision of information would be much less effective than a flexible model tailored to the individual.[7] Therefore the way forward was to develop and test a new

---

[2] R Collier, 'The Dashing of a "Liberal Dream"?—The Information Meeting, The "New Family" and the Limits of Law', 11 *Child and Family Law Quarterly* 257 at 266.

[3] Centre for Family Studies at the University of Newcastle upon Tyne, 'Information Meetings and Associated Provisions within the Family Law Act 1996' (London, Lord Chancellor's Department, 2001) 830.

[4] Lord Irvine, Hansard, House of Lords, 17 June 1999, Col WA 39.

[5] Sarah Bowler, quoted in *BBC News*, above n 1.

[6] Centre for Family Studies, above n 3, 830.

[7] *Ibid*, 830. See also C Dyer, 'Government drops plan for no-fault divorce', *The Guardian*, 2 September 2000; BBC News, 'No-Fault Divorce to be Scrapped', www.bbc.co.uk/news, 16 January 2001; *BBC News*, 'Bishop Regrets Divorce Decision', www.bbc.co.uk/news, 17 January 2001.

model of information meeting prior to full implementation of the Act.[8] This new model would consist in a more personal meeting in which presenters could help attendees select from a range of standard packages that would each allow for the inclusion or exclusion of certain types of information. This meeting would be relevant to all attendees, since it would be closer to a personal interview with a more sensitive script enabling account to be taken of attendees' diverse circumstances. These circumstances would include the circumstances of those who perceived the information meeting 'as an unwelcome intrusion and a hurdle to be got over as speedily as possible.'[9] The researchers' final conclusion was that the evidence from the pilots showed that information provision and the meeting with the marriage counsellor did and could support the principles of the Family Law Act.[10]

These findings raise two questions: first, what the Government found disappointing about the pilot results, and secondly, what the Government's disappointment tells us about the Government's understanding of the purpose of information provision. To answer the first question, the Government was disappointed that 39 per cent of the 7,000 volunteers who attended the information meetings had said that they were more likely to see a solicitor than before, while only seven per cent went on to mediation and 13 per cent to marriage counsellors.[11] To answer the second question, this tells us that for the Government, the purpose of providing information was not to inform but to direct decision-making, and the way to measure its success was to monitor what people decided to do after the information had been provided.[12] This interpretation is supported by the press release that announced that the reform would not be implemented. In this press release, the Lord Chancellor recognised that the research showed that attendees valued the provision of information, but emphasised that the information meetings were not effective in helping most people to save their marriages, tending to incline those who were uncertain about their

---

[8] Centre for Family Studies, above n 3, 836.

[9] *Ibid*, 837. See also Lord Chancellor's Department, 'Divorce', above n 1; Leader, 'Back to the bad old ways', *The Guardian*, 18 January 2001.

[10] Centre for Family Studies, above n 3, 832.

[11] Lord Irvine, Hansard, House of Lords, 17 June 1999, Col WA 39; Baroness Hollis, Hansard, House of Lords, 6 July 1999, Col 781; Lord Chancellor's Department, Information Meetings, above n 1, vii; *BBC News*, above n 1; Gibb, 'Irvine forced', above n 1; Gibb, 'Irvine will', above n 1; Dyer, above n 1.

[12] Collier, above n 2; J Walker, 'Whither the Family Law Act, Part II?' in M Thorpe and E Clarke (eds), *No Fault or Flaw: The Future of the Family Law Act 1996* (Bristol, Jordan Publishing, 2000) 10.

marriage towards divorce.[13] The purpose that the Lord Chancellor attributed to information provision and the method that he adopted to measure its success are even more remarkable because the research into the information meetings and the pilots had not been designed to test what people did with the information. Instead, they had been designed to examine different ways of providing information. Consideration of the subsequent behaviour of the attendees had been just one, albeit significant, element in the evaluation of the meetings.[14] According to one commentator:

> Information meetings do not only have the objective, however, of satisfying those who attend them. They should also influence the behaviour of those who attend them, by helping them to save their marriages where possible and by encouraging the mediated settlement of disputes where marriages cannot be saved.[15]

Judged by this criterion, the results were clearly disappointing and the information meetings could be regarded as a failure, as the researchers themselves recognised in the 'Final Thoughts' of the final Report:

> Our research demonstrates beyond doubt that separating and divorcing families need better information than is currently available, that those who attended information meetings on a voluntary basis in the pilots appreciated the information provided, and that the MWMC [meeting with the marriage counsellor] is capable of helping people with a wide variety of agendas to move forward and take the next steps. Information meetings, however they are constructed, are unlikely to be able to change the culture of divorce or people's behaviour in isolation from other reforms.[16]

My argument in this chapter is that the purpose that the Government attributed to providing information, namely to direct decision-making, is the post-liberal approach. While the post-liberal dimensions of the Family Law Act explored in other chapters, namely the post-liberal approach to decision-making, relationships, education and responsi-

---

[13] Lord Chancellor's Department, 'Divorce', above n 1. See also C Dyer, 'Divorce Law Reform Ditched', *The Guardian*, 17 January 2001; K Ahmed, 'U-Turn Over No-Fault Divorce Law', *The Observer*, 14 January 2001; J Rozenberg, 'Labour to Scrap Tory "No-Fault" Divorces', *The Daily Telegraph*, 17 January 2001; *BBC News*, 'No-Fault', above n 7; BBC News, 'Bishop', above n 7.

[14] Collier, above n 2, 266.

[15] W Arnold, 'Implementation of Part II of the Family Law Act 1996: The Decision Not to Implement in 2000 and Lessons Learned From The Pilot Meetings' in Thorpe and Clarke, above n 12, 16–17.

[16] Centre for Family Studies, above n 3, 860.

bility, were present from the inception of the divorce proposals, post-liberal information was a later addition. The reason is that the post-liberal approach to information represents the most coercive aspect of post-liberalism and, as I have argued throughout the book, the slide towards increasing coercion occurred only during the progression of the Family Law Act. In the next section, I examine the tacking on of the post-liberal approach to information and the corresponding drive towards coercion that this signified in the Family Law Act, first in relation to the information meetings and then more generally.

POST-LIBERAL INFORMATION IN THE FAMILY LAW ACT

Information Meetings

> The modern citizen envisaged by the Family Law Bill was the fact-gathering, rational, caring parent who would make decisions on the basis of knowledge. . . . The aim of governance would be to produce [this] citizen.[17]

It is remarkable that almost nobody took exception to what was arguably the heart of the scheme, namely the period of reflection and consideration, while the collapse of the entire edifice was caused by an aspect that was itself only added after inception. The information meetings were not present at all in the original Law Commission report in 1990.[18] They first entered the picture in the 1993 Government Consultation Paper, which envisaged a personal interview with the overall aim of ensuring only:

> . . . that the parties were better informed generally about divorce and its consequences and also about the availability of mediation services, and were offered every encouragement to use mediation.[19]

Two years later in the 1995 White Paper the purpose of what had become group information sessions had shifted considerably. At this point, couples were seen as needing 'a better understanding of the con-

---

[17] C Smart, 'Divorce in England 1950–2000: A Moral Tale?' in S Katz *et al* (eds), *Cross Currents: Family Law and Policy in the United States and England* (New York, Oxford University Press, 2000) 377.

[18] Law Commission, *The Ground for Divorce* (London, HMSO, 1990).

[19] Lord Chancellor's Department, *Looking to the Future: Mediation and the Ground for Divorce* (London, HMSO, 1993) 62.

sequences of divorce and the effects of divorce on children'.[20] During the Committee stage of the Family Law Bill, the Government accepted an amendment providing that couples would have to be made fully aware of both the effect of divorce on their children and the financial implications of the break-up.[21] Unsurprisingly:

> This extension from information about legal principles, divorce procedures and marriage guidance services to information about 'the consequences of divorce and the effects of divorce on children' creates much wider scope for the use of value-based persuasion.[22]

During the Parliamentary debates on the information meetings, it is arguable that the mid-point in their development from informing to influencing had been reached. Lord Mackay accordingly expressed an ambivalent attitude to the purpose of information provision at this stage:

> The emphasis should be that we provide them with all the information that they need, as effectively as we can, and then leave them to use it, and use it to the best advantage that they see from their point of view.[23]

For reasons that will be explored in the next section, the post-liberal approach to information became Government policy in 1997 with the election of the Labour Government. In relation to the information meetings, this is evidenced by the proposal in Supporting Families to introduce two meetings. The first would have concentrated on information to help the parties consider whether their marriage was really over, while the second would have provided information about ancillary issues at a stage when the parties were already clear that they wanted a divorce. The idea behind having two meetings was explicitly that the first would have a realistic prospect of changing the parties' minds about their marriage.[24] The proposal:

---

[20] Lord Chancellor's Department, *Looking to the Future: Mediation and the Ground for Divorce* (London, HMSO, 1995) 56.

[21] S 8(9)(c) and (d) Family Law Act 1996; J Copley, 'Ministers Forced to Climb Down on Divorce', *The Daily Telegraph*, 1 May 1996.

[22] J Eekelaar, 'Family law: keeping us "on message" ', 11 *Child and Family Law Quarterly* 387 at 389.

[23] Lord Mackay, Hansard, House of Lords, 23 January 1996, Col 997.

[24] Home Office, *Supporting Families: A Consultation Document* (London, HMSO, 1998) 35.

. . . indicates a 'mindset' which fails to perceive divorce as a means *an individual* might choose to protect his or her interests, but rather sees it as an opportunity to try to control the behaviour of both parties to the marriage.[25]

The information meetings shifted from being non-existent in 1990 to being a minor detail in 1993 to being described by the Lord Chancellor, when he announced in 2001 that the divorce scheme would not be implemented, as central to Part II of the Family Law Act.[26] This was partly because their significance was no longer limited to their practical import: according to the Final Evaluation Report, the information meeting was by then symbolic of concerns about the importance of respecting the dignity of marriage.[27] More importantly though, it was particularly easy for the coercive slide from informing to influencing decision-making to occur in relation to the information meetings for four reasons. First, in very practical terms it was extremely difficult for one meeting both to inform and to influence.[28] Secondly, the results that the Government was hoping for from the pilots straddled the division between method and result, and as we have seen throughout the book, adopting the right method of decision-making was a feature of the Family Law Act from the beginning. It is at least possible that had the majority of attendees decided to attend mediation or to see a marriage counsellor, the Government would have implemented Part II of the Family Law Act, even if these attendees had still left the process more sure that they wanted a divorce. Attending mediation or marriage counselling is part of the *method* of making the decision, which is whether or not to divorce, and it may well be that the Government would not have demanded a fall in the divorce rate as a measure of success of the Family Law Act. The third, more general, reason is that it is difficult if not impossible to measure the decision-making process and much easier to measure what people do.[29] Measuring the extent to which people reflect is a hopeless task: measuring how many people attend mediation or marriage counselling is arguably the nearest approximation. Finally, we saw in chapter four that one of the principal mechanisms for educating divorcing couples was mediation –

[25] Eekelaar, above n 22, 390.

[26] Lord Chancellor's Department, 'Divorce', above n 1. See also Baroness Hollis, Hansard, House of Lords, 6 July 1999, Col 781; P Johnston and T Shaw, 'Divorce White Paper: Lord Mackay's Way to Mend a Marriage', *The Daily Telegraph*, 28 April 1995; Dyer, above n 13; Rozenberg, above n 13.

[27] Centre for Family Studies, above n 3, 830.

[28] J Walker, 'Whither the Family Law Act, Part II?' in Thorpe and Clarke, above n 12, 6.

[29] See ch 6, p 235.

mediation was one of the main ways of informing people how to behave – and that a subsidiary lesson to be learnt was the importance of considering reconciliation.[30] When divorcing couples declined to attend either mediation or marriage guidance, this made a considerable dent in the Government's education programme. We can now fully appreciate why Baroness Hollis, when asked to explain the Government's 1999 decision to postpone implementation, emphasised that the original intention of the information meetings was definitely not that far more attendees would choose to see a solicitor than a mediator or marriage guidance counsellor.[31]

Period of Reflection and Consideration

Let us now move away from the information meetings themselves and examine the slide towards increasing coercion more broadly, beginning with the heart of the scheme, the period of reflection and consideration. We saw in chapters two and four that during progression of the divorce proposals the purpose of the period of reflection and consideration switched from being purely evidentiary to creating an opportunity to reflect to imposing an obligation to reflect.[32] However, if we go further back still to interpretations of the Law Commission Consultation Paper in 1988,[33] it is possible to find even less interventionist objectives for the period of reflection and consideration than to provide evidence that the marriage had irretrievably broken down. For example, a New Law Journal editorial argued in 1988 that, rather than regarding divorce as being available on the basis of a process over time, there should be official acknowledgement that divorce was to be available on demand subject only to a prescribed time scale.[34] Even as late as 1993, a leading academic was arguing that the Law Commission proposals[35] were attempting to disguise the reality that divorce would be available on unilateral demand, albeit deferred for a year.[36] However by 1996, the proposals were being described as 'more a

[30] See pp 149–52.
[31] Baroness Hollis, Hansard, House of Lords, 6 July 1999, Col 781.
[32] See pp 71–73 and 147–48.
[33] Law Commission, *Facing the Future: A Discussion Paper on the Ground for Divorce* (London, HMSO, 1988).
[34] P Brown, 'Divorce—The Fault Fiction', 138 *New Law Journal* 377.
[35] Law Commission, above n 18.
[36] S Cretney, 'Divorce on Demand', *The Times*, 14 December 1993.

conservative attempt at social engineering rather than the liberal measure it was once portrayed as being.'[37]

Mediation

I examined the way that the provision of mediation was used as a method of education in chapter four.[38] The increasing slide to coercion occurred here in that mediation became less and less voluntary as the proposals made their way through the stages of discussion. In particular, the Family Law Act itself attempts to steer legally aided parties into mediation by requiring them to attend a meeting with a mediator prior to making an application for legal aid to be represented by a lawyer in family matters.[39] During the Parliamentary debates Lord Mackay assured that:

> If, despite such a meeting [with a mediator], parties remain unconvinced, they will have been made fully aware of mediation and at least will be making an informed decision not to attempt mediation. It is important that parties are put in a position of fully understanding mediation and how it might help them.[40]

Moreover, the Act merely states that if mediation appears suitable then the mediator will help the person applying for representation to decide whether to apply instead for mediation.[41] However:

> The notion of the mediator 'helping' the person 'to decide whether to apply instead for mediation' barely conceals the persuasive role of the mediator, and, while it remains possible for a person to ask for legal aid for a lawyer after seeing a mediator, the Legal Aid Board will take into account the opinion of the mediator.[42]

The final version of the Family Law Act also contained a power to adjourn court proceedings to enable the parties to attempt mediation.[43]

[37] PW Davies, 'Concessions for the Right, Deals With the Left . . . Divorce Law Ushers In A New Era For Wives', *The Independent*, 18 June 1996.

[38] See p 149.

[39] S 15(3F) Legal Aid Act 1988, inserted by s 29 Family Law Act 1996. This is in Part III of the Family Law Act, which has been implemented.

[40] Lord Mackay, Hansard, House of Lords, 4 March 1996, Col 96.

[41] S 15(3F)(b) Legal Aid Act 1988, inserted by s 29 Family Law Act 1996.

[42] Eekelaar, above n 22, 391. For a similar view, see Lord Irvine, Hansard, House of Lords, 4 March 1996, Col 92.

[43] S 14(1)(a) Family Law Act 1996. For concern about the coercive character of this provision, see Lord Irvine, Hansard, House of Lords, 4 March 1996, Col 42.

Most dramatically, having arranged financial matters became a condition of obtaining a divorce, subject to certain well-defined exceptions.[44] Not only did the Law Commission not propose this condition in their 1990 Report, but they even discussed and positively rejected the suggestion.[45] However, the 1995 White Paper abandoned the Law Commission position on this question, recommending instead that the settling of arrangements be a pre-condition of divorce.[46] This condition fitted snugly with the development of the post-liberal approach to information in the Family Law Act, in that part of the purpose of this condition was to bring home to the parties the implications of divorce in the hope that they might change their minds.[47]

Marriage-saving

> . . . the revelation that the Lord Chancellor regards it as 'disappointing' that many people, after having been informed about some of the realities of divorce, now wish to consult a solicitor, presumably in order to safeguard their interests, is deeply disturbing, especially since people seem to have expressed the desire to do this in the face of some kind of attempt to persuade them otherwise. What conclusion will the Lord Chancellor draw from this? Will it be that the 'message' is not getting through, and must be reinforced? Or that people are simply 'not responsible', because they do not agree with the message? And if this is so regarding mediation, may it not also be true regarding the other matters, in particular, saving marriages?[48]

Far and away the clearest example of the development of the post-liberal approach to information is the increasing emphasis on saving marriages.[49] As we saw in chapter four, marriage-saving was barely present as an aim in the early stages of the scheme.[50] Shortly after publication of the Law Commission Report in 1990, Lord Mackay went so far as to say that he appreciated that there was a strong feeling that the Law Commission had not sufficiently clearly recognised the need to

---

[44] S 3(1)(c), s 9 and Schedule 1 Family Law Act 1996.
[45] Law Commission, above n 18, 40–41.
[46] Lord Chancellor's Department, above n 20, 29.
[47] J Dewar, 'The Normal Chaos of Family Law' 61 *Modern Law Review* 467 at 477.
[48] Eekelaar, above n 22, 392.
[49] See Dewar, above n 47, 477; P Mansfield, 'From Divorce Prevention to Marriage Support' in Thorpe and Clarke, above n 12, 30.
[50] Pp 145–52.

strengthen the institution of marriage.[51] By the 1995 White Paper, marriage-saving had become one element in the proposals, so that the White Paper acknowledged that:

> The current system provides little incentive or opportunity for reflection as to whether . . . with appropriate help, the couple might wish to attempt to save the marriage.[52]

Once the Family Law Bill entered Parliament, the emphasis on marriage-saving increased exponentially. During the Committee stage, the Government accepted an amendment to Part I of the Act that courts would have regard to the principle that couples were to be encouraged to take all practical steps to save the marriage, by counselling or otherwise.[53] This was described at the time as making marriage counselling a key element of the scheme.[54] Other even more coercive amendments that pulled in the same direction were seriously considered but ultimately rejected. For example, Lord Mackay was reported as being sympathetic to cross-party demands that couples should have to meet with a marriage guidance counsellor before being allowed to make a statement that their marriage had broken down.[55] Even though this amendment was not included in the Family Law Act, the suggestion was tested in the pilot project along with attendance at information meetings.[56]

Part of the reason that marriage-saving is the clearest example of the development of the post-liberal approach to information is that it had cross-party support. Moves to enhance marriage-saving were driven by a coalition between the then Labour Opposition and the right-wing pro-marriage wing of the Conservative Party.[57] The successful amendment mentioned above was proposed by a former Conservative Minister, and welcomed by the chairman of the Conservative Family

---

[51] Lord Mackay, quoted in K Standley, *Family Law* (Basingstoke, Hampshire, London, Macmillan, 1993) 97.

[52] Lord Chancellor's Department, above n 20, 8.

[53] S 1(b) Family Law Act 1996, which has been implemented; R Smithers, 'Ministers Agree Counselling Change to Family Law Bill', *The Guardian*, 1 May 1996; Copley, above n 21.

[54] Smithers, above n 53.

[55] G Jones, 'Mackay Bows to Divorce Defeat', *The Daily Telegraph*, 26 April 1996.

[56] See Centre for Family Studies, above n 3, ch 13.

[57] 'Brutish and Longer', *The Guardian*, 17 February 1999; Dyer, above n 7; Leader, above n 9; C Sarler, 'Let's Hear it For Divorce', *The Observer*, 21 January 2001; Gibb, 'Irvine Forced', above n 1; Gibb, 'Irvine Will', above n 1; R Smithers, 'Tory Divorce Bill Rebels Rally Allies', *The Guardian*, 20 April 1996.

Campaign because it would go 'some way further in trying to put the
emphasis in the Bill on saving marriages',[58] but it was also supported
by Labour back-benchers.[59] The unsuccessful amendment that couples
should be compelled to attend a meeting with a marriage guidance
counsellor, nevertheless tested in the pilot schemes, was in contrast
proposed by Labour.[60] Indeed, before the Third Reading, Paul Boateng
used his closing address to warn the Government that it could not rely
on Labour's support for the Bill unless the Government agreed to inject
a new emphasis on reconciliation and better to support the institution
of marriage.[61] The clearest example of the alliance is provided by the
compulsory waiting period between attending the information meeting
and making the statement of marital breakdown, which was proposed
by Labour but passed with the support of Conservatives. The only difference was that Labour originally suggested a wait of one month,
which Conservative rebels managed to increase to three months.[62] It
was because the drive towards marriage-saving was supported by this
alliance that its momentum was irresistible.

LABOUR'S MOTIVATION

The cross-party alliance lobbying for the development of a post-liberal
approach to information raises the question of the motivation of the
allies. The motivation of the conservative wing is easy to discern: since
they were anti-divorce and pro-marriage, they were keen to accentuate
the conservative elements of the Family Law Bill.[63] As we will see in

---

[58] Julian Brazier, quoted in Copley, above n 21.

[59] Copley, above n 21; Smithers, above n 53.

[60] Leader, 'Labour Joins The Right: Divorced From Reality', *The Independent*,
29 May 1996.

[61] 'MPs Threaten to Mangle Divorce Bill', *The Independent*, 26 April 1996; 'Four
Cabinet Ministers Vote For Divorce Defeat', *The Guardian*, 25 April 1996; 'Four Cabinet
Ministers Join Divorce Revolt', *The Times*, 25 April 1996; P Mansfield, 'From Divorce
Prevention to Marriage Support' in Thorpe and Clarke, above n 12, 30.

[62] S 8(2) Family Law Act 1996; Smithers, above n 53; Smithers, above n 57; 'Ministers
Defy Tory Pressure to Ditch Divorce Bill', *The Independent*, 26 April 1996.

[63] See Lord Moran, Hansard, House of Lords, 29 February 1996, Col 1648; Lord
Moran, Hansard, House of Lords, 30 November 1995, Col 764; Lord Jakobovits,
Hansard, House of Lords, 30 November 1995, Col 721; Lord Simon, Hansard, House of
Lords, 30 November 1995, Col 747; 'Brutish', above n 57; Dyer, above n 7; Leader, above
n 9; Gibb, 'Irvine Forced', above n 1; Gibb, 'Irvine Will', above n 1.

detail in chapter six, they had never been converted to post-liberal conceptions of autonomy and responsibility.[64]

Labour's motivation bears more discussion. It is clear that Labour were uncomfortable with the procedural nature of the obligations from early on. For example, during the debates Paul Boateng worried: 'We have somehow to build into what we are doing some messages about values'[65] and promised: 'Labour will seek to put a new focus on reconciliation.'[66] However, it has been suggested that this stance was adopted only because Labour was afraid to alienate the moral lobby by opposing marriage-saving measures pre-election.[67] This explanation is inconsistent with the fact that it was with the election of the Labour Government in 1997 that the post-liberal approach to information became official Government policy.

It is relatively uncontroversial that a feature of the Labour Government has been a more marked concentration on the presentation of policies rather than the policies themselves. It has been argued that one consequence of the concentration on 'spin' that has been less remarked upon is the risk that government itself will become the victim of its own belief in the importance of appearances so that:

When policies are criticised, or even when they seem to be rejected by the public, it is common for ministers to react by saying that they are failing to 'get their message across', as if the criticisms or rejection are all the result of some dreadful misunderstanding – a failure of communication – rather than actual opposition to the policies in question.[68]

It has been pointed out that this depends on the persuader's having a firm belief in the correctness of his or her position. If he or she is sure that he or she is right then people could fail to agree only through a flaw either in the way that he or she has presented his or her argument or in the understanding of the audience.[69] It has been argued that this mindset, although not exclusive to any one political party, is most closely associated with the Labour Government and can accordingly be seen in a number of recent Government policies, specifically Labour's approach to Part II of the Family Law Act.[70]

[64] See particularly pp 205–8.
[65] Paul Boateng, Hansard, House of Commons, 24 April 1996, Col 483.
[66] Smithers, above n 57.
[67] 'Brutish', above n 57.
[68] Eekelaar, above n 22, 387.
[69] *Ibid*, 387.
[70] *Ibid*.

However, there was another difference in the Labour Government's attitude to Part II of the Family Law Act which seems to contradict, but is in fact consistent with, their adoption of a post-liberal approach to information. At the same time as Labour became more concerned to influence behaviour, Labour also became more concerned about being *seen* to influence behaviour. It was with the election of the Labour Government that anxiety started to be evinced that Part II of the Family Law Act was a nannying piece of legislation.[71] Labour was anxious to be seen as concerned with saving marriages, at the same time as Labour was anxious not to be seen to be interfering in people's private lives.[72] The latter anxiety was evident in the forewords to Supporting Families, in which the Home Secretary recognised that families 'do not want to be lectured or hectored, least of all by politicians'[73] and to the strategy proposed by the Lord Chancellor's Advisory Group on Marriage and Relationship Support, Moving Forward Together, in which the Lord Chancellor assured that '[t]he Government has no desire to tell people how to live their lives.'[74] These two concerns run together because, given that there is something inherently patronising in a system that offers marriage counselling to those seeking divorce, anxiety about being perceived as nannying was bound to increase alongside the burgeoning emphasis on marriage-saving.[75] Nannying was a particular worry in relation to divorce given, first, the vast numbers of divorcing couples and, secondly, their social make-up. It is difficult if not impossible to treat divorcing couples in the same manner as social security claimants or parents of truanting children, given that the élite contains at least its fair proportion of divorcees.[76]

[71] W Arnold, 'Implementation of Part II of the Family Law Act 1996: The Decision Not to Implement in 2000 and Lessons Learned from The Pilot Meetings' in Thorpe and Clarke, above n 12, 15.

[72] Ahmed, above n 13.

[73] Home Office, above n 24, 2.

[74] Lord Chancellor's Advisory Group on Marriage and Relationship Support, 'Moving Forward Together: A Proposed Strategy for Marriage and Relationship Support for 2002 and Beyond' (London, Lord Chancellor's Department, 2002).

[75] W Arnold, 'Implementation of Part II of the Family Law Act 1996: The Decision Not to Implement in 2000 and Lessons Learned from The Pilot Meetings' in Thorpe and Clarke, above n 12, 23.

[76] See M Phillips, 'A Pause at the Parting of the Ways', *The Guardian*, 2 November 1990; 'Brutish', above n 57.

POST-LIBERAL INFORMATION

Gone is the idea that the role of law is to facilitate and implement private decisions: it now seeks to influence the decisions themselves.[77]

At the end of the Introduction, I highlighted an apparent contradiction that I suggested could stand as a preliminary illustration of the post-liberal dimension of the Family Law Act. This was that the Family Law Act seemed to emphasise both party control and a more intervention-ist divorce procedure. While this looks contradictory from a liberal perspective, I claimed that by the end of the book, I would have shown that this coupling made sense on a post-liberal reading of the Act, because tempering party control with behaviour modification is almost a definition of the post-liberal approach to autonomy.[78] While resolv-ing this contradiction has been a theme throughout the book, in this section I explore it further.

Illusory Autonomy

It has been argued that post-liberalism, specifically civic-republicanism, starts with the relatively uncontroversial empirical observation that social interactions of every sort mould individuals. From this premise post-liberalism surmises that individual values are products of the social matrix. But then post-liberals:

> . . . leap to the normative conclusion that society should shape its citizens' individual personalities intentionally, with precise goals in mind, rather than permit individual personalities to be defined at random through the complex intersection of many different social influences. After all, the argu-ment goes, if the social shaping of the individual is inevitable, we may as well take control of the process to ensure that the shaping is done correctly. This series of empirical and normative determinations produces the central theme of civic republican thought: the government should act aggressively to mold individuals in socially beneficial ways.[79]

---

[77] Dewar, above n 47, 477. See also J Dewar, 'Family Law and Its Discontents', 14 *International Journal of Law, Policy and the Family* 59 at 79.
[78] See p 12.
[79] S Gey, 'The Unfortunate Revival of Civic Republicanism', 141 *University of Pennsylvania Law Review* 801 at 813.

Throughout the book a theme has been that there is an almost inevitable slide towards more authoritarian, coercive strains of post-liberalism that require a particular decision as well as a particular method of decision-making: we can now spell out why. This is because there is only party control, and there is no party control. The subject must make his or her own decisions, but they are not real decisions and so do not deserve respect. Within a post-liberal framework all that the law can do is to cajole, to ask us to examine our consciences and check that what we are doing is really right for us, but the law can do this without shame. Modification of behaviour must inevitably replace prohibitions on behaviour, but modification can be unbridled. Choice is an illusion therefore manipulation of choice is unexceptionable. Two leading family law academics have rightly commented that:

> . . . we seem to be developing a fuzzy area of law where the Family Law Act exhorts rather than prescribes, by offering information . . .[80]

Post-liberalism almost inevitably slides towards the requirement of a particular result and towards regarding the purpose of providing information as being to achieve that result because post-liberalism regards the subject's untutored preferences as worthless. The coercive character of information provision within post-liberalism is taken to its limit by one leading civic republican who argues that when bad decision-making is a result of absence of information, it is not clear-cut whether government should provide the information or ban the decision. This is because the information may be too complex to communicate easily, rendering information provision costly or ineffective. In these circumstances:

> . . . a flat prohibition – justified on the ground that informed people would not engage in the transaction – may be far simpler to administer[81] [therefore] government may either provide the relevant information or under some circumstances ban the decision altogether.[82]

The bracketing together of providing information and banning the decision as equivalents is as startling as it is informative. While a liberal

---

[80] M Maclean and M Richards, 'Parents and Divorce: Changing Patterns of Public Intervention' in A Bainham *et al* (eds.), *What is a Parent? A Socio-Legal Analysis* (Oxford, Hart Publishing, 1999) 269.

[81] CR Sunstein, 'Legal Interference with Private Preferences', 53 *University of Chicago Law Review* 1129 at 1166–67.

[82] *Ibid*, 1139.

sees a gulf between providing information and coercing behaviour, because for a post-liberal the sole purpose of providing information is to ensure that people make the right decision, the liberal gulf becomes a post-liberal small step.

Downgrading Freedom from Interference

The post-liberal approach to information is both cause and effect of two important and inter-related points that have been made already but can now be further explored. The first is that the post-liberal conception of freedom devalues freedom from interference,[83] concentrating instead on the importance of helping people to become autonomous. This is because to a post-liberal, the fullest conception of freedom is freedom to develop oneself, therefore individual freedom is to be understood not as the capacity for free choice but as an activity of self-development.[84] We have already seen that while the liberal individual who chooses his or her ends must have a fundamental preference for conditions that facilitate choice, the post-liberal subject who discovers his or her ends will have a preference for conditions that enable self-knowledge. Within post-liberalism, since our ends are part of our selves, our lives go better not by having the conditions necessary to select and revise our projects but by having those needed to come to an awareness of our constitutive ends.[85] The condition best suited for protecting choice is negative freedom, or being left alone, but this is not the condition best suited to self-knowledge.

Being left alone does not best enable self-knowledge for two reasons. The first is that, as we saw in chapter four, within post-liberalism, rather than being a quality attributed to everyone through their humanity, autonomy is a matter of degree.[86] Therefore autonomy is capable of being either promoted or stifled:[87]

---

[83] See pp 132–6.

[84] C C Gould, *Rethinking Democracy: Freedom and Social Cooperation in Politics, Economy and Society* (Cambridge, Cambridge University Press, 1988).

[85] P 67.

[86] P 133.

[87] R Fallon, 'Two Senses of Autonomy', 46 *Stanford Law Review* 875 at 890; R Beiner, 'What's the Matter with Liberalism?' in A Hutchinson and L Green (eds), *Law and the Community: The End of Individualism?* (Toronto, Carswell, 1989) 47.

Each of us is the product of material and cultural forces; we may flourish or wither depending on the education we receive, the range of options open to us, and the treatment we get from others.[88]

Arguably, feminism takes this furthest. From feminism comes the suggestion that because we are thrown into a world that we do not choose but that inevitably shapes us, personhood is vulnerable in that we can be crushed in our efforts to become our own persons. Therefore we need to recognise explicitly that personhood is a project that needs legal, political, ethical and moral recognition if it is to be effectively maintained.[89] We cannot assume that a human is free, because the freedom to struggle to become a person is no more than a chance or opportunity that depends on a prior set of conditions and that has to be protected legally.[90] The legal system does not merely recognise, but also actively constitutes and confirms, who is to be valued and who is to matter. Because the self depends on the law for recognition, there can never be any simple freedom from intervention.[91] People are entitled not so much to protection from interference but more to the means for them to become autonomous.[92]

The second reason that being left alone does not best enable self-knowledge is that, as we saw in chapter one, self-knowledge can fail for inner reasons as well as external ones.[93] The personal nature of obligations within post-liberalism has been emphasised in order to draw the conclusion that post-liberalism implies that choices are best made and moral questions answered by the person himself or herself since he or she has the truest insight into his or her own values.[94] In fact, the opposite is the case. The person himself or herself is not the final authority on the question whether he or she is free because he or she is not the final authority on whether his or her desires are authentic, but may be wrong or mistaken.[95] For the process of self-examination to be meaningful, the agent must have a clear sense of the basis on which he or she

---

[88] Fallon, above n 87, 899.

[89] D Cornell, *At the Heart of Freedom: Feminism, Sex and Equality* (Princeton, New Jersey, Princeton University Press, 1998) 63.

[90] D Cornell, *The Imaginary Domain: Abortion, Pornography and Sexual Harassment* (New York, Routledge, 1995) 5.

[91] *Ibid*, 42.

[92] For discussion, see J Friedman, 'The Politics of Communitarianism', 8 *Critical Review* 299 at 299.

[93] See pp 16–18.

[94] C Schneider, 'Marriage, Morals and the Law', 1994 *Utah Law Review* 503 at 531.

[95] P 17.

decides to carry forward or repudiate his or her identity. Non-interference makes it impossible for others to probe sufficiently closely to decide whether the self has substituted a new identity reflectively or simply on a whim.[96] Since we cannot rule out second-guessing,[97] negative freedom does not enable self-realisation.[98] Even if the subject is better placed than anyone else to decide what is right for him or her, he or she can certainly be aided in deciding this correctly:

> While there is a tendency to stress the importance of the inner voice . . . communitarians recognize the basic fact that without continual external reinforcement, the conscience tends to deteriorate.[99]

Instrumental communitarians, discussed in chapter one,[100] link the changing conception of freedom with social change. They argue that freedom in the sense of being left alone was plausible when life could be lived predominantly on one's own homestead, but now that society is more interactive, freedom must exist within and be guaranteed by institutions.[101] On this view, an institution guides and sustains individual identity in the same way as a family, forming individuals by enabling or disabling certain ways of behaving and relating to others, so that each individual's possibilities depend on the opportunities opened up within the institution to which the person belongs.[102]

So self-knowledge, unlike choice, is not best enabled by freedom from interference. Conversely, self-knowledge, in contrast to choice, may be positively enhanced by external mechanisms and enforced procedures. Accordingly, according to post-liberalism, 'we find ourselves numbed into passivity by the absence of opportunities for meaningful deliberation.'[103] We can now understand why Lord Mackay was unembarrassed by his proclamation that:

---

[96] R Beiner, 'Revising the Self', 8 *Critical Review* 247 at 249. For discussion, see W Kymlicka, *Contemporary Political Philosophy: An Introduction* (Oxford, Oxford University Press, 1990) 208.

[97] C Taylor, 'What's Wrong with Negative Liberty?' in C Taylor, *Philosophy and the Human Sciences: Philosophical Papers 2* (Cambridge, Cambridge University Press, 1985) 228.

[98] *Ibid*, 212.

[99] A Etzioni, 'The Good Society', 7 *Journal of Political Philosophy* 88 at 93.

[100] Pp 25–8.

[101] R Bellah *et al*, *The Good Society* (New York, Knopf, 1991) 9.

[102] *Ibid*, 40.

[103] R Beiner, 'What's the Matter with Liberalism?' in Hutchinson and Green, above n 87, 53.

... people may need help to become reconciled; they may need help with reflection; they may need help in a number of ways.[104]

Lord Habgood was unabashed by his belief that '[t]he Bill gives a couple the gift of time, and the help to use it.'[105] The White Paper unashamedly announced that couples needed to be encouraged and helped to take responsibility,[106] so that the law had to provide mechanisms to create an opportunity for reflection and reconsideration.[107] Most strongly put:

> ... without participatory institutions to permit such discovery [of his real needs through the intervening discovery of himself] it is not permissible to regard 'all expressed wants' as reflecting 'real needs'.[108]

It has been rightly observed that the post-liberal:

> ... will 'improve' us against our will, but therapeutically, not coercively – helping us to become explicitly what we already are latently.[109] ... The claim that others can sometimes know what is good for us better than we know it ourselves may be dangerous even when it is not always false.[110]

Trusting the State

> ... the ideal of socialised self-realization ... always implies gentle superintendence by the political power.[111] ... [It is] an inadvertent collusion with everything in modern life that leads to the growth of the power of the state.[112]

The second cause and effect of the post-liberal approach to information, inter-related to the dismissive attitude to freedom from interference, is a lack of suspicion of the state.[113] It has been argued that

[104] Lord Mackay, Hansard, House of Lords, 25 January 1996, Col 1198.

[105] Lord Habgood, Hansard, House of Lords, 29 February 1996, Col 1646.

[106] Lord Chancellor's Department, above n 20, 31. For general discussion, see N Lacey and L Zedner, 'Discourses of Community in Criminal Justice', 22 *Journal of Law and Society* 301 at 301–2.

[107] Lord Chancellor's Department, above n 20, 17–18.

[108] C Berry, *The Idea of a Democratic Community* (Hemel Hempstead, Harvester Wheatsheaf, 1989) 56.

[109] S Holmes, 'The Permanent Structure of Antiliberal Thought' in N Rosenblum (ed), *Liberalism and the Moral Life* (Cambridge, Massachusetts, Harvard University Press, 1989) 236.

[110] *Ibid*, 239.

[111] G Kateb, 'Democratic Individuality and the Meaning of Rights' in Rosenblum, above n 109, 202.

[112] *Ibid*, 203.

[113] For discussion, see Gey, above n 79.

post-liberals from across the political spectrum are increasingly advocating state intervention and social engineering under terms that they can share, such as community, empowerment and the promotion of autonomy. New forms of control are being advanced at work, in education and in the home, justified by various ends such as equal opportunity or quality control.[114] We have already explored two reasons for post-liberal trust of public power in chapter four. First, we saw that while the liberal prioritises rights over the good, the post-liberal reverses this prioritisation.[115] It is the rights-based notion of separate individuals that needs a neutral state:[116]

> For Kantian liberals, it is precisely because we are freely choosing, independent selves that we need a neutral framework, a framework of rights that refuses to choose among competing values and ends.[117]

Since post-liberalism disputes the disjuncture between self and community, individual safeguards against a collectivist state make little sense.[118] Secondly, we saw that freedom requires the identity of citizens to be defined partly by civic responsibilities;[119] a neutral state may therefore erode rather than enhance our autonomy.[120]

The most fundamental reason, though, for lack of suspicion of the state is that, as we have seen, within post-liberalism autonomy is regarded as illusory. Since we are constructed out of social forces, state power is at worst just one more of these influences. The individual cannot complain about governmental manipulation because individual autonomy is viewed as nugatory, inevitably at the mercy of collective manipulation in any case:[121]

> To remove, on libertarian grounds, limits set by the public, far from enhancing autonomy, merely leaves individuals subject to all the other influences,

---

[114] B Almond, 'The Retreat from Liberty', 8 *Critical Review* 235.

[115] Pp 130–1.

[116] M Sandel, 'Morality and the Liberal Ideal', *New Republic*, 7 May 1984, 15 at 17; B Frohnen, *The New Communitarians and the Crisis of Modern Liberalism* (Lawrence, University Press of Kansas, 1996) 201.

[117] M Sandel, *Democracy's Discontent: America in Search of a Public Philosophy* (Cambridge, Massachusetts, Belknap Press, 1996) 12. See also Beiner, above n 96.

[118] Beiner, above n 96. For discussion, see Gey, above n 79, 803; Almond, above n 114, 244.

[119] Pp 135–7.

[120] Sandel, above n 117, 27.

[121] R Beiner, 'What's the Matter with Liberalism?' in Hutchinson and Green, above n 87, 47; C R Sunstein, *Free Markets and Social Justice* (New York, Oxford, Oxford University Press, 1997); Sunstein, above n 81. For discussion, see Gey, above n 79, 831.

which reach them not as information or environmental factors they can analyze and cope with, but as invisible messages of which they are unaware and that sway them in nonrational ways.[122]

If the state could remain neutral, neutrality would still be a mirage because the wider social order is not neutral, but it is not in any case possible for the state or the legal system to remain neutral because social practices including law inevitably significantly influence people's preferences and choices.[123] These preferences and choices do not even exist independently of the state or legal system.[124] Therefore there is no good reason falsely to constrain the state with the requirement of neutrality. Post-liberals regard it as fully legitimate for government and law to try to shape preferences because social life as a whole is partial to particular ways of life and preferences:[125]

> Typically, we find ourselves barbarized by an empty public culture, intimidated by colossal bureaucracies . . . inflated by absurd habits of consumption, deflated by the Leviathans that surround us, and stripped of dignity by a way of living that far exceeds a human scale. We live in societies that embark upon the grandest and most hubristic collective projects, while granting their citizens only the feeblest opportunities for effective say over the disposal of their own destiny. To speak of autonomous moral agency and the ethical prerogatives of free choice-making individuals in this context is nothing short of a grotesque insult.[126]

However, post-liberalism goes much, much further than seeing the state as just one more influence on us. Rather, post-liberalism regards the state as a helpful, counteracting antidote to distortions of our autonomy by other social sources. Post-liberals depict liberalism as stubbornly maintaining that the state alone poses a threat to autonomy, so that if state neutrality can be secured this is a sufficient safeguard. Liberalism, they suggest, measures autonomy in inverse relation to *government* interference with private action, and this can only be explained by an ideologically charged distrust of government and

---

[122] A Etzioni, *The New Golden Rule: Community and Morality in a Democratic Society* (New York, Basic Books, 1998) 21.

[123] Sunstein, above n 121, 5; J Singer, 'The Privatization of Family Law', 71 *Wisconsin Law Review* 1443 at 1539; Beiner, above n 96, 256.

[124] Singer, above n 123, 1539.

[125] R Beiner, 'What's the Matter with Liberalism?' in Hutchinson and Green, above n 87, 47; Sunstein, above n 121, 5.

[126] R Beiner, 'What's the Matter with Liberalism?' in Hutchinson and Green, above n 87, 53.

relative complacency about the effects of private power.[127] In fact it is post-liberalism that proclaims that the state alone does *not* pose a threat to autonomy:[128]

> . . . the state might be needed to render individuals *more* autonomous – for instance, by removing or inhibiting the power of other social forces to captivate and bewitch individuals without directly coercing them.[129]

There are three main reasons that post-liberals exempt government alone from the charge of distorting autonomy. The first reason depends on coupling the lack of particular suspicion of the state with the necessity for a collective actor.[130] We saw in chapter one that individual actors are generally powerless to change norms that do not serve them well[131] and in chapter four that the only way that true autonomy can be achieved is through a collective process.[132] Putting these points together, this means that collective action is necessary to enable norms to be changed in a direction that is consistent with people's underlying aspirations and judgements, so that it promotes rather than undermines freedom for a collective process to discover and counter distortions.[133] Once a neutral attitude to state power has been adopted, the government is clearly the natural coordinator and compiler of community decisions;[134] government is the most efficient and effective collective actor.[135]

Secondly, government is seen as more likely to represent the public interest than are private bodies because it represents wider interests.[136] In contrast, private non-governmental power is characterised as a cognitive distortion indefensible on any ground other than self-interest,[137]

---

[127] R Beiner, *What's the Matter with Liberalism?* (Berkeley, California, University of California Press, 1992) 26; R Beiner, 'What's the Matter with Liberalism?' in Hutchinson and Green, above n 87, 46–47; Fallon, above n 87, 882–83.

[128] Beiner, above n 127, 26; R Beiner, 'What's the Matter with Liberalism?' in Hutchinson and Green, above n 87, 46; Fallon, above n 87, 882–83; Sunstein, above n 81, 1145. For discussion, see Gey, above n 79, 803.

[129] Beiner, above n 127, 26. See also R Beiner, 'What's the Matter with Liberalism?' in Hutchinson and Green, above n 87, 47; Fallon, above n 87, 882.

[130] For discussion, see Gey, above n 79, 827.

[131] P38.

[132] Pp 134–6.

[133] Sunstein, above n 81; Sunstein, above n 121.

[134] For discussion, see Gey, above n 79, 842.

[135] *Ibid*, 843.

[136] *Ibid*, 844.

[137] Sunstein, above n 81, 1153–54.

providing a strong basis for governmental intervention when these distortions can be identified:[138]

> Civic-republicans view 'private preferences' as especially susceptible to distortion by non-governmental collective forces within society. The civic-republican response to this problem is to give the community and its government the power to control and revise presumptively 'nonautonomous' individual preferences.[139]

The third reason again depends on the coupling of lack of particular suspicion of state power, this time with the necessity of relationships for autonomy, explored in chapter three.[140] It follows from this coupling that relationships with state agents potentially foster autonomy, although of course post-liberals recognise that, just like the spousal relationship, our relationship with the state may either foster or undermine autonomy:

> If we understand autonomy as made possible by relationship rather than exclusion, we can better understand the genuine problem of autonomy in the modern state. Our central problem today is not maintaining a sphere into which the state cannot penetrate but fostering autonomy where people are already within the sphere of state control or responsibility.[141]

Ultimately, post-liberals perceive a straight choice between private power and state power, and choose state power. Any other choice, they fear, would lead to the embracing of the status quo as neutral and natural.[142] This is a common feminist criticism of liberalism: liberal neutrality is recast as substantive misogyny. The argument is that in the face of existing sexual inequality, a politics that refuses to take sides with women in the name of neutrality is in reality taking sides with men as the more powerful sex, allowing them to maintain their dominance through a state policy of non-interference.[143] For example, government regulation of speech aimed at stopping private manipulation of speech

---

[138] Sunstein, above n 81, 1158.

[139] Gey, above n 79, 833.

[140] Pp 96–8.

[141] J Nedelsky, 'Law, Boundaries, and the Bounded Self', 30 *Representations* 162 at 169.

[142] Beiner, above n 127, 26; R Beiner, 'What's the Matter with Liberalism?' in Hutchinson and Green, above n 87, 46–47; Fallon, above n 87, 882–83.

[143] P Weiss, 'Feminism and Communitarianism: Comparing Critiques of Liberalism' in P Weiss and M Friedman (eds), *Feminism and Community* (Philadelphia, Temple University Press, 1995) 178.

is not itself seen as a manipulative interference with freedom of speech.[144]

It is true that communitarianism in particular distinguishes itself from conservatism partly by preferring to rely on 'the moral voice of the community, education, persuasion and exhortation'[145] rather than law enforcement by the state[146] and accordingly seeking to draw a clear line between the moral voice and law.[147] However, this line becomes blurry or even non-existent once we see, as we did in chapter four, that law enforcement by the state *becomes* the moral voice of the community, as happened in the Family Law Act. Within communitarianism, because of the lack of suspicion of state influence, the law and the state are able to blend into the community, presenting themselves as just one more voice to listen to. Etzioni for one is quite clear that the only factor that distinguishes state coercion from other exercises of power is the threat or use of force. Therefore when he draws a line between legitimate and illegitimate action, the only actions that are even potentially on the illegitimate side are government dictates, because they are backed up by force and leave no options to the actor. There is nothing illegitimate about the articulation of a moral voice, by the state or the community, since this leaves the ultimate choice with the individual. Moreover, the best way to minimise the need for government coercion is to foster rather than diminish the moral voice. Etzioni argues that individualists who dispute this division are relying on an ambiguity in the term 'coercion', using it to cover a wide range of behaviour, from imprisonment to psychological pressure,[148] whereas in fact:

> . . . a measure of psychological pressure is contained in most, if not all, social relations, and most assuredly in the voice of the community.[149]

In addition, communitarians of a civic republican slant believe that since it is not possible for the law to remain neutral, it is legitimate for the state to shape preferences not only through education but also through laws.[150]

---

[144] Fallon, above n 87, 882.

[145] Etzioni, above n 122, 16–17.

[146] *Ibid*; B Woodhouse, ' "It All Depends on What You Mean By Home": Toward a Communitarian Theory of the "Nontraditional" Family', 1996 *Utah Law Review* 569 at 586–87.

[147] Etzioni, above n 122, 139.

[148] Etzioni, above n 122, 131–32. For discussion, see Frohnen, above n 116.

[149] Etzioni, above n 122, 131–32.

[150] See e.g. Sunstein, above n 121, 5.

Therefore it could be suggested that the tenets of post-liberal theory deny access to any significant theoretical limitations on governmental power:[151]

> . . . the nature and extent of these malfunctions will support considerable legislative and judicial intrusion into private preference structures.[152] . . . Even outside of the traditional category of harm to others, the legal system does and should attempt to shape private choices. Whether the ultimate goal is liberty or welfare, there will be often important gains from collective action that decides on ends rather than simply implements them.[153]

Moreover, there is no boundary to governmental intrusion.[154] Government can legitimately intervene in 'areas of individual ideology, beliefs, attitudes, and private consensual behavior.'[155] This intervention is legitimated if not required by the concept of civic virtue, alongside the disdain for private preferences that have not come under governmental supervision.[156] Since the post-liberal state has far more to achieve than the liberal state, it will inevitably be far more intrusive.[157] More specifically, if divorce law is to perform a behaviour-modifying function then it will inevitably be far more interventionist:[158]

> When equipped with a definition of freedom that amounts to the absence of freedom, or a notion like 'coercion understood as consent' the civic republicans can justify virtually any governmental intrusion into the individual persona, while simultaneously disavowing any intent to interfere with personal preferences they deem legitimate.[159]

THE ÉLITE

We have seen at several points in the book that post-liberalism is inevitably an élitist theory, despite its protestations to the contrary.

---

[151] Gey, above n 79, 857.

[152] Sunstein, above n 81, 1172.

[153] *Ibid*, 1173.

[154] See J Nolan, *The Therapeutic State: Justifying Government at Century's End* (New York, New York University Press, 1998) 38.

[155] See Gey, above n 79, 862.

[156] *Ibid*, 863.

[157] See S Holmes, 'The Permanent Structure of Antiliberal Thought' in Rosenblum, above n 109, 230; Nolan, above n 154, 292.

[158] See Dewar, above n 47, 478.

[159] Gey, above n 79, 826. W Galston, *Liberal Purposes: Goods, Virtues, and Diversity in the Liberal State* (New York, Cambridge University Press, 1991) 86.

Clearly, once the post-liberal approach to information had been adopted, there was no escape from the élitist nature of post-liberalism: if decisions are to be directed, then someone must be capable of direction. The post-liberal character of Part II of the Family Law Act both enabled and was enabled by the fact that the divorce proposals were very definitely an élitist reform. There was neither popular dissatisfaction with the Matrimonial Causes Act nor popular support for Part II of the Family Law Act.[160] Specifically, there was little popular enthusiasm for the complete removal of fault that would have been effected by the Family Law Act. On the contrary, it has been shown empirically that divorcees in particular are deeply concerned about issues of blame, which colour their perceptions of fairness and their ideas about justice:

> . . . faced with the loss that divorce inevitably entails, as well as the need to build a new life, the imputation of blame can feature prominently on the psychological agendas of divorcing people.[161]

It has been argued that most divorcees struggle to make sense of what went wrong with their marriage and that making sense of the past is a necessary part of negotiating a new reality to replace the shared reality of their marriage. The need to rewrite the story of the marriage is so important that couples compete for their own version to be accepted as the true one.[162]

More generally, it has been suggested that family legislation from 1960 to about 1990 was a response to wider social and economic changes that produced widespread dissatisfaction with the law and hence public pressure for changes in the law. However, since the late 1980s, there has been a shift from the permissive approach of the late 1960s towards social engineering designed to mitigate harms perceived as generated by the previous era. It has been argued that the Children Act 1989 is the watershed in this respect. Accordingly, the Family Law Act, along with other 1990s reforms such as the Child Support Act 1991, was imposed by government explicitly to mould family practices:

---

[160] W Arnold, 'Implementation of Part II of the Family Law Act 1996: The Decision Not to Implement in 2000 and Lessons Learned from the Pilot Meetings' in Thorpe and Clarke, above n 12, 15.

[161] SD Sclater and C Piper, 'The Family Law Act 1996 in Context' in SD Sclater and C Piper (eds), *Undercurrents of Divorce* (Aldershot, Ashgate, 1999) 6. See also G Davis and M Murch, *Grounds for Divorce* (Oxford, Clarendon Press, 1988).

[162] J Brown and SD Sclater, 'Divorce: A Psychodynamic Perspective' in Sclater and Piper, above n 161, 155.

The essential difference between important legislative changes to family law up to the 1990s and during that decade is that in the former case changes were 'from the bottom up' while more recently they have been 'from the top down'. Moreover, they have been 'from the top down' within the context of a very clear agenda about family life.[163]

Recognition that Part II of the Family Law Act was a 'top down' reform has led to an optimistic reading of its failure, namely that it was brought down by the resistance of ordinary people:

People do not just passively accept the roles society provides for them. Rather, they are more likely to play an active role in evaluating what is best for them, in all the circumstances of their own lives. As a result, they will negotiate, or even actively challenge and resist, the normative prescriptions that are implicit in policies, laws and professional practices. Examples of such resistance have already been found in research on divorce mediation and the information meetings piloted in relation to section 8 of the FLA.[164]

It is true that the divorce scheme failed at least partly because people didn't do what the Government meant them to do. They gladly took the information but rather than being influenced by the information, they were merely informed by it, and rather than drawing the conclusion that they should attend mediation or marriage counselling, or perhaps even stay married, they drew the conclusion that they needed better legal advice.[165] But it would be wrong to describe this as resistance. Admittedly, there was no popular support for Part II of the Family Law Act; however as we saw in chapter four, people did and do generally accept, if not support, the crucial tenet of post-liberalism that they need help to make decisions. More strongly put, citizens naturally comply with programmes and policies based on therapeutic rationales, because they seem obviously plausible.[166] What we witnessed with the collapse of Part II of the Family Law Act was that, rather than resisting, divorcees unwittingly drew the opposite results from the ones that Government wanted them to draw, while agreeing all the while with the underlying rationale on which Part II was based.[167] In other words, divorcees accepted that they needed help and that they could not

---

[163] C Smart and B Neale, *Family Fragments?* (Cambridge, Polity Press, 1999) 175.

[164] SD Sclater and C Piper, 'Re-moralising the Family?—Family Policy, Family Law and Youth Justice', 12 *Child and Family Law Quarterly* 135 at 149–50.

[165] SM Cretney and J M Masson, *Principles of Family Law* 6th edn (London, Sweet & Maxwell, 1997) 381. See also Dewar, above n 77, 79.

[166] Nolan, above n 154, 298.

[167] Sclater and Piper, above n 164, 151.

manage their divorces themselves, but simply chose a different form of help from the one that the Government was advocating.

If decisions are to be directed, someone must do the directing. The question is who. We have already seen that the shift from freedom as choice to freedom as self-realisation leads to a growth in state power, and to a certain extent the state is the élite:

> . . . socialized self-realization . . . is almost indistinguishable from thera-peutic and paternalistic condescension to ordinary persons who are secretly thought by theorists to be no better than a plebs. Who but the state can ultimately administer, or at least supervise, therapeutic and paternalist dis-ciplines to a whole society . . . ?[168]

However, the élite is also far broader than the state. Acceptance of the idea that divorcees can no longer manage their divorces themselves has given rise to an élite class of experts and:

> . . . new industries of advice giving. In the field of divorce the new experts are, of course, the mediators and conciliators who should be added to the more established ranks of politicians, judges, marriage guidance counsellors and the child psychologists.[169]

Accordingly, '[t]herapists became the teachers and norm-setters in marriage and then, later, in the dissolution of marriage.'[170] The ten-dency to see family law problems in medical terms[171] leads the law to listen to specialists from other disciplines, such as medicine, psychiatry and psychology, relying on their recommendations and even confiding direct power to them.[172] Because behaviour is increasingly interpreted in terms of health not morality, the role of therapeutic practitioners is even more essential:[173]

> These psychologists, psychiatrists, counselors, therapists, and social work-ers have been granted a high level of prestige and social recognition in American society for their ability to help individuals make sense of life in the modern world. They interpret individual behavior and social interactions

---

[168] G Kateb, 'Democratic Individuality and the Meaning of Rights' in Rosenblum, above n 109, 203.

[169] C Smart and B Neale, 'Good Enough Morality? Divorce and Postmodernity', 17 *Critical Social Policy* 3 at 8.

[170] BD Whitehead, *The Divorce Culture: Rethinking Our Commitments to Marriage and the Family* (New York, Knopf, 1997) 49.

[171] See p 89.

[172] C Schneider, 'Moral Discourse and the Transformation of American Family Law', 83 *Michigan Law Review* 1803 at 1854.

[173] Nolan, above n 154, 9.

with an authority that was once conferred on individuals associated with other vocations in American society.[174]

More generally, experts on civic consciousness, or facilitators, are the new élite.[175] If people are shaped into radically different forms by social institutions then the élite are those who have the power to shape and reinterpret these institutions.[176]

So power within post-liberalism is diffuse.[177] It has been recognised that the dispersal of control ultimately leads to the expansion of social control.[178] Changes that seem to weaken hierarchies of power may actually establish new channels through which they can be expressed or even strengthened.[179] State involvement may be less, but intervention more pervasive:[180]

> Looked at superficially such changes (it is better not to call them 'reforms') might appear to weaken hierarchies of power. In reality what they do is make control more intrusive, more pervasive and more effective. . . . We find rampant interventionism, a system of indirect controls and pervasive reliance on professional expertise.[181]

We will see in more detail in chapter six that in relation to divorce in particular post-liberal responsibility was inevitably more intrusive and interventionist than the preceding liberal form of responsibility.[182] We can note here that this is doubly disguised because at the same time as suspicion of the state has receded, overt state intervention in the family has been replaced by more diffuse intrusion, so that 'the governance of citizens *through* the family may now have achieved unprecedented

---

[174] Nolan, above n 154, 8.

[175] Frohnen, above n 116.

[176] *Ibid*, 198.

[177] G Kateb, 'Democratic Individuality and the Meaning of Rights' in Rosenblum, above n 109, 203.

[178] MDA Freeman, 'Down with informalism: Law and lawyers in family dispute resolutions' 2 *Family Law Journal* 67 at 71; MDA Freeman, 'Questioning the Delegalization Movement in Family Law: Do We Really Want a Family Court?' in J Eekelaar and SN Katz (eds), *The Resolution of Family Conflict: Comparative Legal Perspectives* (Toronto, Butterworths, 1984) 18; Nolan, above n 154, 298–99.

[179] MDA Freeman, 'Questioning the Delegalization Movement in Family Law: Do We Really Want a Family Court?' in Eekelaar and Katz, above n 178, 8.

[180] *Ibid*, 9; Freeman, above n 178, 71.

[181] MDA Freeman, 'Questioning the Delegalization Movement in Family Law: Do We Really Want a Family Court?' in Eekelaar and Katz, above n 178, 19. See also Freeman, above n 178, 71.

[182] Pp 235–38.

heights'.[183] It has been argued that this feeds back to the state itself, to provide the state with a new system of indirect control.[184]

THE END OF POST-LIBERAL INFORMATION?

In chapter four I argued that divorce had become primarily an educative process. In this chapter we have seen that while divorcing couples agreed that they needed educating, they chose different lessons from the ones that the Government was recommending, opting for legal advice rather than mediation or marriage counselling. This was interpreted by the Government as a generalised failure to learn the moral lessons of divorce. Such failure was particularly unfortunate given, as we saw in chapter four, that the definition of a moral agent has become someone who accepts that he or she needs moral education: it is impossible to act morally while rejecting moral assistance.[185] Accordingly, the Government had no option but to abandon the education programme represented by Part II of the Family Law Act. Nevertheless, according to the current Lord Chancellor, Part II of the Family Law Bill was 'a kind of a prolegomenon for a new philosophy.'[186] The collapse of Part II of the Family Law Act does not signify the end of the post-liberal approach to information, either in relation to divorce or more generally.

Post-Liberal Information on Divorce

To examine divorce first, the Government has made clear that it intends to postpone implementation of Part II of the Family Law Act indefinitely and to ask Parliament to repeal it when an opportunity arises.[187] However, it has also confirmed that this is because it does not believe that Part II of the Act fulfils the principles and premises of the Act, to which the Government remains wedded:

> The Government is committed to supporting marriage and to supporting families when relationships fail, especially when there are children involved.

[183] SD Sclater, *Divorce: A Psychosocial Study* (Aldershot, Ashgate, 1999) 17.
[184] *Ibid*, 185.
[185] Pp 154–55.
[186] Lord Irvine, Hansard, House of Lords, 23 January 1996, Col 985.
[187] Lord Chancellor's Department, 'Divorce', above n 1.

But this very comprehensive research, together with other recent valuable research in the field, has shown that Part II of the Family Law Act is not the best way of achieving those aims.[188]

Accordingly, a spokesman for the Lord Chancellor's Department recently confirmed that that there were other ways, apart from new legislation, of implementing the principles of the Family Law Act.[189] True to their word, the day before announcing that Part II of the Family Law Act would not be implemented, the Lord Chancellor's Department announced that the Government would be supporting a national advertising campaign to promote mediation to divorcing and separating couples. As well as advertisements in national publications, a leaflet on mediation services would be available in doctors' surgeries, health clinics, social services departments, family courts and court welfare services. People responding to the advertisements would get information about mediation services in their area.[190] Other proposals to impart information are afoot; for example, last year the Lord Chancellor's Department and Home Office's Family Policy Committee were reported to be supporting a book advising couples on the perfect marriage.[191] More ambitious is the piloting of new Family Advice and Information Networks, which specifically build on the experience of piloting information meetings and are intended to provide tailored information similar to that which would have been provided by the information meetings. They would enable people to access services such as information, legal advice, mediation and counselling from a single point of reference, their aim being to help couples resolve disputes and consider saving their relationship. They would inform couples about the effects of separation on children, how to avoid these effects and the help that is available in this regard. The Networks would explicitly promote mediation, and marriage and relationship counselling. They would offer support to parents in talking to their

---

[188] *Ibid.* See also Dyer, above n 13; *BBC News*, 'No-fault', above n 7; *BBC News*, 'Bishop', above n 7; Sclater and Piper, above n 164, 145.

[189] R Verkaik, 'Lawyers Attack Misery of "Fault Game" Divorces', *The Independent*, 2 January 2002. See also Lord Chancellor's Department, 'Divorce', above n 1; *BBC News*, 'No-Fault', above n 7; Lady Justice Hale OBE, 'The Way Forward' in Thorpe and Clarke, above n 12, 146; 'Brutish', above n 57.

[190] Lord Chancellor's Department, 'The Government Supports Publicity Campaign to Increase Awareness of Family Mediation', 15 January 2001. See also Rozenberg, above n 13.

[191] Ahmed, above n 13.

children and to children who were specifically referred.[192] While the collapse of Part II of the Family Law Act means that couples will not have to make financial arrangements before divorcing,[193] this may benefit divorcing couples less than they might expect. This is because the Lord Chancellor announced in May 2000 that the Children Act 1989 might be amended so that couples would have to settle arrangements for the children before divorcing.[194]

Post-Liberal Information on Marriage

We saw in chapter four that since divorce is no longer equivocally bad, marriage is no longer equivocally good, but rather is now, like divorce, a moral staging post, a lesson that needs to be learnt in order to be beneficial.[195] It is no coincidence that Supporting Families proposed the first restrictions on marriage since marriage was initially regulated by the 1753 Marriage Act, some of which have been successfully implemented, as we saw in chapter four.[196] Interestingly, the Government has made more relative headway with post-liberal marriage than post-liberal divorce. During the debates on the Family Law Act, the Duke of Norfolk argued that marriage counselling:

. . . should continue after the engagement, during the marriage and once there are children. Marriage counselling and help should continue throughout a marriage. . . . We should increase the assistance that is given to married couples from the very start to the very end of their marriage.[197]

Lord Mackay endorsed this:

I believe that the earlier the service is available the better. That is why, like my noble friend the Duke of Norfolk, I attach a great deal of importance to the preparation for marriage.[198] . . . the sooner help can be asked for the better.[199]

---

[192] Legal Services Commission, *Developing Family Advice and Information Services* (London, Legal Services Commission, 2002); Legal Services Commission, *Family Advice and Information Networks* (London, Legal Services Commission, 2001).

[193] See p 176.

[194] M Dearle, 'Making a "Dog's Dinner" Out of Divorce Reforms', *The Times*, 5 September 2000; Ahmed, above n 13; Gibb, 'Irvine Will', above n 1; Leader, 'The Family Way', *The Times*, 18 December 2000.

[195] Pp 160–62.

[196] Home Office, above n 24; pp 161–62.

[197] Duke of Norfolk, Hansard, House of Lords, 22 January 1996, Col 834.

[198] Lord Mackay, Hansard, House of Lords, 22 January 1996, Col 837.

[199] *Ibid*, Col 884.

This approach was supported by Moving Forward Together, published in April 2002, which suggested that the time had come to move 'to a more long-term, proactive, positive and preventative approach.'[200] Already, since the Lord Chancellor announced in 1999 that Part II of the Family Law Act was to be postponed, he has increased funding to organisations offering support for marriages and relationships by two-thirds. Early in 2001 the Lord Chancellor announced that this would be spent on improving existing marriage and relationship services, researching into the most effective forms of intervention and disseminating good practice.[201] Just as with marriage-saving in the context of divorce, other proposals have been considered before being ultimately rejected; for example, Lord Northbourne moved an unsuccessful amendment to the Marriage Ceremony (Prescribed Words) Act 1996, which would have made couples spell out their commitment to their children in the marriage ceremony. His justification for this was that there was:

> . . . a need to encourage young couples who are contemplating marriage to consider carefully the nature of the engagement they are entering into.[202]

Post-Liberal Information in Family Law

An outstanding recent example of the continuing influence of post-liberal information within family law is provided by Making Contact Work, a report from the Children Act Sub-Committee of the Advisory Board on Family Law, published in February 2002.[203] In this report, the Board's starting point was recognition that when the primary carer disobeys a contact order requiring him or her to allow contact between the child and another adult, generally the other parent, enforcing the

[200] Lord Chancellor's Advisory Group on Marriage and Relationship Support, above n 74, 19.

[201] Lord Chancellor's Department, 'Lord Chancellor Announces Marriage and Relationship Support Funding', 16 January 2001. See also Lord Chancellor's Department, 'Divorce', above n 1; Dyer, above n 13; Ahmed, above n 13; Rozenberg, above n 13; *BBC News*, 'No-fault', above n 7; *BBC News*, 'Bishop', above n 7; Gibb, 'Irvine Will', above n 2; Leader, above n 194.

[202] Lord Northbourne, Hansard, House of Lords, 2 July 1996, Col 1426.

[203] Lord Chancellor's Advisory Board on Family Law: Children Act Sub-Committee, 'Making Contact Work: A Report to the Lord Chancellor on the Facilitation of Arrangements for Contact Between Children and their Non-Residential Parents and the Enforcement of Court Orders for Contact' (Lord Chancellor's Department, London, 2002).

contact order by fining or imprisoning the carer is both crude and ineffective.[204] The main reason is that it is hard to justify such punishment
as being in the child's best interests.[205] Their conclusion was that the
Government should legislate to provide the courts with a range of
therapeutic remedies in such cases,[206] so that fines or imprisonment
would be genuinely the last resort only when education, therapy and
persuasion had failed.[207]

The Report regarded better information to both parents at the earliest possible stage in the breakdown of their relationship and preferably
before they had parted,[208] as of crucial importance in making contact
work.[209] There were four pieces of information that the Board considered particularly necessary. The first was the importance to children of
maintaining contact wherever possible with the parent with whom
they are not living. Secondly, parents needed to know how difficult
successful post-separation parenting is for both parents. Thirdly, they
needed information about the serious harm caused to children by
continuing acrimony between their parents. Finally, they needed to be
aware of the services available to help resolve difficulties over contact.[210] More broadly, there was a need to promote general understanding of the importance of the involvement of both parents in the
upbringing of their children.[211] The directive nature of this information is too obvious to be dwelt on.

The importance placed on information in the Report was also
clearly founded on the assumption that if parents were fully informed
then they would be inexorably driven to the right result, which was
that the primary carer would allow conflict-free contact:

> Whilst it is in no sense a panacea, we are strongly of the view that if parents
> have ready access to high quality information about the effects of their sep-
> aration on themselves and on their children; about the difficulties involved
> in post separation parenting; and about the effect of continuing parental
> hostility on their children, then their views on contact will be much better
> informed. An understanding of the traumatic process through which both

---

[204] *Ibid*, 13 and 97.
[205] *Ibid*, 13.
[206] *Ibid*, 13.
[207] *Ibid*, 14 and 97.
[208] *Ibid*, ch 1 and p 22.
[209] *Ibid*, 11 and 22.
[210] *Ibid*, 11.
[211] *Ibid*, 22.

adults and children are going is likely to help make contact easier for both adults and for children.[212]

Some of the responses to the Consultation Paper suggested far earlier information, recalling the discussion in chapter four.[213] The Oxfordshire Children and Family Court Advisory and Support Service team proposed that a leaflet detailing the implications of parental responsibility should be given or sent to both parents when they registered the birth of their child. The Tavistock and Portman NHS Trust suggested discussion of parental responsibility at ante-natal classes, as well as information to be included in primary and secondary school education.[214]

The Report envisaged plenty of opportunities for providing information, recommending that courts should have the power to compel parents to attend a range of meetings, including a meeting with a mediator, similar to the one that would have been implemented by Part II of the Family Law Act.[215] The range of meetings included information meetings, conciliation meetings, psychological or psychiatric assessments, meetings with a counsellor, parenting classes designed to persuade parents to obey the contact order and, if the parents were in breach of an order, education programmes or perpetrator programmes.[216] In addition, the Report recommended giving courts the power to place parents on probation, with a condition of treatment or attendance at a particular class or programme, and the power to impose a community service order to include programmes specifically designed to address the default in contact.[217]

We have already seen that at the coercive end of post-liberalism, little difference is perceived between providing information and coercing behaviour.[218] The Report shows that the converse is also true: classically punitive measures are seen as less necessary when information provision becomes directive.[219] However, this point should not be

[212] Lord Chancellor's Advisory Board on Family Law: Children Act Sub-Committee, 'Making Contact Work: A Report to the Lord Chancellor on the Facilitation of Arrangements for Contact Between Children and their Non-Residential Parents and the Enforcement of Court Orders for Contact' (Lord Chancellor's Department, London, 2002) 22.
[213] Pp 160–64.
[214] Lord Chancellor's Advisory Board on Family Law, above n 203, 30.
[215] *Ibid*, 43; p 175.
[216] Lord Chancellor's Advisory Board on Family Law, above n 203, 89, 90, 98 and 99.
[217] *Ibid*, 14, 89 and 99.
[218] Pp 182–83.
[219] See more generally Nolan, above n 154, 298.

misunderstood as seeking to diminish the punitive nature of post-liberal information provision. In this respect, it is instructive to note the difference that the Report envisaged between punitive and non-punitive remedies. The Report recommended that there should be two stages, the first being essentially non-punitive. At this non-punitive stage:

> The resident parent could, for example, be directed to attend an information meeting, or a parenting programme designed to address intractable contact disputes or required to seek psychiatric advice.[220]

At the punitive stage, the only difference would be that the court could impose an order with a penal sanction, such as community service or regular attendance at parenting classes.[221]

The Government has accepted the substance of the recommendations in the Report and has begun to implement those that do not require new legislation.[222] A programme board has been established to consider how to achieve the objectives of the Report[223] and a working group has been set up to develop 'a communication and information strategy'.[224] Leaflets have been issued and parenting plans are being promoted. Funding, which is to be distributed in part through the National Association for Contact Centres, has been allocated to supporting mediation and sponsoring the National Children's Home website, Itsnotyourfault.[225] Moreover, the post-liberal approach to information has been dramatically adopted in a recent contact dispute, *Re H*.[226] In this case the Court of Appeal disagreed with the trial judge's view that every avenue had been explored to enable contact between the father and his child, and accordingly ordered that a consultant child psychiatrist see every member of the family.

---

[220] Lord Chancellor's Advisory Board on Family Law, above n 203, 98.

[221] *Ibid*, 98. See Lord Chancellor's Advisory Board on Family Law, 'Government's Response to the Report of the Children Act Sub-Committee of the Lord Chancellor's Advisory Board on Family Law, "Making Contact Work"' (Lord Chancellor's Department, London, 2002) 9 for concerns about this proposal.

[222] Lord Chancellor's Advisory Board on Family Law, 'Government's Response to the Report of the Children Act Sub-Committee f the Lord Chancellor's Advisory Board on Family Law, "Making Contact Work"' (Lord Chancellor's Department, London, 2002).

[223] *Ibid*, 2.

[224] *Ibid*, 4.

[225] *Ibid*, 4. See also Lord Chancellor's Department, 'Making Contact Work—Further Government Investment in Services', 6 August 2002; 'Parenting Plan: PLANNING FOR YOUR CHILDREN'S FUTURE' at www.lcd.gov.uk/family/leaflets/parentplan+english/default.htm.

[226] [2001] 1 FCR 59.

A final example is the treatment of newly unemployed lone mothers, who were originally encouraged to attend an interview to be given advice and assistance about returning to work.[227] At this stage, the proposal was not coercive: lone mothers were to be penalised neither for failing to go back to work nor even for failing to attend an interview, but merely given information about job opportunities and presumably the advantages of employment. Inevitably the post-liberal slide to coercion occurred: lone mothers were to be required to attend an interview as a condition of receiving benefit. The language used by the Secretary of State for Social Security to describe this proposal has been examined.[228] Specifically, it has been noted that he referred to the *responsibility* to take up the guidance offered in the interview and to there being *no excuse* for failing to take up the opportunity of work.[229] The almost inevitable development of the post-liberal approach to information provision has rightly been interpreted as follows:

> People are at one and the same time treated *as if* they were independent, responsible and autonomous individuals, with the freedom of choice that entails, but, because of the persuader's belief that he holds the only rational view, they are effectively denied any real choice at all.[230]

---

[227] Eekelaar, above n 22, 387–88.
[228] *Ibid*, 388.
[229] *Ibid*, 388.
[330] *Ibid*, 388.

6

Divorcing Responsibly

DIFFERENT CONCEPTIONS OF RESPONSIBILITY

URING DISCUSSION OF the Family Law Bill there was clear and uniform agreement that one of the principal aims of a civilised divorce law was to encourage responsible behaviour on divorce. However, disagreement emerged at a less abstract level: opponents of the reform argued that Part II of the Family Law Act would detract from responsible behaviour;[1] proponents responded that responsibility

---

[1] Eg Baroness Young, Hansard, House of Lords, 30 November 1995, Col 733; Baroness Young, Hansard, House of Lords, 11 January 1996, Col 325; Baroness Young, Hansard, House of Lords, 11 January 1996, Col 351; Baroness Young, Hansard, House of Lords, 22 January 1996, Col 862; Baroness Young, Hansard, House of Lords, 29 February 1996, Col 1638; Baroness Young, Hansard, House of Lords, 29 February 1996, Col 1640; Bishop of Prelate, Hansard, House of Lords, 29 February 1996, Col 1638; Lord Stoddart, Hansard, House of Lords, 29 February 1996, Col 1641; Lord Stoddart, Hansard, House of Lords, 29 February 1996, Col 1651; Lord Ashbourne, Hansard, House of Lords, 29 February 1996, Col 1642; Lord Ashbourne, Hansard, House of Lords, 30 November 1995, Col 772; Lord Ashbourne, Hansard, House of Lords, 5 July 1996, Col 1752; Lord Ashbourne, Hansard, House of Lords, 6 July 1999, Col 788; Lord Clifford, Hansard, House of Lords, 29 February 1996, Col 1662; Lord Stallard, Hansard, House of Lords, 29 February 1996, Col 1651; David Alton, Hansard, House of Commons, 17 June 1996, Col 562; Angela Rumbold, Hansard, House of Commons, 24 April 1996, Col 451; Angela Rumbold, Hansard, House of Commons, 24 April 1996, Col 469; John Patten, Hansard, House of Commons, 17 June 1996, Col 575; John Patten, Hansard, House of Commons, 25 March 1996, Col 759; Jill Knight, Hansard, House of Commons, 17 June 1996, Col 560; Edward Leigh, Hansard, House of Commons, 24 April 1996, Col 454. See also M White, 'Rebel Lords Hit Divorce Bill', *The Guardian*, 1 March 1996; M Phillips, 'Death Blow To Marriage', *The Observer*, 7 May 1995; M Phillips, 'Unhappy Families on the Marry-Go-Round', *The Observer*, 29 October 1995; Charles Colchester, quoted in S Ward, 'Ministers Plan Divorce Reform Retreat: Christian Pressure Group Thrust to Centre of Debate', *The Independent*, 1 November 1995; R Deech, 'Divorce Law and Empirical Studies', 106 *Law Quarterly Review* 229 at 243; J Gorecki, 'Moral Premises of Contemporary Divorce Laws: Western and Eastern Europe and the United States' in JM Eekelaar and SN Katz (eds), *Marriage and Cohabitation in Contemporary Societies: Areas of Legal, Social and Ethical Change: An International and Interdisciplinary Study* (Toronto, London, Butterworths, 1980) 129; A Morse, 'Fault: A Viable Means of Re-injecting Responsibility in Marital Relations', 30 *University of Richmond Law Review* 605 at 651; C Schneider, 'Moral Discourse and the Transformation of American Family Law', 83 *Michigan Law Review* 1803 at 1809.

would be enhanced.[2] For example, Baroness Young, who spearheaded opposition to the Bill in the House of Lords argued:

> The removal of fault undermines individual responsibility. By removing it, the state is actively discouraging any concept of lifelong commitment to marriage, to standards of behaviour, to self-sacrifice, to duty, to any thought for members of the family. It declares that neither party has any responsibility for the breakdown of marriage.[3]

More recently, Lord Ashbourne lamented the enactment of the Family Law Bill:

> It is fundamentally unjust that people who are victims of their spouse's betrayal or irresponsibility should be further penalised by losing their

---

[2] Eg Lord Habgood, Hansard, House of Lords, 29 February 1996, Col 1645; Lord Irvine, Hansard, House of Lords, 24 March 1999, Col 1322; Tony Blair, quoted in S Boseley and P Wintour, 'Blair Backs "Stable" Two-Parent Families', *The Guardian*, 30 March 1995; B Hoggett, 'Family Law Reform: Where Will it End?' 3 *King's College Law Journal* 64; Lord Mackay, 'Family Law Reform', 128 *Law and Justice* 3 at 9 and 10–11; Lord Mackay, quoted in L Hodgkinson, 'The Beginning of a Whole New Life Apart', *The Guardian*, 20 July 1990; Lord Mackay, quoted in C Dyer, 'Mackay Defends Move to No-Fault Divorce', *The Guardian*, 20 January 1996; Lord Mackay, Hansard, House of Lords, 30 January 1996, Col 1414; Lord Mackay, Hansard, House of Lords, 4 March 1996, Col 24; Lord Mackay, quoted in G Davis, 'The Law Can't Save Marriages', *The Independent*, 11 May 1990; Lord Mackay, Hansard, House of Lords, 30 November 1995, Col 701; Lord Mackay, Hansard, House of Lords, 30 November 1995, Col 703; Lord Mackay, Hansard, House of Lords, 11 January 1996, Cols 307; Lord Mackay, Hansard, House of Lords, 11 January 1996, Col 308; Lord Mackay, Hansard, House of Lords, 11 January 1996, Col 312; Lord Mackay, Hansard, House of Lords, 22 January 1996, Col 841; Lord Mackay, Hansard, House of Lords, 22 January 1996, Col 842; Lord Mackay, Hansard, House of Lords, 22 January 1996, Col 847; Lord Mackay, Hansard, House of Lords, 22 January 1996, Col 848; Lord Mackay, Hansard, House of Lords, 22 January 1996, Col 874; Lord Mackay, Hansard, House of Lords, 25 January 1996, Col 1116; Lord Mackay, Hansard, House of Lords, 25 January 1996, Col 1177; Lord Mackay, quoted in 'Couples to Attend Mediation', *The Times*, 7 December 1993; Chris Davies, Hansard, Commons, 17 June 1996, Col 767; Law Commission, *Facing the Future: A Discussion Paper on the Ground for Divorce* (London, HMSO, 1988) 42; Law Commission, *The Ground for Divorce* (London, HMSO, 1990) 17; Lord Chancellor's Department, *Looking to the Future: Mediation and the Ground for Divorce* (London, HMSO, 1995) vi, 10, 18, 25, 26, 31, 37, 43; Nigel Shepherd, quoted in J Copley, 'Ministers "to Join Revolt on Divorce"', *The Daily Telegraph*, 24 April 1996; Leader, 'Labour Join the Right: Divorced from Reality', *The Independent*, 29 May 1996; Baroness David, Hansard, House of Lords, 30 November 1995, Col 759; A Coote, *The Guardian*, 26 September 1990; Lord Gisborough, Hansard, House of Lords, 30 November 1995, Col 754; I M Ellman, 'The Misguided Movement to Revive Fault Divorce, and Why Reformers Should Look Instead to the American Law Institute', 11 *International Journal of Law, Policy and the Family* 216 at 229; N Lawson, 'A Cruel Divorce Trick to Play on the Children', *The Times*, 21 February 1996.

[3] Baroness Young, Hansard, House of Lords, 30 November 1995, Col 733.

children and their house simply because justice has decided to be blind to personal responsibility.[4]

This perspective was echoed by commentators outside the Houses of Parliament. For example, Melanie Phillips wrote in the Observer:

> The abolition of fault will virtually kill marriage as a concept with any legal meaning. Fault implies responsibility. Abolishing fault effectively declares that the breakdown of the marriage is no one's responsibility. Moreover, eradicating failure to meet marital obligations eradicates the obligations themselves. Duties such as staying together, being faithful to each other and treating each other reasonably exist in law only by virtue of the fault that accrues to desertion, adultery or unreasonable behaviour. Remove these faults and marriage becomes little more than the smile on the face of the Cheshire cat.[5]

But Lord Mackay replied to the argument in the following way:

> It is a mistake to believe that the present law underlines in any way the idea of responsibility by the use of fault in the ground for divorce. Using fault as a basis for divorce enables a quick exit from marriage, leaving the responsibilities of that marriage behind. Under the new system, couples will consider the responsibilities of their marriage in the period of reflection and consideration. I believe that this new emphasis on couples addressing their responsibilities prior to divorce communicates a clear message about marriage which is not there in the present system, namely that marriage is not to be treated lightly and that the ending of a marriage in divorce is not a trivial matter.[6]

Lord Habgood directly attributed the enhancement of responsibility to the introduction of the period of reflection:

> . . . time is important not just for what can be done in it − . . . Time is important also as a public assertion that marriages are not easily undone. . . . To take time over something is to take a measure of responsibility. . . . the undoing of marriage . . . is a serious business which takes time and reflection and requires the acceptance of responsibility for what is done.[7]

In this approach, the Lords were adopting the tone set by the preceding Government papers. For example, the 1995 White Paper suggested that:

[4] Lord Ashbourne, Hansard, House of Lords, 6 July 1999, Col 788.
[5] Phillips, 'Death blow', above n 1.
[6] Lord Mackay, Hansard, House of Lords, 30 November 1995, Col 701. See also Lord Mackay, quoted in Dyer, above n 2.
[7] Lord Habgood, Hansard, House of Lords, 29 February 1996, Col 1645.

The benefits of these proposals are that they will: . . . encourage couples to meet the responsibilities of marriage and parenthood before the marriage is dissolved.[8] . . . any move towards encouraging and helping couples to take joint responsibility for the breakdown in the marriage and the consequences that flow from it, would be a positive step.[9]

This contrasting attitude to responsibility also found support from outside Parliament:

[The divorce proposals] are designed to ensure that one party cannot simply walk away from the marriage without addressing his (or her) responsibilities to the children or the other spouse.[10]

Given that both sides of the debate believed that responsibility was desirable, a plausible hypothesis is that the disagreement lay in contrasting conceptions of what constitutes responsible behaviour.[11] In particular, it has been suggested that when post-liberals, specifically communitarians, believe that liberals do not emphasise responsibility, it may be because post-liberals and liberals have different conceptions of responsibility.[12] In the last chapter I suggested that the reason that Conservative rebels opposed Part II of the Family Law Bill was that they had never been converted to the post-liberal conception of responsibility.[13] In this chapter I take up this suggestion to argue that opponents of Part II of the Family Law Act, though conservative, were hanging on to a liberal conception of responsibility which is increasingly falling out of favour;[14] the Family Law Act implemented the more fashionable post-liberal conception of responsibility.

In chapter four we saw that the moral distinction is no longer between divorce and marriage but is now between good marriage or divorce and bad marriage or divorce, so that a divorcee who divorces

---

[8] Lord Chancellor's Department, above n 2, v–vi. See also Lord Chancellor's Department, above n 2, 29.

[9] *Ibid*, 31. See also Law Commission, Ground for Divorce, above n 2, 11.

[10] Hoggett, above n 2, 76.

[11] On different meanings of responsibility generally, see J Lucas, *Responsibility* (Oxford, Oxford University Press, 1995), especially 5; J Eekelaar, 'Parental Responsibility: State of Nature or Nature of the State', 1 *Journal of Social Welfare and Family Law* 37; L McClain, 'Rights and Irresponsibility', 43 *Duke Law Journal* 989.

[12] McClain, above n 11, 994; R Eckstein, 'Towards a Communitarian Theory of Responsibility: Bearing the Burden for the Unintended', 45 *University of Miami Law Review* 843 at 896.

[13] Pp 178–79.

[14] C Taylor, 'What is Human Agency?' in T Mischel (ed), *The Self: Psychological and Philosophical Issues* (Oxford, Blackwell, 1977) 129–30.

well may exit his or her marriage with enhanced moral standing. It follows that, while divorcing responsibly would have been an oxymoron in any previous era, it is now a distinct possibility. In this chapter, I begin by drawing out what responsible divorce entails. I then examine post-liberal conceptions of responsibility, which emerge out of the post-liberal conception of autonomy. Towards the end of the chapter, I turn to the implications that procedural responsibility holds, both for divorce law and more generally. In essence, this chapter spells out the implication from the book that responsible divorce is a procedural not a substantive achievement.

THE RESPONSIBLE POST-LIBERAL SUBJECT

The post-liberal subject is able to be neither fully responsible nor fully irresponsible, because there is no action that he or she must take or refrain from taking in order to be responsible. Instead, he or she exhibits the degree of responsibility that he or she has reached by his or her attitude towards his or her actions. The responsible post-liberal subject is judged not by what he or she does but by how he or she approaches his or her actions.

The liberal view of responsibility was clear-cut; there just were certain actions that one should or should not take:

> . . . good behaviour is simple. It is about easy things. The choice may be difficult but the distinction is easy. Stealing is wrong; lying is wrong; telling the truth is right.[15]

This is no longer the case. Instead:

> . . . psychological man must learn not to judge himself, his relationships, or other people according to moral rules; to do so is dysfunctional . . .[16]

Post-liberal responsibility is no longer about discrete decisions; responsible behaviour has become a way of being, a mode of thought;

[15] Lord Elton, Hansard, House of Lords, 12 November 1996, Col 918. For discussion, see C Smart and B Neale, 'Good Enough Morality? Divorce and Postmodernity', 17 *Critical Social Policy* 3 at 4. For examples of the liberal view of responsibility, see Law Commission, 'Reform of the Grounds of Divorce, The Field of Choice' (London, HMSO, 1966); Lucas, above n 11; J Gorecki, 'Moral Premises of Contemporary Divorce Laws: Western and Eastern Europe and the United States' in Eekelaar and Katz, above n 1, especially 129; Deech, above n 1, 243.

[16] Schneider, above n 1, 1848. See also A Etzioni, *The New Golden Rule: Community and Morality in a Democratic Society* (New York, Basic Books, 1998) 135–36.

the focus has shifted from the content of the decision to the process of making the decision. For example, faced with the decision whether to tell a lie, the responsible person is no longer necessarily the one who tells the truth. Now, he or she shows his or her responsibility by the attitude with which he or she approaches the decision and the extent to which he or she reflects on the implications of what he or she chooses. The person who tells the truth without ado is less responsible than the person who lies after having considered the consequences of different courses, learning some important lessons about honesty, and of course about himself or herself, from the experience. An even more responsible person would realise that to tell the truth is complex, perhaps impossible, since it involves understanding ourselves first; he or she would understand that we neither tell the truth nor lie but rather tell the degree of truth of which we are capable:

> In this sense, the very notion of honesty is redefined, because the basis for honesty becomes one's willingness to be in touch with and to express one's feelings. It is not honesty in the sense of truthfulness to an objectively measured empirical reality or an external worldview that enjoins the individual to hold certain things as true and adjust his or her behavior accordingly; nor is it the honesty of intellectual deference to reason or even, in some instances, to conventional protocol.[17]

It has been argued that the new form of responsibility is evident in 'the talk shows . . . which pervade daytime television':[18]

> To be sure, audiences generally contain censorious members. But at least as common – I would say more common – are people who rise to urge the danger of value judgments, the virtues of tolerance, the merits of nonconformity, the power of environmental forces and psychological drives, and the benefits of therapy . . . much of the time their implicit and often explicit position is that 'lifestyles' are matters of personal choice, that criticism of such choices is at least presumptuous and possibly perilous, and that conflict is best resolved therapeutically. . . . [The] experts are . . . professionally committed to avoiding moral discourse. The closest they come to making moral distinctions is when they criticize the audience for judging the guests.[19]

The shift in the meaning of responsibility has exerted a profound impact on family life. It has been argued that because people no longer

---

[17] J Nolan, *The Therapeutic State: Justifying Government at Century's End* (New York, New York University Press, 1998) 6.

[18] C Schneider, 'Marriage, Morals and the Law', 1994 *Utah Law Review* 503 at 548.

[19] *Ibid*, 548. See also M A Glendon, *Abortion and Divorce in Western Law* (Cambridge, Massachusetts, Harvard University Press, 1987) 108.

follow rigid life patterns, and our biographies are no longer pre-given, new types of relationships have supplanted fixed models. Accordingly, a focus on family practices, or doing family, is more instructive than a focus on the following of rules.[20] A recent study of family responsibilities found that even in relation to parent-child responsibilities, interviewees felt that there were no clear rules about what to do. The researchers made a distinction between such rules, which they referred to as substantive issues, and guidelines that indicate how to work out the proper thing to do, or procedural issues. They suggested that in practice people operate with a concept of family obligation that is much more fluid than is implied by the idea of moral rules. This led them to highlight the importance of looking at relationships between people in the context of the family relationships as a whole and at exchanges of assistance as a two-way process. They concluded that their data showed a higher level of agreement over procedures than over the substance of obligations:[21]

> In focusing on the moral dimensions of relationships between kin, we are emphasising the 'how' rather than the 'what' of family life. We are suggesting that *the way* in which one individual interacts with another is just as important – and can be more important – than the substance of the goods and services which they exchange.[22]

People recognised guidelines about how to work out whether it was appropriate to offer assistance to a relative, rather than guidelines that pointed to what to do in concrete terms.[23]

A good illustration of the shift in meaning of responsibility in the specific context of the parent-child relationship is Tony Blair's response to his son's arrest, coupled with the media reaction to the incident. In July 2000, the Prime Minister's 16-year-old son, Euan, was arrested for being drunk and incapable, after police officers found him lying on the ground in Leicester Square. Euan also gave the police a false name, age and address. Five days after the incident, Euan's

---

[20] E Silva and C Smart, 'The "New" Practices and Politics of Family Life' in E Silva and C Smart (eds), *The New Family?* (London, Sage, 1999) 4; D Morgan, 'Risk and Family Practices: Accounting for Change and Fluidity in Family Life' in E Silva and C Smart (eds), *The New Family?* (London, Sage, 1999) 28–29.

[21] J Finch and J Mason, *Negotiating Family Responsibilities* (London, Tavistock / Routledge, 1993).

[22] *Ibid*, 129.

[23] *Ibid*, 166.

headteacher told the *Sunday Telegraph* that it was the responsibility of parents to prevent teenage drinking:

> . . . in the way that adults, parents and society generally exercise responsibility in these areas. That's to be aware of the fact that it's happening and to try to ensure that children don't start drinking too early and that when they do they understand the effects of alcohol and learn to use it responsibly.[24]

This isolated and oblique suggestion that Tony Blair had lacked responsibility as a father was universally condemned.[25] Tony Blair's own verdict on the incident, given in a speech at the Faith in the Future conference the day after Euan's arrest, was far more in tune with current notions of parental responsibility:

> The values you represent are the values we all share. Respect, tolerance, the family, trying to bring up children properly. . . . Being a Prime Minister can be a tough job, but I always think that being a parent is probably tougher. Sometimes you don't always succeed, but to me the family is more important than anything else.[26]

In this passage, Tony Blair showed that he understood that being a good parent did not mean succeeding but did mean trying hard; he demonstrated that he was aware that parenting was both arduous and crucial. He revealed awareness that it was neither how he acted as a parent nor what decisions he made in his capacity as a parent that determined his level of responsibility. Rather, his success as a parent depended on his attitude. The following description from a journalist indicates that Tony Blair was successful in demonstrating that his attitude was responsible: 'Honest, contrite and above all extremely emotional, the Prime Minister gave possibly the most personal speech of his career.'[27] In the resulting media coverage, Tony Blair was universally praised for having rightly realised that the virtues of parenting were procedural not substantive, one commentator confirming that

[24] John McIntosh, quoted in C Milmo, 'Head Accused of Playing Politics Over Euan Blair', *The Independent*, 10 July 2000.

[25] See *ibid*.

[26] Tony Blair, quoted in P Waugh, 'Honest, Contrite and Above All Emotional, Blair Faces Up to the Morning After the Night Before', *The Independent*, 7 July 2000. See also 'Blair's Son Says Sorry After "Drunk and Incapable" Arrest', *The Guardian*, 6 July 2000; BBC News, 'Blair's Son "Drunk and Incapable"', www.bbc.co.uk/news, 6 July 2000; N Watt, 'Emotional PM Talks of Faith and Family', *The Guardian*, 7 July 2000; M White and N Watt, 'Blair Shows Strain After Son's Arrest', *The Guardian*, 7 July 2000; A Grice and P Waugh, 'Being a Prime Minister Can be Tough, But Being a Parent is Sometimes Tougher', *The Independent*, 7 July 2000.

[27] Waugh, above n 26.

'[t]he only real skills of value are compassion, openness and emotional literacy.'[28] The stance adopted by Tony Blair and the media echoed that adopted two and a half years earlier, when William Straw, the 17-year-old son of Jack Straw, then Home Secretary, was cautioned for dealing cannabis. Jack Straw commented:

> William is now learning the lessons of this episode and he has of course my full support in doing so.[29]

BBC News delivered the general media verdict on the incident, which was that Jack Straw had 'won admiration for his honest approach to the family crisis.'[30]

Another recent study found that the absence of predetermined obligations was more pronounced in same-sex relationships than heterosexual relationships because they are constructed and maintained outside conventional institutional systems, but this study otherwise replicated the findings of the study mentioned above:

> Within this sort of ethos, terms such as duty or obligation tended to be avoided by our subjects, having, as one gay man said, 'a negative connotation'... Duty is 'like some kind of moral code that people use to put on you. ... I don't think I need that kind of external thing put on me'... These terms were compared unfavourably with the concepts of responsibility and mutual care and commitment.[31]

There is some support in this body of research for the view that the term 'responsibility' is being successfully redefined by the post-liberal camp. The researchers in the first study mentioned regarded the word 'responsibility' as more appropriate for procedural considerations than 'obligations' or 'duties', since 'responsibility' seemed to imply more fluidity than the latter terms.[32] Above all, this body of research certainly supports the assertion that the premise of family life is increasingly that 'the vessel of family shouldn't be filled with substantive moral content.'[33]

---

[28] R Coward, 'Kids and Kidology', *The Observer*, 9 July 2000.

[29] *BBC News*, 'Cabinet Minister's Son Cautioned', www.bbc.co.uk/news, 12 January 1998.

[30] *BBC News*, 'A History of Christmas Scandal Past', www.bbc.co.uk/news, 22 December 1998.

[31] J Weeks *et al*, 'Everyday Experiments: Narratives of Non-Heterosexual Relationships' in Silva and Smart, above n 20, 95.

[32] Finch and Mason, above n 21, 166.

[33] MC Regan, *Family Law and the Pursuit of Intimacy* (New York, New York University Press, 1993) 2.

For the first time ever, it is possible to divorce responsibly. Indeed, the White Paper informed us that:

> The Government is encouraged by the recent research which demonstrates that increasing numbers of couples are seeking to dissolve their marriage as responsibly as is possible.[34]

However, in referring to responsible divorce, the legislature was thinking in terms of post-liberal responsibility. It was clear from the language used in the Family Law Act debates to describe responsibility that being responsible was an attitude that existed along a continuum, rather than a quality that the divorcee either had or lacked. Specifically, the divorcee was exhorted to adopt the following approaches to responsibility: have a sense of,[35] address,[36] consider,[37] carefully consider,[38] undertake,[39] take,[40] take into account,[41] take seriously,[42] recognise,[43] acknowledge,[44] face,[45] face up to,[46] face up

---

[34] Lord Chancellor's Department, above n 2, 43.

[35] Lord Simon, Hansard, House of Lords, 29 February 1996, Col 1660; Tony Blair, quoted in Boseley and Wintour, above n 2.

[36] Lord Mackay, 'Family Law', above n 2, 9; Hoggett, above n 2.

[37] Lord Mackay, 'Family Law', above n 2, 10–11.

[38] Lord Mackay, Hansard, House of Lords, 22 January 1996, Col 875; Lord Mackay, Hansard, House of Lords, 23 January 1996, Col 956.

[39] Lord Mackay, Hansard, House of Lords, 4 March 1996, Col 24.

[40] Law Commission, *Facing the Future*, above n 2, 42; Lord Chancellor's Department, *Looking to the Future: Mediation and the Ground for Divorce* (London, HMSO, 1993) 17; Lord Chancellor's Department, above n 2, 10, 31 and 43; Nigel Shepherd, quoted in Copley, above n 2; Leader, above n 2.

[41] Lord Mackay, Hansard, House of Lords, 25 January 1996, Col 1177.

[42] Lord Mackay, quoted in Hodgkinson, above n 2.

[43] Law Commission, *Ground for Divorce*, above n 2, 17.

[44] Lord Chancellor's Department, above n 2, 43; Lord Chancellor's Department, above n 40, 17.

[45] Lord Mackay, Hansard, House of Lords, 22 January 1996, Col 841; Lord Mackay, Hansard, House of Lords, 22 January 1996, Col 847; Lord Mackay, Hansard, House of Lords, 25 January 1996, Col 1177; Lord Mackay, quoted in 'Couples to Attend Mediation', *The Times*, 7 December 1993; Chris Davies, Hansard, House of Commons, 17 June 1996, Col 767; Baroness Young, Hansard, House of Lords, 11 March 1996, Col 666; Lord Chancellor's Department, above n 2, v.

[46] Lord Mackay, Hansard, House of Lords, 11 January 1996, Col 308; Lord Mackay, Hansard, House of Lords, 11 January 1996, Col 312; Lord Mackay, Hansard, House of Lords, 22 January 1996, Col 841; Lord Mackay, Hansard, House of Lords, 22 January 1996, Col 842; Lord Mackay, Hansard, House of Lords, 22 January 1996, Col 847; Lord Mackay, Hansard, House of Lords, 22 January 1996, Col 848; Lord Mackay, Hansard,

fully to,[47] have regard to,[48] look to,[49] share,[50] accept,[51] meet,[52] deal with,[53] fulfil[54] and discharge.[55]

We have seen that the ways in which the divorcee is supposed to adopt these approaches to responsibility are by reflecting deeply,[56] taking time[57] and learning his or her lesson.[58] Baroness Scotland aptly summed up the Family Law Act as trying 'to put the emphasis back on conciliation, preparation and thought.'[59] More generally, it has been rightly recognised that modern family law is increasingly performing an expressive function, concerned to 'radiate messages'[60] and designed to influence behaviour in a general rather than detailed way:

> . . . recent legislation on divorce . . . is best understood as setting out general aspirations on how to divorce well: adults should be reasonable, self-denying, conciliatory, and fully conscious of the implications of their actions for themselves and for others.[61]

As we have seen, while people still marry with a sense of commitment, the commitment is no longer to permanence; rather the commitment is the procedural one of *trying to make the marriage work*. The new

House of Lords, 22 January 1996, Col 874; Lord Mackay, Hansard, House of Lords, 25 January 1996, Col 1176; Lord Mackay, Hansard, House of Lords, 25 January 1996, Col 1177; Lord Mackay, Hansard, House of Lords, 30 January 1996, Col 1414; Lord Mackay, Hansard, House of Lords, 4 March 1996, Col 24; Lord Mackay, quoted in Davis, above n 2.

[47] Lord Mackay, Hansard, House of Lords, 25 January 1996, Col 1176.

[48] Lord Simon, Hansard, House of Lords, 11 March 1996, Col 637.

[49] Lord Chancellor's Department, above n 2, 18 and 43.

[50] Baroness David, Hansard, House of Lords, 30 November 1995, Col 759; Lord Chancellor's Department, above n 40, 39; Coote, above n 2.

[51] Lord Habgood, Hansard, House of Lords, 29 February 1996, Col 1645; Lord Chancellor's Department, above n 2, 37; Lord Chancellor's Department, above n 40, 41.

[52] Law Commission, *Ground for Divorce*, above n 2, 17; Lord Chancellor's Department, above n 2, vi and 26.

[53] Lord Mackay, Hansard, House of Lords, 4 March 1996, Col 24.

[54] Lord Mackay, Hansard, House of Lords, 30 November 1995, Col 701; Lord Mackay, 'Family Law', above n 2, 3; Lord Chancellor's Department, above n 2, 25.

[55] Lord Mackay, Hansard, House of Lords, 30 November 1995, Col 703.

[56] See ch 2.

[57] See ch 3.

[58] See ch 4.

[59] Baroness Scotland, Hansard, House of Lords, 6 July 1999, Col 788.

[60] J Dewar, 'The Normal Chaos of Family Law', 61 *Modern Law Review* 467 at 483. See also J Dewar, 'Family Law and Its Discontents', 14 *International Journal of Law, Policy and the Family* 59 at 69.

[61] Dewar, 'Chaos', above n 60, 483. See also J Dewar and S Parker, 'English Family Law since World War II: From Status to Chaos' in S Katz *et al* (eds.), *Cross Currents: Family Law and Policy in the United States and England* (New York, Oxford University Press, 2000) 139; Dewar, 'Discontents', above n 60, 68.

marriage has its own new procedural obligations: a concern for permanence and personal virtue has been replaced by the new virtues of honesty, communication and tolerance.[62] Empirical research has confirmed the primacy of these obligations. When interviewed, American married couples insisted on 'the 'obligation' to communicate one's wishes and feelings honestly and to attempt to deal with problems in the relationship.'[63] In contrast, they had few ideas of substantive obligations that could develop between partners in a relationship.[64] The only substantive morality that was acceptable was that whatever the couple agreed to was right:[65]

> As long as there were strict commandments and prohibitions regulating married life and the daily routine, it was fairly obvious to everyone what was correct, pleasing to God and natural. Why bother with big words, complicated questions and long explanations? Each spouse knew the rules and also knew that the other one knew them. (Even those who chose to disobey knew what they were doing: they were violating custom and moral attitudes and rebelling against the norms.) In this respect there has been a fundamental transformation in recent decades, and especially in recent years. The fewer firm regulations there are, the more we are expected to work them out for ourselves, asking 'What's right and what's wrong?' and 'What do you want and what do I want?' and 'What should we do?'.[66]

Crucially, the procedural nature of the new obligations does not weaken their force, a good example of their strength being the following stricture:

> . . . it is a fundamental moral obligation to seek marital therapy when marital distress is serious enough to threaten the marriage. We need a cultural ethic that would make it just as irresponsible to terminate a marriage without seeking professional help as it would be to let someone die without seeking a physician.[67]

[62] Schneider, above n 18; U Beck and E Beck-Gernsheim, *The Normal Chaos of Love* (Cambridge, Polity Press, 1995) 171.

[63] RN Bellah *et al*, *Habits of the Heart: Individualism and Commitment in American Life* (Berkeley, California, University of California Press, 1985) 109. See also J Weeks *et al*, 'Everyday Experiments: Narratives of Non-Heterosexual Relationships' in Silva and Smart, above n 20, 93.

[64] Bellah, above n 63, 109.

[65] *Ibid*, 139. See also Glendon, above n 19, 108; J Weeks *et al*, 'Everyday Experiments: Narratives of Non-Heterosexual Relationships' in Silva and Smart, above n 20.

[66] Beck and Beck-Gernsheim, above n 62, 91.

[67] W Doherty, 'How Therapists Threaten Marriages' in A Etzioni (ed), *The Essential Communitarian Reader* (Lanham, Rowman & Littlefield, 1998) 164–65.

Clearly, the total removal of fault from the divorce process both implies and is implied by post-liberal responsibility: if no actions are prescribed or proscribed then there can be no substantive basis for divorce. The emphasis on mediation is also consistent with the new form of responsibility, since mediation requires the adoption of an attitude rather than any particular decision. It is of the essence in mediation that responsibility remains with the parties themselves and that the role of the mediator is simply to assist them.[68] According to the White Paper, mediation could encourage couples to take responsibility for the breakdown of their marriage and accept responsibility for the ending of their marriage.[69]

This shift in the meaning of responsible divorce has been documented in the etiquette literature. In essence, 'propriety no longer takes the form of right conduct but of good explanations.'[70] Psychological norms have replaced social norms, and therapeutic correctness has become the new standard of good behaviour.[71] This trend is particularly strong when it comes to divorces involving children. While a concern about the effect of divorce on children is constant, the solution has shifted from preserving the marriage for the sake of children to instructions about how best to tell the children about the divorce.[72]

POST-LIBERAL RESPONSIBILITY

Post-liberal rejection of the liberal conception of responsibility stems from the same roots as post-liberal rejection of liberal autonomy. The reason is that according to the liberal conception of responsibility we are entitled to hold someone responsible for his or her actions only if he or she could have chosen otherwise. However, as we saw in chapter two, according to post-liberals, he or she could have chosen otherwise only if the choice had no causal antecedents, and they believe that in order to

---

[68] S Cretney, *Elements of Family Law* 2nd edn (London, Sweet & Maxwell, 1992) 60–62; C Piper, 'Divorce Conciliation in the United Kingdom: How Responsible Are Parents?', 16 *International Journal of Sociology of Law* 477 at 478.

[69] Lord Chancellor's Department, above n 2, 43. See also Lord Chancellor's Department, above n 2, 37–38.

[70] BD Whitehead, *The Divorce Culture: Rethinking Our Commitments to Marriage and the Family* (New York, Knopf, 1997) 69.

[71] *Ibid*, 69.

[72] *Ibid*, 69. For an exception, see W Galston, 'A Liberal-Democratic Case for the Two-Parent Family' in Etzioni, above n 67, 146.

avoid recursion the choice must rest on wants that are ultimately the product of circumstances.[73] Accordingly, the agent is merely matching his or her pre-existing desires to the best means of achieving them and cannot be described as acting responsibly. Because our insights are limited by our experience, failure to understand a certain insight or see the point of some moral advice can be described as irresponsible only if we are attributing responsibility to people in relation to outcomes that they cannot presently avoid.[74] Post-liberals suggest that liberal responsibility is similarly unable to cope with the role that character plays in grounding responsibility. For instance, if someone steals because he or she has a greedy character then he or she is not freely exercising his or her will and so cannot be held responsible in the liberal sense.[75]

As with the post-liberal problem of autonomy, once liberal responsibility has been questioned, the main task becomes to develop a post-liberal conception of responsibility. Perhaps unsurprisingly, a version of the most coherent post-liberal account of autonomy, namely cognitive autonomy, accomplishes this task most coherently as well. Since we can discover our character through deep thought, responsibility falls to us in the sense that fresh insight might alter our evaluations of ourselves for the better. Within the limits of our capacity to change our decisions by fresh insight, we are responsible in the post-liberal sense.[76] Therefore, the only abstract and unconditional responsibility is to monitor who we are becoming, in other words to pay attention to ourselves, and this responsibility does not require any particular action in any particular situation.[77]

In essence, consistently with breaking the link between choice and autonomy, post-liberals also break the link between choice and responsibility, clearly essential in the liberal mindset. Indeed, the importance of character means that, from an Aristotelian perspective, linking choice with responsibility seems not obvious but decidedly odd:

---

[73] P 56.

[74] C Taylor, 'What is Human Agency?' in Mischel, above n 14, 129–30. For discussion, see R Phillips, *Putting Asunder: A History of Divorce in Western Society* (Cambridge, Cambridge University Press, 1989) 566; J Gorecki, 'Moral Premises of Contemporary Divorce Laws: Western and Eastern Europe and the United States' in Eekelaar and Katz, above n 1, 127; Schneider, above n 1, 1853.

[75] M Dan-Cohen, 'Responsibility and the Boundaries of the Self', 105 *Harvard Law Review* 959 at 973.

[76] C Taylor, 'What is Human Agency?' in Mischel, above n 14, 129–30.

[77] V Davion, 'Integrity and Radical Change' in C Card (ed), *Feminist Ethics* (Lawrence, Kansas, University Press of Kansas, 1991) 186.

Surely, the Aristotelian will say, it is a mark of the supremely good person
that his or her character has been so formed by training in and exercise of
the virtues that he or she often could not do or be other than virtuous in his
or her choices and actions.[78] . . . the present state of my judgments, feelings
and thoughts is the outcome of my whole moral history. I am what my past
has made me. Accountability as well as moral substance involves this kind
of reference to the past. For whether I ought to be held accountable now is
always in part a matter of whether I did in the past take appropriate steps to
make myself what I ought to be now or not. The famous example of the
drunk man who may not be able to control his actions now, but can be held
to be accountable for them, if it was in his power not to get drunk at the
appropriate time, needs to be generalized to cases extending over long
periods of time, indeed through the whole of each individual life. The question, that is, of what it is in my power to do cannot be answered except by
inspecting what may be the whole of my moral history. Take away that history and the identity that it presupposes, and there is only the semblance of
a moral agent left.[79]

The most coherent conception of post-liberal autonomy, cognitive
autonomy, has been translated into a post-liberal conception of
responsibility, namely the constitutive paradigm of responsibility.[80]
Since this paradigm weakens the connection between choice and
responsibility, it contrasts itself with responsibility based on choice,
described as the free will paradigm of responsibility:[81]

Whereas the free will paradigm treats responsibility as a matter of what we
choose to do, the constitutive paradigm treats responsibility as a matter of
what and who we are.[82]

According to this theory, the constitutive paradigm does not so much
conflict with the free will paradigm as include the free will paradigm,
since different forms of responsibility draw on different elements of the
self. Volition is one element in our conception of the self, but not
the only element, so volition is one ground of responsibility, but not the
only ground. Accordingly, volitional responsibility is a special case of
constitutive responsibility.[83] Like questions of autonomy under the
model of cognitive autonomy, the constitutive paradigm enables us to

[78] A MacIntyre, 'How Moral Agents Became Ghosts or Why the History of Ethics
Diverged from That of the Philosophy of Mind', 53 *Synthese* 295 at 309.
[79] *Ibid*, 310.
[80] Dan-Cohen, above n 75.
[81] *Ibid*, 960.
[82] *Ibid*, 961.
[83] *Ibid*, 961.

reinterpret disputes about the ascription of responsibility as involving a negotiation over the self's boundaries.[84] So when we assume responsibility for having broken a vase, for example, we perform an act of self-constitution; we identify with some aspect of ourselves by which we are the vase-breaker. This identification is not of course a free and conscious choice but is more likely to take the form of an uncontrollable emotion, for example, shame.[85] This interpretation allows us to affirm responsibility for our will or our character by accepting them as a constituent of our self. Within this paradigm it does not matter that our will or character is not free in the sense of undetermined, because responsibility is validated not by the reality of the choice but by the reality of our identification with the choice.[86]

In chapter two, we saw that a version of cognitive autonomy represented the predominant feminist response to the problem of autonomy.[87] In relation to responsibility, the same pattern emerges. Hoagland's theory of lesbian agency under oppression bears many similarities to the communitarian conceptions of responsibility considered above.[88] She too wants to move away from a rule-bound approach that tells lesbians what to do and reassures them that they did the right thing, no matter what the consequences, and describes the rule-bound approach as patriarchal ethics, which she argues lesbians neglected to challenge when they challenged patriarchal politics.[89] We saw in chapter one that feminists are wary of accepting women's actions as truly autonomous because they are the products of social experiences that are at least partly the cause of male superiority. But we also saw that feminists are concerned to keep some notion of agency in order to retain the possibility of liberating women.[90] Consistently, Hoagland's theory sets out to keep some link between choice and responsibility while entirely breaking the link between blame and responsibility.[91] She argues that if we focus on questions of praise or blame among the oppressed, we are caught between the extremes of blaming the victim

[84] Dan-Cohen, above n 75, 961.

[85] *Ibid*, 969.

[86] *Ibid*, 975.

[87] Pp 63–66.

[88] SL Hoagland, *Lesbian Ethics: Toward New Value* (Palo Alto, California, Institute of Lesbian Studies, 1988); SL Hoagland, 'Why *Lesbian* Ethics?' in C Card (ed), *Adventures in Lesbian Philosophy* (Bloomington, Indiana University Press, 1994).

[89] SL Hoagland, 'Why *Lesbian* Ethics?' in Card, above n 88, 206.

[90] P 29.

[91] SL Hoagland, 'Why *Lesbian* Ethics?' in Card, above n 88, 206.

and victimisation. At one extreme, no account is taken of the context of oppression, so that the victim is blamed not just for her choices but for the whole situation, an example being the belief that women invite rape. At the other extreme, although lesbians can legitimately argue that they cannot be blamed because they are oppressed, this is not helpful because they need to carry on making choices, and this argument leads to their being seen as incapable of doing so.[92] The middle road of blaming lesbians but recognising excuses based on their oppression is also unsatisfactory because it fails to acknowledge that all their decisions are coerced.[93] Therefore:

> Moral accountability as we understand it – centrally focused on 'praise' and 'blame' – does not present us with a viable concept of choice under oppression.[94]

Breaking the link between blame and responsibility, rather than between choice and responsibility, is of course the direct form in which post-liberal responsibility was implemented in the Family Law Act.

For Hoagland, the problem cannot be solved by developing a more sophisticated treatment of praise and blame but only by moving away from these notions entirely. This is partly because of the context of oppression, just discussed. It is also because, as we saw in chapter three, Hoagland's theory adopts a form of relationship-based autonomy, which she describes as autokoenony.[95] Blame is inconsistent with autokoenony because it keeps the focus firmly on one party and away from the interactive nature of the situation, promoting individualism and an attribution of total responsibility, rather than a recognition that everyone involved has some degree of agency. In particular, it allows lesbians to justify their behaviour, rather than facing up to the part that they played in the scenario:

> If I am accountable to you, then the idea is that you judge me on your own terms. If you are accountable to me, then I judge you on my terms.[96] . . . We demand of each other that we be accountable, and yet that demand smacks of expecting someone to stand before a judge and jury to be found guilty or innocent. This, again, involves the perspective of one who has the power to

---

[92] Hoagland, above n 88, 211–12. See also McClain, above n 11; Etzioni, above n 16, 137.

[93] Hoagland, above n 88, 211–12.

[94] *Ibid*, 215.

[95] P 97.

[96] Hoagland, above n 88, 227.

excuse, a judge. It suggests a lesbian must justify her behavior and gain our approval. It requires the illusion of impartial observers. And it encourages us to separate her behavior from ours and so not examine our part. Accountability invites all the pitfalls of focusing on praise and blame which I've been discussing.[97]

When Hoagland turns to the question of what should replace praise, blame and accountability, the close connection between her theory and that of cognitive autonomy becomes even clearer. She suggests that we should place the notion of intelligibility at the centre of moral agency.[98] Hoagland distinguishes firmly between intelligibility, which involves an attempt to clarify, and justification, which involves an attempt to absolve. With intelligibility:

> The idea is not that we make no mistakes or that we never hurt another; the idea is that we understand the full dynamics of our interactions.[99] . . . I am simply suggesting that as we make judgments regarding each other, we focus, not on an antagonistic process of another justifying herself on my terms or of me justifying myself on her terms – the process of judges – but rather on a process that involves both an ability to explain and an ability to understand.[100]

Because intelligibility is founded on being able to explain our choices, intelligibility depends crucially on the post-liberal virtues of self-understanding and self-examination.[101]

Intelligibility seems to involve not just self-understanding but also willingness to work at understanding other lesbians' choices, especially those that we disagree with. But on closer inspection, in Hoagland's theory as in the discussion in chapter three, duties to others are subordinated to duties to the self. Hoagland explains that we try to understand other lesbians' choices as a route to understanding our part in their choices and how such choices are or could be our own. Hoagland is quite clear that at least part of the point of understanding others is that we thereby gain a better understanding of ourselves, by understanding how we could have made any number of the choices that they have made:

[97] Hoagland, above n 88, 221.
[98] *Ibid.* See also McClain, above n 11, 453.
[99] Hoagland, above n 88, 223.
[100] *Ibid,* 228.
[101] *Ibid,* 223.

Within ethics we lean more toward labeling someone a liar, for example, and less toward understanding the process and interaction of lying. When we talk about 'liars', we focus more on one who has the character of a liar, who is essentially through and through a liar. As a result, when we've been lied to, we are less tempted to ask whether we realized we were being lied to, and if not, what that means. We are less likely to ask what our part was in the lying. Our concern more often is to define and fix what she is. Yet understanding another's choices includes understanding our part in them.[102]

Clearly, Hoagland's theory is also consistent with the general outline of the post-liberal responsible subject given near the beginning of the chapter.[103] For her, the responsible person is certainly not necessarily the one who tells the truth but is the one who best understands the dynamics and complexities of the process of lying and being lied to.

Intelligibility also fits better with autokoenony than does blame, because intelligibility is a two-way process, held together by cooperation:

Within the framework of intelligibility . . . if you are trying to explain something to me, I try to situate myself in such a way that your choices become intelligible to me. Intelligibility involves both of us trying to reach each other, to connect, at some level.[104]

The concept of lesbian moral agency focuses on judgements in the realm of intelligibility not accountability because such a focus is founded on cooperation not antagonism.[105]

So within post-liberalism what we do is less important than how we feel about it. In professing a value we do not acknowledge an objective demand but rather say something about the shape that we have given our life. The connection with substantive conduct is not entirely lost because there is an 'ironic caveat': one cannot have self-esteem if one is behaving dysfunctionally according to community standards, the assumption being that if we value ourselves then we will behave as society expects us to behave.[106] Conversely, if we criticise the conduct of others then their self-esteem will be further diminished, which in turn

---

[102] *Ibid*, 224.

[103] Pp 209–10.

[104] Hoagland, above n 88, 227.

[105] *Ibid*. For a similar account, see V Davion, 'Integrity and Radical Change' in Card, above n 77.

[106] For discussion, see J Purdy, 'Age of Irony', 39 *The American Prospect* 84; Glendon, above n 19, 108; Nolan, above n 17, 172.

will further undermine their conduct.[107] The coercive consequences of attributing people's bad behaviour to low self-esteem and then equating high self-esteem with conformity to the values of a post-liberal society are plain. They can be added to the inexorable drive to coercion that we have witnessed throughout this book:

> . . . self-esteem programs further the communitarian agenda. They bring together groups of individuals, led by professionals 'expert' at making us feel good. They encourage us to tolerate and support one another, punishing only cynics and doomsayers with public disapproval. They seem to impose no rules but in fact seek, through the pressures of group opinion and the authority of scientific expertise, to shape our conduct and character along communitarian lines.[108]
>
> What matters is not that we construct a paradise of equality and authenticity, but that we constantly strive to do so. Indeed, paradise in a significant sense consists, for communitarians, of the collective pursuit of paradise. It is only in striving that we can assert ourselves and find within ourselves the capacities and talents that make us unique and allow us to flourish . . .[109]

Within post-liberal theory, the fact that we are the products of our decisions has necessitated a shift in the meaning of responsibility to parallel the shift in the meaning of autonomy. If we are created by our decisions then we cannot be held to account for our decisions, but we can be for the care that we have taken over them. Responsibility is therefore measured not by our level of self-control but by our level of self-awareness; the person who is the most responsible is the one with the greatest capacity for self-knowledge; the more we know ourselves, the better a person we can be:

> The self-command that is measured in the first case in terms of the scope and reach of my will is determined in the second by the depth and clarity of my self-awareness.[110]

It is the displacement of the old responsibility by the new responsibility that has led so many commentators, not least the opponents of Part II of the Family Law Act discussed above,[111] to observe a decline

---

[107] For discussion, see Etzioni, above n 16, 136.

[108] B Frohnen, *The New Communitarians and the Crisis of Modern Liberalism* (Lawrence, University Press of Kansas, 1996) 170.

[109] *Ibid*, 178.

[110] M Sandel, *Liberalism and the Limits of Justice* (Cambridge, Cambridge University Press, 1998) 59. See also C Smart and B Neale, *Family Fragments?* (Cambridge, Polity Press, 1999) 114.

[111] Pp 206–7.

in morality.[112] To some extent, whether there has been a decline or a shift in morality is a definitional dispute. As we saw in chapter three, post-liberalism struggles to recognise duties to others because the subject's primary life task has become to develop his or her self, and to many, morality is centrally about duties to others.[113] For example, it has been argued that unless conscience points outside ourselves to a moral law that binds us in spite of our desires, conscience loses its coherence and becomes just one impulse among many.[114] That this is primarily a definitional dispute is illustrated by the modified claim that it is neither that family law has become less moral nor that family lawmakers do not have moral reasons for their decisions. It is rather, as we saw in chapter three, that the language is increasingly drawn from psychology or medicine, not morality;[115] for example, within therapeutic culture moral faults are seen as illnesses while feeling guilty about one's authentic actions is now seen as unhealthy.[116] The adoption of a neutral stance towards divorce law, specifically the shift from fault to breakdown as the basis for divorce, has been seen as a paradigm of the law's withdrawal from moral language, or morality.[117]

In contrast, defenders of post-liberal responsibility seek to 'tease out new styles of moral thinking in intimate life'.[118] On this view, there has not been an abnegation of moral values but simply a shift in moral focus.[119] Likewise, there has been a diminution only in one type of moral discourse, for example that relating to fault,[120] and a change in the vocabulary of morality does not translate into a decrease in moral language.[121]

[112] For discussion, see Smart and Neale, above n 15, 4.
[113] For example, Schneider, above n 18, 526; Frohnen, above n 108, 211; Glendon, above n 19, 108.
[114] Frohnen, above n 108, 211.
[115] P 89; Schneider, above n 18, 505–6.
[116] For discussion, see Glendon, above n 19, 108; Schneider, above n 1, 1853–54; Nolan, above n 17, 9.
[117] Schneider, above n 18, 505–6; Schneider, above n 1; Ellman, above n 2, 228–29.
[118] Smart and Neale, above n 110, 16.
[119] D Rhode and M Minow, 'Reforming the Questions, Questioning the Reforms: Feminist Perspectives on Divorce Law' in S Sugarman and H Hill Kay, *Divorce Reform at the Crossroads* (New Haven, Connecticut, Yale University Press, 1990) 210.
[120] N Cahn, 'The Moral Complexities of Family Law', 50 *Stanford Law Review* 225.
[121] *Ibid*, 244; K O'Donovan, 'Love's Law: Moral Reasoning in Family Law' in D Morgan and G Douglas, *Constituting Families: A Study in Governance* (Stuttgart, Germany, Steiner (Franz) Verlag Wiesbaden GmbH, 1994) 43–44; K O'Donovan, *Family Law Matters* (London, Boulder, Colorado, Pluto Press, 1993) 112; R Chadwick, 'Moral Reasoning in Family Law—A Response to Katherine O'Donovan' in D Morgan and G Douglas, *Constituting Families: A Study in Governance* (Stuttgart, Germany, Steiner (Franz) Verlag Wiesbaden GmbH, 1994) 53.

More specifically, comparing the Law Commission paper preceding the 1969 divorce reform with the papers preceding the 1996 reform reveals a shift from a confident moral statement to reliance on the language of consumerism, efficiency and pragmatism; but the question remains whether the later language is any less moral.[122] It has even been argued that post-liberal societies are more profoundly moral than traditional societies: because there are ever fewer straightforward rules or religious certainties to follow, rather than follow custom we are obliged to realise our responsibility and become more conscious of moral choices.[123] The liberal approach to morality is seen as impoverished because the only aspect of an action that is morally relevant is which side of the line the action falls, permitted or prohibited. Since the line is the same for all agents, what is morally relevant has no specific connection with the characteristics of any particular agent but is instead completely impersonal.[124]

Whether a decline or a shift in morality is perceived, there is no question that moral values and specifically responsibility are now generally defined in terms of procedure rather than substance.[125] As we have seen already, because our obligations are now principally procedural, the State would be quite wrong to prevent divorce, because it is possible to divorce responsibly. However the State is well within its rights to ask a prospective divorcee whether he or she has kept his or her commitment to *work at the marriage*. In chapters two, three and four we discussed three different ways in which the divorcee is required to work at the marriage. We can now pull these together to re-state that the procedural requirements of thinking, delaying and learning the lesson are not optional: they are the new virtues:

> Because this self-resolution is something we do, when we do it, we can be
> called responsible for ourselves; and because it is within limits always up to

[122] K O'Donovan, 'Love's Law: Moral Reasoning in Family Law' in Morgan and Douglas, above n 121, 43–44; O'Donovan, above n 121, 110–12; R Chadwick, 'Moral Reasoning in Family Law—A Response to Katherine O'Donovan' in Morgan and Douglas, above n 121, 53.

[123] Smart and Neale, above n 110, 118; Smart and Neale, above n 15, 6; E Silva and C Smart, 'The 'New' Practices and Politics of Family Life' in Silva and Smart, above n 20, 12.

[124] MacIntyre, above n 78, 311.

[125] K O'Donovan, 'Love's Law: Moral Reasoning in Family Law' in Morgan and Douglas, above n 121, 43–44; O'Donovan, above n 121, 112; R Chadwick, 'Moral Reasoning in Family Law—A Response to Katherine O'Donovan' in Morgan and Douglas, above n 121, 53. See J Dewar, 'Reducing Discretion in Family Law', 11 *Australian Journal of Family Law* 309 at 310 and Dewar, 'Discontents', above n 60, for the contrasting view that within post-liberal family law prescriptive rules are more prominent than within liberal family law.

us to do it, even when we don't . . . we can be called responsible . . . whether
we undertake this radical evaluation or not.[126]

. . . families come in all shapes and sizes and therefore so, too, do family values, or perhaps one might call them family responsibilities.[127]

The modern form of responsibility is relativistic in two ways. First, it
recognises and even applauds diverse family forms.[128] Secondly, as we
have seen, being responsible no longer involves doing anything nor
refraining from doing anything. More concretely, we have seen that
under Part II of the Family Law Act it would no longer have been necessary for divorcing couples to prove fault; they would have decided
themselves using their own criteria whether their marriage had broken
down. More generally, modern family law does not regard its mission
as to effect a substantive moral vision.[129] According to the Law
Commission, '[t]he complexities of family life are no longer capable of
being reduced to simple certainties.'[130]
One family law commentator has warned that while the retreat from
prescription could be welcomed as making way for pluralism, it takes
place in the name of pragmatism not liberty.[131] This warning becomes
apt when we notice that the new mode of responsibility is relative as well
as relativistic, also in two senses. First, and ironically, post-liberals end
up reclaiming the original objection to liberal responsibility by arguing

[126] C Taylor, 'What is Human Agency?' in Mischel, above n 14, 133.
[127] Baroness Hamwee, Hansard, House of Lords, 30 November 1995, Col 777.
[128] For example, Cahn, above n 120, 238; SM Okin, *Justice, Gender and the Family*
(New York, Basic Books, 1989) 125; Hoggett, above n 76, 76; E Silva and C Smart, 'The
'New' Practices and Politics of Family Life' in Silva and Smart, above n 20, 12; D Morgan,
'Risk and Family Practices: Accounting for Change and Fluidity in Family Life' in Silva
and Smart, above n 20, 29; J Weeks *et al*, 'Everyday Experiments: Narratives of Non-
Heterosexual Relationships' in Silva and Smart, above n 20, 84; A Bainham, 'Family Law
in a Pluralistic Society' in N Lowe and G Douglas (eds), *Families Across Frontiers* (The
Hague, Martinus Nijhoff Publishers, 1996) 306; Lord Addington, Hansard, House of
Lords, 12 November 1996, Col 919.
[129] MC Regan, 'Market Discourse and Moral Neutrality in Divorce Law', 1994 *Utah
Law Review* 605 at 606–607; Regan, above n 33, 36. See also Dewar, 'Discontents', above
n 60, 79.
[130] Law Commission, *Ground for Divorce*, above n 2, 11.
[131] K O'Donovan, 'Love's Law: Moral Reasoning in Family Law' in Morgan and
Douglas, above n 121, 44; O'Donovan, *Family Law Matters*, above n 121, 112.

that since the capacity for moral agency is shaped by a variety of factors, people are not equal in this capacity.[132] Secondly, in relation to a particular person's responsibility, 'the capacity for reflection enables the self . . . to arrive at a self-understanding less opaque if never perfectly transparent.'[133] Any inquiry under the new approach to responsibility is inevitably even more obscure and baffling than the traditional investigation into fault. It has been suggested that this is because there is no social understanding of what procedural responsibility requires,[134] but it can be argued at least as plausibly that part of the reason for the shift from substantive to procedural responsibility was the collapse in consensus over what substantive responsibility entails.[135] In fact, it is not because there is no such consensus that the inquiry is nebulous but rather because, while under the old conception of responsibility it was possible to be responsible, under the new conception, responsible behaviour is a continuum. Now one can be more or less considered, cautious and reflective about one's decisions, but one can never think carefully enough, delay long enough or learn the lesson well enough. Post-liberals are quite clear that if we take the commitment to monitor ourselves seriously, 'it involves a great deal of work.'[136]

In relation to divorce, the demanding nature of post-liberal responsibility is well illustrated by the Law Commission's argument for requiring people to begin the divorce process by making a statement that they believed that the marriage had broken down. The argument was that this form of wording placed:

> . . . a greater personal responsibility on initiators by requiring them to express a view about the state of their relationship rather than merely recite

[132] MacIntyre, above n 78, 309. For discussion, see Schneider, above n 18, 531.

[133] Sandel, above n 110, 153.

[134] Schneider, above n 18, 531; R Smith, 'Parental Responsibility—and an Irresponsible State?', 71 *Childright* 7 at 8.

[135] See generally Regan, above n 129, 608; Regan, above n 33, 39; Frohnen, above n 108, 46; K O'Donovan, 'Love's Law: Moral Reasoning in Family Law' in Morgan and Douglas, above n 121, 44; O'Donovan, above n 121, 111; S Benhabib, 'Autonomy, Modernity and Community: Communitarianism and Critical Social Theory in Dialogue' in S Benhabib, *Situating the Self: Gender, Community and Postmodernism in Contemporary Ethics* (Cambridge, Polity, 1992) 75; Dewar, above n 125; Smart and Neale, above n 15, 4; Purdy, above n 106; J Eekelaar, *Family Law and Social Policy* 2nd edn (London, Weidenfeld and Nicolson, 1984) 43; Glendon, above n 19, 108; Finch and Mason, above n 21. In relation to divorce in particular, see Law Commission, *Ground for Divorce*, above n 2, 11; Dewar, 'Chaos', above n 60, 485.

[136] V Davion, 'Integrity and Radical Change' in Card, above n 77, 186. See also M Griffiths, *Feminisms and the Self: The Web of Identity* (London, New York, Routledge, 1995) 187.

a statutory ground which may bear no resemblance to what they are thinking or feeling.[137]

According to Lord Mackay:

> . . . the obligations of marriage do not stop with the obligation not to com-
> mit adultery – I believe that there is a good deal more to the marriage rela-
> tionship than that – nor do those obligations stop at the obligation not to be
> guilty of unreasonable conduct. I believe that the obligations of marriage, as
> set out in the *Book of Common Prayer* and in the scriptures on which I
> believe that that book is soundly based, are much more far reaching and inti-
> mate . . . It cannot be reduced to a list of contractual conditions.[138]

Given that as a result of their relative character, post-liberal responsibilities are more nebulous and therefore more demanding, let us investigate how this works in relation to divorce in particular. In questioning the
description of the move to no-fault divorce as a shift away from moral values, it has been argued that no-fault standards should be, and to some
extent are, based on commitments to substantive sexual equality, principles of cooperative care-taking behaviour and a maximisation of children's interests.[139] The last of these principles has been taken
up, to suggest that virtue has become 'doing the right thing for the
children' and vice is now 'ignoring the children's interests'.[140] But, unlike
the old fault-based prohibitions on adultery, unreasonable behaviour or
desertion, every divorcee will always transgress against the new aspirational norms of divorcing harmoniously,[141] and otherwise divorcing well:

> . . . of course, few adults match up to this paragon, but this serves merely to
> open up a gap, in which transgressions will be penalised as the system seeks
> to normalise divorcing behaviour in accordance with the legislative ideal.[142]

It has rightly been concluded that these 'normative commitments imply
an expanded concept of responsibility . . . for divorcing spouses and
parents'.[143]

[137] Law Commission, *Ground for Divorce*, above n 2, 27.
[138] Lord Mackay, Hansard, House of Lords, 11 January 1996, Cols 307–308. See also
Lord Mackay, 'Family Law', above n 2, 11.
[139] D Rhode and M Minow, 'Reforming the Questions, Questioning the Reforms:
Feminist Perspectives on Divorce Law' in Sugarman and Hill Kay, above n 119, 210. See
also Cahn, above n 120.
[140] M King, 'Foreword' in SD Sclater and C Piper (eds), *Undercurrents of Divorce*
(Aldershot, Ashgate, 1999) x.
[141] SD Sclater and C Piper, 'The Family Law Act 1996 in Context' in *ibid*, 6.
[142] Dewar, 'Chaos', above n 60, 484. See also Dewar, 'Chaos', above n 60, 485; Dewar,
'Discontents', above n 60, 79
[143] D Rhode and M Minow, 'Reforming the Questions, Questioning the Reforms:
Feminist Perspectives on Divorce Law' in Sugarman and Hill Kay, above n 119, 210.

The expansive nature of post-liberal responsibilities has been documented in family law outside divorce. For example, recent exhortations to exercise parental responsibility have prioritised feelings over facts and focused on the amount and type of parental communication;[144] it is the quality of the parental relationship and the attitudes of the parents that are deemed essential, rather than physical care and financial support.[145] It has been argued that the absence of any definition of parental responsibility seriously undermines the child's ability to call parents to account. However, when this argument leads to an attempt to define parental responsibility more closely, it is noteworthy that the example given is procedural, vague, extensive and insidious, namely that it should be an explicit parental responsibility not to transmit racist attitudes or convey them in stereotypes to children.[146] With respect to family relations generally, concern has turned away from the structure towards the substance; there is now less preoccupation with the form of family in which people choose to live and more with 'moral' aspects of responsibility in relationships.[147] Family life is seen less as an arrangement of roles and more as a relationship of persons behind the roles.[148] It has been rightly recognised that the focus on 'doing' family as opposed to 'being' family demands constant participation and commitment from each member of the family.[149] It is hard to disagree with one commentator's conclusion that 'by prescribing inner states rather than behaviour, modern standards of family perfection make success almost impossible to achieve.'[150]

Moreover, not only is our level of responsibility graded against our level of self-awareness, but responsible behaviour also depends on the

[144] Piper, above n 68, 480.

[145] *Ibid*, 488; M Sandel, *Democracy's Discontent: America in Search of a Public Philosophy* (Cambridge, Massachusetts, Belknap Press, 1996) 113.

[146] Smith, above n 134, 8.

[147] D Morgan and G Douglas, 'The Constitution of the Family: Three Waves for Plato' in Morgan and Douglas, above n 121; Smart and Neale, above n 110, 31; Cahn, above n 120; Whitehead, above n 70, 148; J Stacey, 'Dan Quayle's Revenge: The New Family Values Crusaders', 259 *The Nation* 119 at 120; D Morgan, 'Risk and Family Practices: Accounting for Change and Fluidity in Family Life' in Silva and Smart, above n 20, 29.

[148] Sandel, above n 145, 113.

[149] E Silva and C Smart, 'The 'New' Practices and Politics of Family Life' in Silva and Smart, above n 20, 8.

[150] Piper, above n 68, 488. See also Dewar, 'Discontents', above n 60, 79. See M Minow and M L Shanley, 'Relational Rights and Responsibilities: Revisioning the Family in Liberal Political Theory and Law', 11 *Hypatia* 4 for a similar point at a more abstract level. See Schneider, above n 1, for the opposite view that modern norms in family law are less aspirational.

vulnerabilities of the person towards whom the behaviour is directed. Within post-liberal theory there is no abstract individual whom we can treat fairly and objectively; it is impossible to construe all obligations as universal duties.[151] Instead, there is a continuum of obligations. At one end there is the universalistic commitment to every human as worthy of universal moral respect, which reflects principles of justice. At the other end there is the standpoint of the concrete other, which is relevant in personal relationships:

> To be a family member, a parent, a spouse, a sister or a brother means to know how to reason from the standpoint of the concrete other. One cannot act within these ethical relationships in the way in which standing in this kind of a relationship to someone else demands of us without being able to think from the standpoint of our child, our spouse, our sister or brother, mother or father.[152]

The standpoint of the concrete other:

> requires us to view each and every rational being as an individual with a concrete history, identity, and affective-emotional constitution . . . [who] . . . is entitled to expect and to assume from the other forms of behavior through which the other feels recognized and confirmed as a concrete, individual being with specific needs, talents, and capacities.[153]

At this end of the continuum, the norms of interaction are friendship, love and care. These norms require far more than the simple assertion of rights and duties in the face of the other's needs. In treating another person as the concrete other, we confirm not only their *humanity* but also their *individuality*.[154] If the standpoint of the generalised and the concrete others exist along a continuum from universal respect for all as moral persons at one end, to the care demanded in close relationships on the other, then, contrary to traditional liberal theory, we should not privilege relationships of justice.[155]

---

[151] Sandel, above n 145, 14; K O'Donovan, 'Love's Law: Moral Reasoning in Family Law' in Morgan and Douglas, above n 121, 44. For discussion, see Frohnen, above n 108, 176.

[152] S Benhabib, 'Introduction' in Benhabib, above n 135, 10.

[153] S Benhabib, 'The Generalized and the Concrete Other' in EF Kittay and DT Meyers (eds), *Women and Moral Theory* (Totowa, New Jersey, Rowman & Littlefield, 1987) 164.

[154] S Benhabib, 'The Generalized and the Concrete Other' in *ibid*, 164.

[155] S Benhabib, 'Introduction' in Benhabib, above n 135, 10; EF Kittay and DT Meyers, 'Introduction' in *ibid*, 10.

Others have pursued this idea at a more concrete level. It has been argued that the internal stance towards marriage requires sensitivity to individuals in their particularity, not simply by virtue of their status as human beings.[156] This calls for appreciation of shifting balances of power and vulnerability, different forms of responsiveness and evolving patterns of need and obligation.[157] These obligations are triggered not by consent to marriage but from shared experience with another. As we saw in chapter three, the sense of responsibility that arises out of the internal stance reflects the awareness of a historical self whose sense of identity emerges from the formation and maintenance of attachments over time:

> Awareness of this character of attachments, the vulnerability that they create, and the trust that they require can produce a sense of constraint with respect to a particular attachment that an agent acting from the external stance would not experience.[158]

As we have seen, from the internal stance, the past has a moral weight in decision-making that it does not have for a person who adopts the external stance.[159] The internal stance is 'a narrative of marriage in which responsibility arises from the demands of interdependence and history.'[160] Similarly in relation to friendship, it has been argued that the obligations friendship attracts are voluntary only in the sense that we choose our friends. Having done so, we fall under special nonvoluntary requirements that we are also not at liberty to renege on.[161]

Outside the specific contexts of marriage and friendship, while the liberal self can only recognise chosen obligations (the capacity to choose being the most essential aspect of liberal personhood),[162] as we saw in chapter four, post-liberalism holds that we are commonly unable to regard ourselves as separate from unchosen obligations.[163] This is because we are encumbered selves, already claimed by certain

[156] MC Regan, *Alone Together: Law and the Meanings of Marriage* (New York, Oxford University Press, 1998) 12.

[157] MC Regan, 'Spousal Privilege and the Meanings of Marriage', 81 *Virginia Law Review* 2045 at 2083.

[158] *Ibid*, 2086.

[159] Ch 3.

[160] Regan, above n 157, 2156.

[161] M Friedman, *What are Friends For?: Feminist Perspectives on Personal Relationships and Moral Theory* (Ithaca, New York, Cornell University Press, 1993) 216.

[162] P 13.

[163] P 132.

commitments the moral force of which consists partly in the fact that they are inseparable from our understanding ourselves as the particular persons that we are:[164]

> . . . as members of this family or community or nation or people, as bearers of this history, as sons and daughters of that revolution, as citizens of this republic.[165] . . . to some I owe more than justice requires or even permits, not by reason of agreements I have made but instead in virtue of those more or less enduring attachments and commitments which taken together partly define the person I am. To imagine a person incapable of constitutive attachments such as these is not to conceive an ideally free and rational agent, but to imagine a person wholly without character, without moral depth. For to have character is to know that I move in a history I neither summon nor command, which carries consequences none the less for my choices and conduct. It draws me closer to some and more distant from others.[166]

Because, as we saw in chapter three, liberalism defines interdependence narrowly by limiting the importance of common connections, it also defines responsibility narrowly by limiting our obligations to one another.[167] In contrast:

> Building on communitarian notions of mutuality . . . [leads to] a more expansive notion of responsibility, a broader range of enforceable duties to and from our institutions.[168]

Empirical research has supported this approach by finding that in order to understand people's attitudes towards their responsibilities it is necessary to understand their present actions in the light of their biographies. Moreover, the research found that people's identities as moral beings are bound up with these responsibilities, so that people are constructed and reconstructed as moral beings through negotiations about giving and receiving assistance. This has an impact on whether they continue with their commitments.[169] For example:

---

[164] Sandel, above n 145, 13–14. For discussion, see D Phillips, *Looking Backward: A Critical Appraisal of Communitarian Thought* (Princeton, New Jersey, Princeton University Press, 1993) 182; A Buchanan, 'Assessing the Communitarian Critique of Liberalism', 99 *Ethics* 852 at 874.

[165] Sandel, above n 110, 179. See also Sandel, above n 145; SM Okin, 'Humanist-Liberalism' in N Rosenblum (ed), *Liberalism and the Moral Life* (Cambridge, Massachusetts, Harvard University Press, 1989) 49.

[166] Sandel, above n 110, 179.

[167] Eckstein, above n 12, 845.

[168] *Ibid*, 847.

[169] Finch and Mason, above n 21.

If the image of 'a caring sister' is valued as part of someone's personal identity then it eventually becomes too expensive to withdraw from those commitments through which that identity is expressed and confirmed.[170]

The related argument has been made that responsibility in general is based on vulnerability, so that responsibility between spouses in particular is not based on the exchange of vows, which is merely the external embodiment of an ethical bond. Instead, responsibility is based on the fact that spouses have placed themselves in each other's power emotionally, and 'from such extraordinary vulnerabilities follow strong responsibilities'.[171] Moreover, where peculiar sensitivities are concerned, 'it is the actor/chooser's responsibility to pick up the signals, however weak they may be.'[172] Since some of the most important vulnerabilities have to do with feelings, this responsibility extends to people's psychological as well as physical sensitivities.[173] It has been left to even more conservative communitarians to recognise that:

> . . . the relentless insistence on consciousness and the endless scanning of one's own and others' feelings while making moment-by-moment calculations of the shifting cost/benefit balances is so ascetic in its demands as to be unendurable.[174]

It is paradoxical that post-liberalism begins with the soothing premise that we cannot be held responsible for our actions because choice is not real, but ends with more insidious and demanding responsibilities than liberalism. One post-liberal theorist has found it unnecessary to jump through these hoops, arguing instead that because choice is not real, the court's emphasis on motive and intention is misplaced, so that we can be held responsible for our actions even if we did not choose them. Focusing on court practice, she argues that courts follow a liberal model of responsibility that places the individual ahead of the group and prioritises separateness over communal ties. Under this model, the court ignores connections among people and protects individualistic values, such as motive and intent:

---

[170] Finch and Mason, above n 21, 170.

[171] Robert Goodin, *Protecting the Vulnerable: A Reanalysis of Our Social Responsibilities* (Chicago, University of Chicago Press, 1985) 79. See also Okin, above n 128, 136.

[172] Goodin, above n 171, 123.

[173] *Ibid.*

[174] Bellah, above n 63, 139.

When the Court insists on a showing of motive, it protects the defendant from responsibility for anything she has not chosen and meant to do as an individual. The Court denies that an individual, a part of a community . . . owes a duty to that community that stems from something other than motive, and rejects duties arising from a community's needs and values. By emphasizing motive, the Court liberates individuals from responsibility for structural problems they did not mean to cause, and negates an affirmative responsibility for attitudes and behavior that hurt other individuals in the institution.[175]

She argues that the centrality of motive in the court's jurisdiction reflects the emphasis on individualism and autonomy. The liberal vision that it embodies presumes that individuals are responsible only for themselves and their own intentions, not for the systemic problems of their institutions. This emphasis on individualism is at best incomplete in that duties should also be imputed that stem from something outside individual motive and intention. But the emphasis may also be incoherent in that when we are removed from our ties to others, we are dislocated and so incapable of making choices. As well as individual duties, we have duties to those around us that stem from the fact that we all benefit from each other. Effects should be emphasised alongside motive, so that individuals' commonality may be protected as well as their individuality.[176] The court's jurisdiction is impoverished because it speaks only to a part of our experience, namely our yearning for autonomy. The court is wrong to emphasise separateness over connectedness, the individual over the community and ultimately wrong to emphasise individual choice over collective ends.[177]

CONCLUSION

It is clear that the post-liberal approach leads to more far-reaching, diverse and nebulous responsibilities. Responsibility in post-liberal theory extends infinitely; it is therefore impossible to define, impossible to fulfil and, crucially, virtually impossible to regulate.[178] Attempts by the law to do so are inevitably uniquely interventionist for several

---

[175] Eckstein, above n 12, 846.
[176] *Ibid*, 847.
[177] *Ibid*, 907.
[178] See generally Schneider, above n 18, 531; See in relation to divorce SM Cretney and JM Masson, *Principles of Family Law* 6th edn (London, Sweet & Maxwell, 1997) 381.

reasons.[179] First, since only the individual concerned is even remotely capable of knowing whether he or she has tried his or her best,[180] a legal investigation into this question is bound to be intense, intensive and deeply personal:[181]

> . . . the state becomes involved not only in the evaluation of behavior but in an assessment of the internal processes of individual psyches. Therapeutic experts testify as to the inner cognitive and emotional processes of the individual. Therapeutic codes and symbols therefore provide the state with the tools whereby it can continue to expand into new, formerly private areas of societal life.[182]

Secondly, as we saw in chapter four, law needs to inculcate the necessary character traits as a prerequisite to post-liberal responsible behaviour.[183] Thirdly, because post-liberal responsibility presents itself as mere procedure, demanding that people neither do nor refrain from doing anything substantive but merely follow a method, it wears a deeper disguise than its predecessor.[184]

According to the Government White Paper:

> The divorce process is only capable of assessing fault in the crudest possible way. The law is ill-suited to engaging in the complex and sensitive factual and moral judgments which, if achievable, would be necessary accurately to reflect the relative blameworthiness of the parties.[185]

It is ironic that one of the principal arguments for the abolition of fault was that it was intrusive to investigate the private arena of marital wrongdoing.[186] In reality, the abolition of fault opened the door to increased state intervention:

> However strong its appeal, the idea of breakdown has dangerous shortcomings. If under the matrimonial offense system a specified offense was

---

[179] McClain, above n 11, 994.
[180] Schneider, above n 18, 531.
[181] Nolan, above n 17, 292.
[182] *Ibid*, 297.
[183] P 138.
[184] K O'Donovan, 'Love's Law: Moral Reasoning in Family Law' in Morgan and Douglas, above n 121, 48.
[185] Lord Chancellor's Department, above n 2, 7.
[186] For examples, see *ibid*, 20; Law Commission, *Facing the Future*, above n 2, 17; Law Commission, *Ground for Divorce*, above n 2, 11; Patrick Nicholls, Hansard, House of Commons, 24 April 1996, Col 459; Glendon, above n 19, 79; L Weitzman and R Dixon, 'The Transformation of Marriage Through No-Fault Divorce: The Case of the United States' in Eekelaar and Katz, above n 1, 148. For disagreement, see Phillips, 'Death blow', above n 1. For discussion, see Schneider, above n 1, 1809.

committed, obtaining a divorce constitutes a right of the innocent spouse. Breakdown of marriage is, on the other hand, a notion vague enough to make pronouncement of divorce a judicial privilege rather than a citizen right. The vagueness opens doors for judicial arbitrariness . . .[187]

Throughout this book, we have seen that post-liberalism includes a coercive drive. In chapter one we saw that the only way that post-liberalism could provide a truly coherent account of autonomy was by abandoning relativism. The constructed nature of the self meant *both* that we can achieve truly autonomous choices only if the élite makes them for us *and* that there is little to prevent the élite doing so: our preferences are not real and so they are not sacrosanct. In chapter two, we saw that the cognitive approach to autonomy could not rescue post-liberalism from the slide to coercion; in fact, the approach contributed to this slide, because failure to impose desirable norms left people at the mercy of their pre-existing characteristics. Chapter four explored the implication of accepting that autonomy could only be achieved if desirable social norms were in place. The implication was that the good citizen had an obligation to maintain post-liberal society not only by participating but also by allowing virtue to be inculcated into him or her through civic education. When translated into divorce law, this meant that the good divorcee had to submit to experiencing his or her divorce as an educative experience and in particular had to accept that he or she needed help. In chapter four I built on the ambivalent attitude to divorce that I identified in chapter three, to conclude that the divorcee's reward for submitting to the educative experience was to be allowed to exit his or her marriage with his or her head held even higher than before. In chapter five the end point of the drive to coercion caused by the illusory nature of autonomy was reached, namely to treat information provision as a means of directing rather than informing people's decisions, so that at the extreme post-liberalism sees little difference between providing information and coercing behaviour. It was when this end point was reached that post-liberalism fell on its own sword. While divorcees accepted the crucial premises of post-liberalism, specifically that they needed help, they treated the information as information, and chose a different form of help from the types that the Government was pushing.

[187] J Gorecki, 'Moral Premises of Contemporary Divorce Laws: Western and Eastern Europe and the United States' in Eekelaar and Katz, above n 1, 126. See also L Weitzman and R Dixon, 'The Transformation of Marriage Through No-Fault Divorce: The Case of the United States' in Eekelaar and Katz, above n 1, 148.

Crucially, as we saw at the end of chapter five, the failure of Part II of the Family Law Act does not signify the end of the post-liberal approach to information. Nor does such failure signify the end of the post-liberal approach to law in general. This book has shown that post-liberalism can pave the way for coercion, evident in the post-liberal conception of responsibility just examined. In relation to divorce specifically, we have just seen that the theoretical shift in the meaning of responsibility enabled Part II of the Family Law Act to be uniquely intrusive and judgemental, because every divorcing couple, on being held up to scrutiny, was found lacking. While Part II failed, this chapter has also demonstrated that the post-liberal approach to responsibility is well established and widespread outside formal legislation. However, the failure of Part II of the Family Law Act also demonstrates that implementation of post-liberal law is problematic, not least because it comes up against obstacles from within post-liberal theory. If post-liberalism continues to gain authority then we can expect more attempts at post-liberal lawmaking. The measure of success that such attempts will achieve remains an open question.[188]

---

[188] See Dewar, 'Discontents', above n 60, 79, for the view that the failure of Part II Family Law Act 1996 is a sign of hope that such attempts will not work.

Bibliography

Abrams, K, 'Ideology and Women's Choices', 24 *Georgia Law Review* 761
——'Kitsch and Community', 84 *Michigan Law Review* 941
——'Law's Republicanism', 97 *Yale Law Journal* 1591
——'Title VII and the Complex Female Subject', 92 *Michigan Law Review* 2479
——'Redefining Women's Agency: A Response to Professor Williams', 72 *Indiana Law Journal* 459
Albert, ME, (1988) 'In the Interest of the Public Good? New Questions for Feminism' in C Reynolds and R Norman (eds), *Community in America: The Challenge of Habits of the Heart* (California University Press, Berkeley, California)
Almond, B, 'The Retreat from Liberty', 8 *Critical Review* 235
Andrews, G, (1990) 'Introduction' in G Andrews (ed), *Citizenship* (Lawrence & Wishart, London)
Arnold, W, (2000) 'Implementation of Part II of the Family Law Act 1996: The Decision Not to Implement in 2000 and Lessons Learned From the Pilot Meetings' in M Thorpe and E Clarke (eds), *No Fault or Flaw: The Future of the Family Law Act 1996* (Jordan Publishing, Bristol)
Avineri, S and de-Shalit, A, (1992) 'Introduction' in S Avineri and A de-Shalit (eds), *Communitarianism and Individualism* (Oxford University Press, Oxford, New York)
Bainham, A, (1996) 'Family Law in a Pluralistic Society' in N Lowe and G Douglas (eds), *Families Across Frontiers* (Martinus Nijhoff Publishers, The Hague, London)
Bainham, A, *et al* (eds), (1999) *What is a Parent? A Socio-Legal Analysis* (Hart Publications, Oxford)
Barber, B, (1984) *Strong Democracy: Participatory Politics for a New Age* (University of California Press, Berkeley)
——(1998) 'A Mandate for Liberty: Requiring Education-Based Community Service' in A Etzioni (ed), *The Essential Communitarian Reader* (Rowman & Littlefield, Lanham)
Bauman, R, (1989) 'The Communitarian Vision of Critical Legal Studies' in A Hutchinson and L Green (eds), *Law and the Community: The End of Individualism?* (Carswell, Toronto)
BBC News, (1998) 'Cabinet Minister's Son Cautioned', www.bbc.co.uk/news, 12 January
——(1998) 'A History of Christmas Scandal Past', www.bbc.co.uk/news, 22 December
——(1999) 'Divorce Reforms Hit the Rocks', www.bbc.co.uk/news, 17 June
——(2000) 'Blair's Son "Drunk and Incapable"', www.bbc.co.uk/news, 6 July

BBC News, (2001) 'No-Fault Divorce to be Scrapped' , www.bbc.co.uk/news, 16 January

——(2001) 'Bishop Regrets Divorce Decision', www.bbc.co.uk/news, 17 January

Beck, U, (1992) *Risk Society: Towards a New Modernity* (Sage Publications, London)

——(1994) 'The Reinvention of Politics' in U Beck, A Giddens and S Lash, *Reflexive Modernization: Politics, Tradition and Aesthetics in the Modern Social Order* (Polity Press, Cambridge)

Beck, U and Beck-Gernsheim, E, (1995) *The Normal Chaos of Love* (Polity Press, Cambridge, Blackwell, United Kingdom, Cambridge, Massachusetts, USA)

Beiner, R, 'Revising the Self', 8 *Critical Review* 247

——(1989) 'What's the Matter with Liberalism?' in A Hutchinson and L Green (eds), *Law and the Community: The End of Individualism?* (Toronto, Carswell)

——(1992) *What's the Matter with Liberalism?* (University of California Press, Berkeley, California)

Bellah, RN, *et al,* (1985) *Habits of the Heart: Individualism and Commitment in American Life* (University of California Press, Berkeley, California)

——*et al,* (1991) *The Good Society* (Knopf, New York)

Benhabib, S and Cornell, D, (1987) 'Beyond the Politics of Gender' in S Benhabib and D Cornell (eds), *Feminism as Critique: Essays on the Politics of Gender in Late-Capitalist Societies* (Polity, Cambridge)

Benhabib, S, (1987) 'The Generalized and the Concrete Other: The Kohlberg-Gilligan Controversy and Moral Theory' in E F Kittay and D T Meyers (eds), *Women and Moral Theory* (Rowman & Littlefield, Totowa, New Jersey)

——(1992) 'Autonomy, Modernity and Community: Communitarianism and Critical Social Theory in Dialogue' in S Benhabib, *Situating the Self: Gender, Community and Postmodernism in Contemporary Ethics* (Polity, Oxford)

——(1992) 'Introduction' in S Benhabib, *Situating the Self: Gender, Community and Postmodernism in Contemporary Ethics* (Polity, Oxford)

Berger, P and Kellner, H, 'Marriage and the Construction of Reality', 46 *Diogenes* 1

Berry, C, (1989) *The Idea of a Democratic Community* (Harvester Wheatsheaf, Hemel Hempstead)

Booth Committee (1985) *Report of the Matrimonial Causes Procedure Committee* (HMSO, London)

Brest, P, 'Further Beyond the Republican Revival: Toward Radical Republicanism', 97 *Yale Law Journal* 1623

Brown, G, 'A View from the Temple', 128 *Law and Justice* 35

Brown, J, and Sclater, SD, (1999) 'Divorce: A Psychodynamic Perspective' in Sclater, SD and Piper, C (eds), *Undercurrents of Divorce* (Ashgate, Aldershot)

Brown, P, 'Divorce—The Fault Fiction', 138 *New Law Journal* 377

Buchanan, A, 'Assessing the Communitarian Critique of Liberalism', 99 *Ethics* 852

Cahn, NR, 'The Moral Complexities of Family Law', 50 *Stanford Law Review* 225

Caney, S, 'Liberalism and Communitarianism: A Misconceived Debate', 40 *Political Studies* 273

Card, C (ed), (1991) *Feminist Ethics* (University Press of Kansas, Lawrence, Kansas)

Centre for Family Studies at the University of Newcastle upon Tyne, (2001) 'Information Meetings and Associated Provisions within the Family Law Act 1996' (Lord Chancellor's Department, London)

Chadwick, R, (1994) 'Moral Reasoning in Family Law – A Response to Katherine O'Donovan' in D Morgan and G Douglas (eds), *Constituting Families: A Study in Governance* (Steiner (Franz) Verlag Wiesbaden GmbH, Stuttgart, Germany)

Cheal, D, (1991) *Family and the State of Theory* (Harvester Wheatsheaf, London)

Clulow, C, (2000) 'Supporting Marriage in the Theatre of Divorce' in M Thorpe and E Clarke (eds), *No Fault or Flaw: The Future of the Family Law Act 1996* (Jordan Publishing, Bristol)

Cochran, C, 'The Thin Theory of Community: The Communitarians and their Critics', 37 *Political Studies* 422

Colker, R, (1991) 'Feminism, Sexuality and Authenticity' in MA Fineman and NS Thomadsen (eds), *At the Boundaries of Law: Feminism and Legal Theory* (Routledge, New York, London)

Collier, R, 'The Dashing of a "Liberal Dream"?—The Information Meeting, The "New Family" and the Limits of Law', 11 *Child and Family Law Quarterly* 257

Cornell, D, (1995) *The Imaginary Domain: Abortion, Pornography and Sexual Harassment* (Routledge, New York)

——(1998) *At the Heart of Freedom: Feminism, Sex and Equality* (Princeton University Press, Princeton, New Jersey)

——'Institutionalization of Meaning, Recollective Imagination and The Potential for Transformative Legal Interpretation', 136 *University of Pennsylvania Law Review* 1135

——'Two Lectures on the Normative Dimensions of Community in the Law', 54 *Tennessee Law Review* 327

Crawford, A, 'The Spirit of Community: Rights, Responsibilities, and the Communitarian Agenda', 23 *Journal of Law and Society* 247

Cretney, S, (1992) *Elements of Family Law* 2nd edn (Sweet & Maxwell, London)

Cretney, SM and Masson, JM, (1997) *Principles of Family Law* 6th edn (Sweet & Maxwell, London)

Daily Telegraph, (1995) P Johnston and T Shaw, 'Divorce White Paper: Lord Mackay's Way to Mend a Marriage', 28 April

——(1996) J Copley, 'Ministers "to Join Revolt on Divorce"', 24 April

——(1996) G Jones, 'Mackay Bows to Divorce Defeat', 26 April

——(1996) J Copley, 'Ministers Forced to Climb Down on Divorce', 1 May

——(2000) M Kallenbach and A Sparrow, 'Peers Back Guidelines on Sex Education in Schools', 19 July

——(2001) J Rozenberg, 'Labour to Scrap Tory "No-Fault" Divorces', 17 January

Damico, A, (1986) 'Introduction' in A Damico (ed), *Liberals on Liberalism* (Rowman & Littlefield, Totowa, New Jersey)

Dan-Cohen, M, 'Responsibility and the Boundaries of the Self', 105 *Harvard Law Review* 959

Davion, V, (1991) 'Integrity and Radical Change' in C Card (ed), *Feminist Ethics* (University Press of Kansas, Lawrence, Kansas)

Davis, G and Murch, M, (1988) *Grounds for Divorce* (Clarendon Press, Oxford)

Deech, R, 'Divorce Law and Empirical Studies', 106 *Law Quarterly Review* 229

Demaine, J, (1996) 'Beyond Communitarianism: Citizenship, Politics and Education' in J Demaine and H Entwistle (eds), *Beyond Communitarianism: Citizenship, Politics and Education* (Macmillan, Basingstoke)

Dewar, J, 'Reducing Discretion in Family Law,' 11 *Australian Journal of Family Law* 309

——'The Normal Chaos of Family Law,' 61 *Modern Law Review* 467

——(1992) *Law and the Family* 2nd edn (Butterworths, London)

Dewar, J and Parker, S, (2000) 'English Family Law since World War II: From Status to Chaos' in S Katz *et al* (eds), *Cross Currents: Family Law and Policy in the United States and England* (Oxford University Press, New York)

DiFonzo, JH, (1997) *Beneath the Fault Line: The Popular and Legal Culture of Divorce in Twentieth-Century America* (University Press of Virginia, Charlottesville, London)

Doherty, W, (1988) 'How Therapists Threaten Marriages' in A Etzioni (ed), *The Essential Communitarian Reader* (Rowman & Littlefield, Lanham, Oxford)

Eckstein, R, 'Towards a Communitarian Theory of Responsibility: Bearing the Burden for the Unintended', 45 *University of Miami Law Review* 843

Eekelaar, J, 'Family law: keeping us "on message"', 11 *Child and Family Law Quarterly* 387

——'Family Law: The Communitarian Message', 21 *Oxford Journal of Legal Studies* 181

——'Parental Responsibility: State of Nature or Nature of the State', 1 *Journal of Social Welfare and Family Law* 37

——(1984) *Family Law and Social Policy* 2nd edn (Weidenfeld and Nicolson, London)

——(1991) *Regulating Divorce* (Clarendon Press, Oxford)

Eekelaar, J and Katz, SN (eds), (1980) *Marriage and Cohabitation in Contemporary Societies: Areas of Legal, Social and Ethical Change: An International and Interdisciplinary Study* (Butterworths, Toronto, London)

——(eds), (1984) *The Resolution of Family Conflict: Comparative Legal Perspectives* (Butterworths, Toronto)

Ellman, MI, 'The Misguided Movement to Revive Fault Divorce, and Why Reformers Should Look Instead to the American Law Institute', 11 *International Journal of Law, Policy and the Family* 216

Elshtain, JB and Buell, J, 'Families in Trouble', 28 *Dissent* 262

Elshtain, JB, 'Feminism, Family and Community', 29 *Dissent* 442

Etzioni, A, 'The Good Society', 7 *Journal of Political Philosophy* 88

——(ed), (1993) *The Spirit of Community: Rights, Responsibilities and the Communitarian Agenda* (Random House, New York)

——(1988) 'Introduction' in A Etzioni (ed), *The Essential Communitarian Reader* (Rowman & Littlefield, Lanham, Oxford)

——(1998) *The New Golden Rule: Community and Morality in a Democratic Society* (Basic Books, New York)

Fallon, R, 'Two Senses of Autonomy', 46 *Stanford Law Review* 875

Ferrara, A, (1990) 'universalisms: procedural, contextualist and prudential' in D Rasmussen (ed), *Universalism vs. Communitarianism: Contemporary Debates in Ethics* (MIT Press, Cambridge, Massachusetts, London)

Finch, J and Mason, J, 'Divorce, Remarriage and Family Obligations', 38 *The Sociological Review* 219

——(1993) *Negotiating Family Responsibilities* (Routledge, London, Tavistock)

Fowler, RB, (1991) *The Dance with Community: the Contemporary Debate in American Political Thought* (Kansas University Press, Kansas)

Frazer, E, (1999) *The Problems of Communitarian Politics: Unity and Conflict* (Oxford University Press, Oxford)

Frazer, E and Lacey, N, (1994) *The Politics of Community: A Feminist Critique of the Liberal-Communitarian Debate* (University of Toronto Press, Buffalo, New York)

Freeman, MDA, 'Down with informalism: Law and lawyers in family dispute resolutions', 2 *Family Law Journal* 67

——(1984) 'Questioning the Delegalization Movement in Family Law: Do We Really Want a Family Court?' in J Eekelaar and SN Katz (eds), *The Resolution of Family Conflict: Comparative Legal Perspectives* (Butterworths, Toronto)

Friedman, J, 'The Politics of Communitarianism', 8 *Critical Review* 229

Friedman, M, (1991) 'The Social Self and the Partiality Debates' in C Card (ed), *Feminist Ethics* (University Press of Kansas, Lawrence, Kansas)

——(1993) *What are Friends For?: Feminist Perspectives on Personal Relationships and Moral Theory* (Cornell University Press, Ithaca, New York, London)

——'Feminism and Modern Friendship: Dislocating the Community', 99 *Ethics* 275

Frohnen, B, (1996) *The New Communitarians and the Crisis of Modern Liberalism* (University Press of Kansas, Lawrence)

Fudge, J, (1989) 'Community or Class: Political Communitarians and Workers' Democracy' in A Hutchinson and L Green (eds), *Law and the Community: The End of Individualism?* (Carswell, Toronto)

Galston, M, 'Taking Aristotle Seriously: Republican-Oriented Legal Theory and the Moral Foundation of Deliberative Democracy', 82 *California Law Review* 331

Galston, W, (1991) *Liberal Purposes: Goods Virtues, and Diversity in the Liberal State* (Cambridge University Press, New York)

——(1998) 'A Liberal-Democratic Case for the Two-Parent Family' in A Etzioni (ed), *The Essential Communitarian Reader* (Rowman & Littlefield, Lanham)

Gardbaum, S, 'Law, Politics and the Claims of Community', 90 *Michigan Law Review* 685

——'Liberalism, Autonomy and Moral Conflict', 48 *Stanford Law Review* 385

——'Why the Liberal State can Promote Moral Ideals After All', 104 *Harvard Law Review* 1350

Gey, S, 'The Unfortunate Revival of Civic Republicanism', 141 *University of Pennsylvania Law Review* 801

Giddens, A, (1991) *Modernity and Self-Identity: Self and Society in the Late Modern Age* (Polity Press, Cambridge)

——(1992) *The Transformation of Intimacy: Sexuality, Love and Eroticism in Modern Societies* (Polity, Cambridge)

——(1994) 'Living in a Post-Traditional Society' in U Beck, A Giddens and S Lash, *Reflexive Modernization: Politics, Tradition and Aesthetics in the Modern Social Order* (Polity Press, Cambridge)

Gilligan, C, (1982) *In a Different Voice: Psychological Theory and Women's Development* (Harvard University Press, Cambridge, Massachusetts, London)

Glendon, MA, (1987) *Abortion and Divorce in Western Law* (Harvard University Press, Cambridge, Massachusetts, London)

Goodin, R, (1985) *Protecting the Vulnerable: A Reanalysis of Our Social Responsibilities* (University of Chicago Press, Chicago)

——(1998) 'Permissible Paternalism: In Defence of the Nanny. State' in A Etzioni (ed), *The Essential Communitarian Reader* (Rowman & Littlefield, Lanham)

Gorecki, J, (1980) 'Moral Premises of Contemporary Divorce Laws: Western and Eastern Europe and the United States' in JM Eekelaar and SN Katz (eds), *Marriage and Cohabitation in Contemporary Societies: Areas of Legal, Social and Ethical Change: An International and Interdisciplinary Study* (Butterworths, Toronto, London)

Gould, CC, (1988) *Rethinking Democracy: Freedom and Social Cooperation in Politics, Economy and Society* (Cambridge University Press, Cambridge)

Greschner, D, (1989) 'Feminist Concerns with the New Communitarians: We Don't Need Another Hero' in A Hutchinson and L Green (eds), *Law and the Community: The End of Individualism?* (Carswell, Toronto)

Griffiths, M, (1995) *Feminisms and the Self: The Web of Identity* (Routledge, London, New York)

Guardian (1990) L Hodgkinson, 'The Beginning of a Whole New Life Apart', 20 July

——(1990) A Coote, 26 September

——(1990) C Dyer, '"Quickie" Divorces Face Axe as Law Commission Urges 12-month Cooling Off Period for Couples', 2 November

——(1990) M Phillips, 'A Pause at the Parting of the Ways', 2 November

——(1994) M D'Antonio, 'The Next Big Idea', 23 June

——(1994) G Mulgan, 'Our Built-in Moral Sense is the Basic We Should Go Back To', 4 August

——(1994) S Milne, 'Everybody's talking about', 7 October

——(1995) 'Just a Social Crowd of Folk', 18 February

——(1995) S Holmes, 'The Ku Klux Klan are a Close-knit Bunch Too', 18 February

——(1995) M Walker, 'Community Spirit', 13 March

——(1995) S Boseley and P Wintour, 'Blair Backs "Stable" Two-Parent Families', 30 March

——(1995) C Dyer, 'Law and Church Welcome End to Quickie Divorces' 28 April

——(1995) M Freely, 'Mediation Isn't Always the Right Message', 28 April

——(1996) M White, 'Rebel Lords Hit Divorce Bill', 1 March

——(1996) R Smithers, 'Tory Divorce Bill Rebels Rally Allies', 20 April

——(1996) 'Four Cabinet Ministers Vote For Divorce Defeat' 25 April.

——(1996) R Smithers, 'Ministers Agree Counselling Change to Family Law Bill', 1 May

——(1996) R Smithers, 'Divorce: A Law Nobody Wants', 18 June

——(1999) 'Brutish and Longer', 17 February

——(2000) 'Blair's Son Says Sorry After "Drunk and Incapable" Arrest', 6 July

——(2000) N Watt, 'Emotional PM Talks of Faith and Family', 7 July

——(2000) M White and N Watt, 'Blair Shows Strain After Son's Arrest', 7 July

——(2000) C Dyer, 'Government drops plan for no-fault divorce', 2 September

——(2000) 'Blow To No-Fault Divorce Hopes', 18 December

——(2001) C Dyer, 'Divorce Law Reform Ditched', 17 January

——(2001) Leader, 'Back to the bad old ways', 18 January

Gutmann, A, 'Communitarian Critics of Liberalism', 14 *Philosophy and Public Affairs* 308

Hafen, B, (1991) 'Individualism and Autonomy in Family Law: The Waning of Belonging', *Brigham Young University Law Review* 1

Hansard, (1995) Baroness Hamwee, House of Lords, 30 November

——(1995) Lord Marsh, House of Lords, 30 November

——(1995) Lord Bishop of Birmingham, House of Lords, 30 November

——(1995) Lord Coleraine, House of Lords, 30 November

——(1995) Baroness David, House of Lords, 30 November

——(1995) Lord Gisborough, House of Lords, 30 November

——(1995) Lord Jakobovits, House of Lords, 30 November

——(1995) Lord Moran, House of Lords, 30 November

——(1995) Lord Simon, House of Lords, 30 November

——(1995) Lord Stallard, House of Lords, 30 November

——(1995) Baroness Young, House of Lords, 30 November

——(1996) Baroness Park, House of Lords, 11 January

——(1996) Lord Irvine, House of Lords, 11 January

——(1996) Lord Mackay, House of Lords, 11 January

——(1996) Lord Stallard, House of Lords, 11 January

——(1996) Baroness Young, House of Lords, 11 January

——(1996) Baroness David, House of Lords, 22 January

——(1996) Lord Mackay, House of Lords, 22 January

——(1996) Duke of Norfolk, House of Lords, 22 January

——(1996) Lord Bishop of Oxford, House of Lords, 22 January

——(1996) Lord Stallard, House of Lords, 22 January

——(1996) Lord Stoddart, House of Lords, 22 January

——(1996) Baroness Young, House of Lords, 22 January

——(1996) Lord Coleraine, House of Lords, 23 January

——(1996) Lord Elton, House of Lords, 23 January

——(1996) Lord Irvine, House of Lords, 23 January

——(1996) Lord Jakobovits, House of Lords, 23 January

——(1996) Lord Mackay, House of Lords, 23 January

——(1996) Lord Mackay, House of Lords, 25 January

——(1996) Baroness Young, House of Lords, 29 January

——(1996) Lord Mackay, House of Lords, 22 February

——(1996) Lord Ashbourne, House of Lords, 29 February

——(1996) Lord Clifford, House of Lords, 29 February

——(1996) Lord Habgood, House of Lords, 29 February

——(1996) Lord Jakobovits, House of Lords, 29 February

——(1996) Lord Moran, House of Lords, 29 February

——(1996) Lord Bishop of Oxford, House of Lords, 29 February

——(1996) Bishop of Prelate, House of Lords, 29 February

——(1996) Lord Simon, House of Lords, 29 February

——(1996) Lord Stallard, House of Lords, 29 February

——(1996) Lord Stoddart, House of Lords, 29 February

——(1996) Lord Mackay, House of Lords, 4 March

——(1996) Lord Mackay, House of Lords, 11 March

——(1996) Lord Jakobovits, House of Lords, 11 March

——(1996) Baroness Strange, House of Lords, 11 March

——(1996) J Patten, House of Commons, 26 March

——(1996) E Leigh, House of Commons, 24 April

——(1996) P Nicholls, House of Commons, 24 April

——(1996) A Rumbold, House of Commons, 24 April

——(1996) D Alton, House of Commons, 17 June

——(1996) J Corston, House of Commons, 17 June

——(1996) C Davies, House of Commons, 17 June

——(1996) J Knight, House of Commons, 17 June

——(1996) J Patten, House of Commons, 17 June

——(1996) Lord Northbourne, House of Lords, 2 July

——(1996) Lord Ashbourne, House of Lords, 5 July

——(1996) Viscount Cranbourne, House of Lords, 5 July

——(1996) Lord Addington, House of Lords, 12 November

——(1996) Lord Elton, House of Lords, 12 November

——(1997) E Leigh, House of Commons, 19 December

——(1999) Lord Craigmyle, House of Lords, 24 March

——(1999) Lord Irvine, House of Lords, 17 June

——(1999) Lord Ashbourne, House of Lords, 5 July

——(1999) Viscount Brentford, House of Lords, 6 July

——(1999) Baroness Hollis, House of Lords, 6 July

——(1999) Lord Jakobovits, House of Lords, 6 July

——(1999) Baroness Scotland, House of Lords, 6 July

Harris, A, 'Race and Essentialism in Feminist Legal Theory', 42 *Stanford Law Review* 581

Hekman, S, (1995) *Moral Voices, Moral Selves: Carol Gilligan and Feminist Moral Theory* (Polity, Oxford)

Hewitt, J, (1989) *Dilemmas of the American Self* (Temple University Press, Philadelphia)

Hirshman, L, 'The Virtue of Liberality in American Communal Life', 88 *Michigan Law Review* 983

Hoagland, SL, (1988) *Lesbian Ethics: Toward New Value* (Institute of Lesbian Studies, Palo Alto, California)

——(1994) 'Why *Lesbian* Ethics?' in C Card (ed), *Adventures in Lesbian Philosophy* (Indiana University Press, Bloomington)

Holmes, S, (1988) 'The Community Trap', *The New Republic,* 28 November, 26

——(1989) 'The Permanent Structure of Antiliberal Thought' in N Rosenblum *Liberalism and the Moral Life* (Harvard University Press, London)

——(1993) *The Anatomy of Antiliberalism* (Harvard University Press, Cambridge, Massachusetts, London)

Home Office, (1998) *Supporting Families: A Consultation Document* (London, HMSO)

Houston, B, (1994) 'In Praise of Blame' in C Card (ed), *Adventures in Lesbian Philosophy* (Indiana University Press, Bloomington)

Hutchinson, A, (1989) 'Talking the Good Life: From Liberal Chatter to Democratic Conversation' in A Hutchinson and L Green (eds), *Law and the Community: The End of Individualism?* (Carswell, Toronto)

Hutchinson, A and Green, L, (1989) 'Introduction' in A Hutchinson and L Green (eds), *Law and the Community: The End of Individualism?* (Carswell, Toronto)

Hutchinson, A and Green L (eds), (1989) *Law and the Community: The End of Individualism?* (Carswell, Toronto)

Independent, (1995) C Brown, 'Mackay Seeks to Calm Unease on Divorce Bill', 25 October

——(1995) P Toynbee, 'Lord Mackay's Well-Intentioned Fiasco' 25 October

——(1995) S Ward, 'Ministers Plan Divorce Reform Retreat: Christian Pressure Group Thrust to Centre of Debate', 1 November

——(1996) Lord Mackay, 'Champions of Marriage Should Back Me', 26 April

——(1996) 'Ministers Defy Tory Pressure to Ditch Divorce Bill', 26 April

——(1996) 'MPs Threaten to Mangle Divorce Bill', 26 April

——(1996) Editorial, 'Labour Joins the Right: Divorced from Reality', 29 May

——(1996) PW Davies, 'Concessions for the Right, Deals With the Left . . . Divorce Law Ushers In A New Era For Wives', 18 June

—— (2000) A Grice and P Waugh, 'Being a Prime Minister Can be Tough, But Being a Parent is Sometimes Tougher', 7 July

——(2000) P Waugh, 'Honest, Contrite and Above All Emotional, Blair Faces Up to the Morning After the Night Before', 7 July

——(2000) 'Head Accused of Playing Politics Over Euan Blair', 10 July

——(2002) R Verkaik, 'Lawyers Attack Misery of "Fault Game" Divorces', 2 January

Jordan, B, Redley, M, James, S, (1994) *Putting the Family First: Identities, Decisions, Citizenship* (UCL Press, London)

Kahn, P, 'Community in Contemporary Constitutional Theory', 99 *Yale Law Journal* 1

Kateb, G, (1989) 'Democratic Individuality and the Meaning of Rights' in N Rosenblum (ed), Liberalism and the Moral Life (Harvard University Press, London)

——(1992) *The Inner Ocean: Individualism and Democratic Culture* (Ithaca, New York, Cornell University Press)

Katz, S, *et al* (eds), (2000) *Cross Currents: Family Law and Policy in the United States and England* (Oxford University Press, New York)

Keller, C, (1986) *From a Broken Web: Separation, Sexism and the Self* (Beacon Press, Boston)

King, M, (1999) 'Foreword' in SD Slater and C Piper (eds), *Undercurrents of Divorce* (Ashgate, Aldershot)

Kittay, EF and Meyers, DT, (1987) 'Introduction' in EF Kittay and DT Meyers (eds), *Women and Moral Theory* (Rowman & Littlefield, Totowa, New Jersey)

Kitwood, T, 'Psychotherapy, Postmodernism and Morality', 19 *Journal of Moral Education* 3

Kymlicka, W, 'Communitarianism, Liberalism, and Superliberalism', 8 *Critical Review* 262

——'Liberalism and Communitarianism', 18 *Canadian Journal of Philosophy* 181

——(1991) *Liberalism, Community, and Culture* (Clarendon Press, Oxford University Press, Oxford, New York)

——(2001) *Contemporary Political Philosophy: An Introduction* 2/e (Oxford University Press, Oxford)

Lacey, N, and Zedner, L, 'Discourses of Community in Criminal Justice', 22 *Journal of Law and Society* 301

Law Commission, (1966) *Reform of the Grounds of Divorce, The Field of Choice* (HMSO, London)

——(1988) *Facing the Future: A Discussion Paper on the Ground for Divorce* (HMSO, London)

——(1990) *The Ground for Divorce* (HMSO, London)

Legal Services Commission, (2001) *Family Advice and Information Networks* (Legal Services Commission, London)

——(2002) 'Developing Family Advice and Information Services' (Legal Services Commission, London)

Lister, R, (1997) *Citizenship: Feminist Perspectives* (Macmillan Press Ltd, Basingstoke, London)

Lord Chancellor's Department Press Release, *Divorce Law Reform—Government Proposes to Repeal Part II of the Family Law Act 1996* (January 2001)

Lord Chancellor's Department, (1993) *Looking to the Future: Mediation and the Ground for Divorce* (London, HMSO)

——(1999) *Information Meetings and Associated Provisions within the Family Law Act 1996: Summary of Research in Progress* (London, Lord Chancellor's Department)

Lord Chancellor's Advisory Board on Family Law: Children Act Sub-Committee, (2002) '*Making Contact Work: A Report to the Lord Chancellor on the Facilitation of Arrangements for Contact Between Children and their Non-Residential Parents and the Enforcement of Court Orders for Contact*' (London, Lord Chancellor's Department)

Lord Chancellor's Advisory Group on Marriage and Relationship Support, (2002) '*Moving Forward Together: A Proposed Strategy for Marriage and Relationship Support for 2002 and Beyond*' (Lord Chancellor's Department, London)

Lord Chancellor's Department, (2002) '*Making Contact Work—Further Government Investment in Services*' 6 August '*Parenting Plan: PLANNING*

FOR YOUR CHILDREN'S FUTURE www.lcd.gov.uk/family/leaflets/ parentplan+english/default.htm

Lucas, J, *Responsibility* (1995) (Oxford University Press, Oxford)

McClain, L, '"Irresponsible" Reproduction', 47 *Hastings Law Journal* 339

——'Rights and Irresponsibility', 43 *Duke Law Journal* 989

Maclean, M and Richards, M, (1999) 'Parents and Divorce: Changing Patterns of Public Intervention' in A Bainham *et al* (eds), *What is a Parent? A Socio-Legal Analysis* (Hart Publications, Oxford)

Macedo, S, (1990) *Liberal Virtues: Citizenship, Virtue and Community in Liberal Constitutionalism* (Clarendon Press, Oxford)

MacIntyre, A, (1985) *After Virtue: a study in moral theory* (Duckworth, London)

——'How Moral Agents Became Ghosts or Why the History of Ethics Diverged from That of the Philosophy of Mind', 53 *Synthese* 295

MacKinnon, C, (1989) *Toward a Feminist Theory of the State* (Harvard University Press, Cambridge, Massachusetts)

Mansfield, P, (2000) 'From Divorce Prevention to Marriage Support' in M Thorpe and E Clarke (eds), *No Fault or Flaw: The Future of the Family Law Act 1996* (Jordan Publishing, Bristol)

Marriage, divorce and adoption statistics: Review of the Registrar General on marriages, divorces and adoptions in England and Wales 2000 (2002) (London, Office for National Statistics)

Martindale, K and Saunders, M, (1994) 'Realizing Love and Justice: Lesbian Ethics in the Upper and Lower Case' in C Card (ed), *Adventures in Lesbian Philosophy* (Indiana University Press, Bloomington)

Meyers, DT, (1989) *Self, Society, and Personal Choice* (Columbia University Press, New York)

——*et al* (eds), (1993) *Kindred Matters: Rethinking the Philosophy of the Family* (Cornell University Press, Ithaca, New York)

Michelman, F, 'Law's Republic', 99 *Yale Law Journal* 1493

Minow, M and Shanley, ML, 'Relational Rights and Responsibilities: Revisioning the Family in Liberal Political Theory and Law', 11 *Hypatia* 4

Minow, M, 'Surviving Victim Talk', 40 *UCLA Law Review* 1411

Moran, M, (1991) 'Introduction' in U Vogel and M Moran (eds), *The Frontiers of Citizenship* (Macmillan, Basingstoke)

Morgan, D and Douglas, G (eds), (1994) *Constituting Families: A Study in Governance* (Verlag Wiesbaden GmbH, Struttgart, Germany, Steiner (Franz))

Morgan, D, (1999) 'Risk and Family Practices: Accounting for Change and Fluidity in Family Life' in E Silva and C Smart (eds), *The New Family?* (Sage, London, Thousand Oaks, New Delhi)

Morse, A, 'Fault: A Viable Means of Re-injecting Responsibility in Marital Relations', 30 *University of Richmond Law Review* 605

Neal, P and Paris, D, 'Liberalism and the Communitarian Critique: A Guide for the Perplexed', 23 *Canadian Journal of Political Science* 419

Nedelsky, J, 'Law, Boundaries, and the Bounded Self', 30 *Representations* 162
——(1989) 'Preconceiving Autonomy: Sources, Thoughts and Possibilities' in
    A Hutchinson and L Green (eds), *Law and the Community: The End of
    Individualism?* (Carswell, Toronto)
Newman, S, (1989) 'Challenging the Liberal Individualist Tradition in
    America: "Community" as a Critical Ideal in Recent Political Theory' in
    A Hutchinson and L Green (eds), *Law and the Community: The End of
    Individualism?* (Carswell, Toronto)
Nolan, J, (1998) *The Therapeutic State: Justifying Government at Century's
    End* (New York University Press, New York, London)
Observer, (1994) M Phillips, 'Father of Tony Blair's Big Idea', 24 July
——(1995) M Phillips, 'The Race to Wake Sleeping Duty', 2 April
——(1995) M Phillips, 'Death blow to Marriage', 7 May
——(1995) M Phillips, 'Unhappy Families on the Marry-Go-Round',
    29 October
——(2000) R Coward, 'Kids and Kidology', 9 July
——(2001) K Ahmed, 'U-turn Over No-fault Divorce Law', 14 January
——(2001) C Sarler, 'Let's Hear It For Divorce', 21 January
O'Donovan, K, (1993) *Family Law Matters* (Pluto Press, London)
——(1994) 'Love's Law: Moral Reasoning in Family Law' in D Morgan and
    G Douglas, *Constituting Families: A Study in Governance* (Steiner (Franz)
    Verlag Wiesbaden GmbH, Stuttgart, Germany)
Okin, SM, (1989) 'Humanist-Liberalism' in N Rosenblum (ed), *Liberalism and
    the Moral Life* (London, Harvard University Press)
——(1989) *Justice, Gender and the Family* (Basic Books, New York)
Oldfield, A, (1990) *Citizenship and Community: Civic Republicanism and the
    Modern World* (Routledge, London)
Parry, G, (1991) 'Paths to Citizenship' in U Vogel and M Moran (eds), *The
    Frontiers of Citizenship* (Macmillan, Basingstoke)
Phillips, D, (1993) *Looking Backward: A Critical Appraisal of Communitarian
    Thought* (Princeton University Press, Princeton, New Jersey)
Phillips, R, (1989) *Putting Asunder: A History of Divorce in Western Society*
    (Cambridge University Press, Cambridge)
Piper, C, 'Divorce Conciliation in the United Kingdom: How Responsible Are
    Parents?' 16 *International Journal of Sociology of Law* 477
Popenoe, D, 'American Family Decline, 1960-1990: A Review and Appraisal',
    55 *Journal of Marriage and the Family* 527
Purdy, J, 'Age of Irony', 39 *The American Prospect* 84
Rasmussen, D (ed), (1990) *Universalism vs. Communitarianism: Contemporary
    Debates in Ethics* (MIT Press, Cambridge, Massachusetts, London)
Regan, MC, (1993) *Family Law and the Pursuit of Intimacy* (New York
    University Press, New York)
——(1994) 'Market Discourse and Moral Neutrality in Divorce Law', *Utah
    Law Review* 605

——(1998) *Alone Together: Law and the Meanings of Marriage* (Oxford University Press, New York)

——'Getting Our Stories Straight: Narrative Autonomy and Feminist Commitments', 72 *Indiana Law Journal* 449

——'Spousal Privilege and the Meanings of Marriage', 81 *Virginia Law Review* 2045

Reiman, J, (1994) 'Liberalism and its Critics' in CF Delaney (ed), *The Liberalism-Communitarianism Debate: Liberty and Community Values* (Rowman & Littlefield, Lanham)

Reynolds, C and Norman, R (eds), (1988) *Community in America: The Challenge of Habits of the Heart* (California University Press, Berkeley, California)

Rhode, D and Minow, M, (1990) 'Reforming the Questions, Questioning the Reforms: Feminist Perspectives on Divorce Law' in S Sugarman and H Hill Kay (eds), *Divorce Reform at the Crossroads* (Yale University Press, New Haven, Connecticut)

Riessman, CK, (1990) *Divorce Talk: Men and Women Make Sense of Personal Relationships* (Rutgers University Press, New Brunswick, New Jersey)

Rodger, J, (1996) *Family Life and Social Control: A Sociological Perspective* (Macmillan, Basingstoke, Hants)

Rosenblum, N, (1987) *Another Liberalism: Romanticism and the Reconstruction of Liberal Thought* (Harvard University Press, Cambridge, Massachusetts)

——(ed), (1989) *Liberalism and the Moral Life* (Harvard University Press, London)

Rourke, N, (1993) 'Domestic Violence: The Challenge to Law's Theory of the Self' in DT Meyers *et al* (eds), *Kindred Matters: Rethinking the Philosophy of the Family* (Cornell University Press, Ithaca, New York, London)

Sandel, M, (1984) 'Morality and the Liberal Ideal', *New Republic*, 7 May

——(1996) *Democracy's Discontent: America in Search of a Public Philosophy* (Belknap Press, Cambridge, Massachusetts)

——(1998) *Liberalism and the Limits of Justice* (Cambridge University Press, Cambridge)

Schneider, C, (1994) 'Marriage, Morals and the Law', *Utah Law Review* 503

——'Moral Discourse and the Transformation of American Family Law' 83 *Michigan Law Review* 1803

Schultz, V, 'Room to Manoeuvre (f)or a Room of One's Own? Practice Theory and Feminist Practice', 14 *Law and Social Inquiry* 123

Sclater, SD, (1999) *Divorce: A Psychosocial Study* (Ashgate, Aldershot)

——'Narratives of Divorce', 19 *Journal of Social Welfare and Family Law* 423

——(1999) 'Experiences of Divorce' in SD Sclater and C Piper (eds), *Undercurrents of Divorce* (Ashgate, Aldershot)

Sclater, SD and Piper, C, (1999) 'Changing Divorce' in SD Sclater and C Piper (eds), *Undercurrents of Divorce* (Ashgate, Aldershot)

——(1999) 'The Family Law Act 1996 in Context' in SD Sclater and C Piper (eds), *Undercurrents of Divorce* (Ashgate, Aldershot)

——(eds), (1999) *Undercurrents of Divorce* (Ashgate, Aldershot)

——'Re-moralising the Family?—Family Policy, Family Law and Youth Justice', 12 *Child and Family Law Quarterly* 135

Scott, ES, 'Rational Decision-making About Marriage and Divorce', 76 *Virginia Law Review* 9

——(1994) 'Rehabilitating Liberals in Modern Divorce Law', *Utah Law Review* 687

Sherry, S, 'Civic Virtue and the Feminine Voice in Constitutional Adjudication' 72 *Virginia Law Review* 543

Shotter, J, (1993) 'Psychology and Citizenship: Identity and Belonging' in B Turner (ed), *Citizenship and Social Theory* (Sage, London)

Silva, E, and Smart C (eds), (1999) *The New Family?* (Sage, London, Thousand Oaks, New Delhi)

Simon, T, (1994) 'The Theoretical Marginalization of the Disadvantaged: A Liberal/Communitarian Failing' in CF Delaney (ed), *The Liberalism-Communitarianism Debate: Liberty and Community Values* (Rowman & Littlefield, Lanham)

Simpson, P, 'Liberalism, State and Community', 8 *Critical Review* 159

Singer, J, 'The Privatization of Family Law', 71 *Wisconsin Law Review* 1443

Skolnick, A, and Rosencrantz, S, 'The New Crusade for the Old Family', 18 *The American Prospect* 59

Smart, C, 'Wishful Thinking and Harmful Tinkering? Sociological Reflections on Family Policy', 26 *Journal of Social Policy* 301

——(1992) 'Unquestionably a moral issue: Rhetorical devices and regulatory imperatives' in L Segal and M McIntosh (eds), *Sex Exposed: Sexuality and the Pornography Debate* (Virago Press Ltd, London)

——(2000) 'Divorce in England 1950-2000: A Moral Tale? in S Katz et al (eds), *Cross Currents: Family Law and Policy in the United States and England* (Oxford University Press, New York)

Smart, C and Neale, B, (1999) *Family Fragments?* (Polity Press, Cambridge)

——'Good Enough Morality? Divorce and Postmodernity', 17 *Critical Social Policy* 3

Smith, R, 'Parental Responsibility — and an Irresponsible State?', 71 *Childright* 7

Stacey, J, 'Dan Quayle's Revenge: The New Family Values Crusaders', 259 *The Nation* 119

——'Families against "The Family": The transatlantic passage of the politics of family values', 89 *Radical Philosophy* 2

Standley, K, (1993) *Family Law* (Macmillan, Basingstoke, Hampshire, London)

Stone, L, (1990) *Road to Divorce: England 1530–1987* (Oxford University Press, Oxford)

Struering, K, 'Feminist Challenges to the New Familialism: Lifestyle Experimentation and the Freedom of Intimate Association', 11 *Hypatia* 135

Sugarman, S and Hill Kay, H (eds), (1990) *Divorce Reform at the Crossroads* (Yale University Press, New Haven, Connecticut)

Sunstein, CR, (1997) *Free Markets and Social Justice* (Oxford University Press, New York, Oxford)

——'Legal Interference with Private Preferences', 53 *University of Chicago Law Review* 1129

——'Preferences and Politics', 20 *Philosophy and Public Affairs* 3

Taylor, C, 'Can Liberalism be Communitarian?' 8 *Critical Review* 257

——(1977) 'What is Human Agency?' in T Mischel (ed), *The Self: Psychological and Philosophical Issues* (Blackwell, Oxford)

——(1985) *Human Agency and Language: Philosophical Papers 1* (Cambridge University Press, Cambridge)

——(1985) 'What's Wrong with Negative Liberty?' in C Taylor, *Philosophy and the Human Sciences: Philosophical Papers 2* (Cambridge University Press, Cambridge)

——(1985) 'Atomism' in C Taylor, *Philosophy and the Human Sciences: Philosophical Papers 2* (Cambridge University Press, Cambridge)

——(1989) 'Cross-Purposes: The Liberal-Communitarian Debate' in N Rosenblum (ed), *Liberalism and the Moral Life* (Harvard University Press, Cambridge, Massachusetts)

——(1989) *Sources of the Self: The Making of the Modern Identity* (Cambridge University Press, Cambridge)

——(1991) *The Ethics of Authenticity* (Harvard University Press, Cambridge, Massachusetts, London)

Tessman, L, 'Who Are My People? Communitarianism and the Interlocking of Oppressions', 27 *International Studies in Philosophy* 105

Thorpe, M, and Clarke, E (eds), (2000) *No Fault or Flaw: The Future of the Family Law Act 1996* (Jordan Publishing, Bristol)

Tomasi, J, 'Community in the Minimal State', 8 *Critical Review* 285

The Times (1993) 'Couples to Attend Mediation', 7 December

——(1993) S Cretney, 'Divorce on Demand', 14 December

——(1996) N Lawson, 'A Cruel Divorce Trick to Play on the Children', 21 February

——(1996) A Thomson, 'Mackay Fails to Pacify Peers on Divorce Reforms', 23 February

——(1996) 'Four Cabinet Ministers Join Divorce Revolt', 25 April

——(1996) L Purves, 'Divorce is About Remorse', 18 June

——(2000) M Dearle, 'Making a "Dog's Dinner" Out of Divorce Reforms', 5 September

——(2000) F Gibb, 'Irvine Will Scrap "No Fault" Divorce', 18 December

——(2000) Leader, 'The Family Way', 18 December

——(2001) F Gibb, 'Irvine Forced to Drop "No-Fault" Divorces', 17 January

——(2001) C Barton, 'Matrimonial Bliss or a Contract for Life?', 23 January

Unger, R, (1975) *Knowledge and Politics* (Free Press, New York)

Walker, J, (2000) 'Whither the Family Law Act, Part II?' in M Thorpe and E Clarke (eds), *No Fault or Flaw: The Future of the Family Law Act 1996* (Jordan Publishing, Bristol)

Walzer, M, 'The Communitarian Critique of Liberalism', 18 *Political Theory* 6

Wardle, L, (1994) 'Divorce Violence and the No-Fault Divorce Culture', *Utah Law Review* 741

Weeks, J, Donovan, C and Heaphy, B, (1999) 'Everyday Experiments: Narratives of Non-Heterosexual Relationships' in E Silva and C Smart (eds), *The New Family?* (Sage, London, Thousand Oaks, New Delhi)

Weiss, P, (1995) 'Feminism and Communitarianism: Comparing Critiques of Liberalism' in P Weiss and M Friedman (eds), *Feminism and Community* (Temple University Press, Philadelphia)

——(1995) 'Feminism and Community' in P Weiss, and M Friedman, (eds), *Feminism and Community* (Temple University Press, Philadelphia)

Weitzman, L and Dixon, R, (1980) 'The Transformation of Marriage Through No-Fault Divorce: The Case of the United States' in J Eekelaar and SN Katz (eds), *Marriage and Cohabitation in Contemporary Societies: Areas of Legal, Social and Ethical Change: An International and Interdisciplinary Study* (Butterworths, Toronto, London)

West, R, (1991) 'The Difference in Women's Hedonic Lives: A Phenomenological Critique of Feminist Legal Theory' in MA Fineman and NS Thomadsen (eds), *At the Boundaries of Law: Feminism and Legal Theory* (Routledge, New York, London)

Whitehead, BD, (1997) *The Divorce Culture: Rethinking Our Commitments to Marriage and the Family* (Knopf, New York)

Williams, S, 'A Feminist Reassessment of Civil Society', 72 *Indiana Law Journal* 417

Woodhouse, B, (1996) '"It All Depends on What You Mean By Home": Toward a Communitarian Theory of the "Nontraditional" Family', *Utah Law Review* 569

Young, IM, (1989) 'The Ideal of Community and the Politics of Difference' in L Nicholson (ed), *Feminism/Postmodernism* (Routledge, London)

Index